THE SUBARCTIC FUR TRADE: NATIVE SOCIAL AND ECONOMIC ADAPTATIONS

THE SUBARCTIC FUR TRADE: NATIVE SOCIAL AND ECONOMIC ADAPTATIONS

edited by Shepard Krech III

UNIVERSITY OF BRITISH COLUMBIA PRESS
VANCOUVER
1984

THE SUBARCTIC FUR TRADE:
NATIVE SOCIAL AND ECONOMIC ADAPTATIONS

This book has been published with the help of a grant from the Social Science Federation of Canada, using funds provided by the Social Sciences and Humanities Research Council of Canada.

Canadian Cataloguing in Publication Data
Main entry under title:
The Subarctic fur trade

Includes bibliographical references and index.
ISBN 0-7748-0186-7
1. Indians of North America - Canada, Northern - Commerce - Addresses,
essays, lectures. 2. Fur trade - Canada, Northern - History - Addresses,
essays, lectures. 3. Indians of North America - Canada, Northern - Economic
conditions - Addresses, essays, lectures. I. Krech, Shepard, 1944-
E98.C7S82 1984   970.004'97   C84-091090-8

International Standard Book Number 0-7748-0186-7

Printed in Canada by Hignell Printing Limited
on acid-free paper.

Contents

Maps and Tables

Introduction

In his epilogue to the Third North American Fur Trade Conference, Glyndwr Williams (1980:315), former general editor of the Hudson's Bay Record Society and a noted historian, summarized his impressions of the strengths of the conference and identified several productive directions for future research. One suggestion that he made was for greater collaboration between anthropologists and historians (and geographers), perhaps for a convergence of their interests in economic history and in the methodology and orientations of ethnohistory. Williams also suggested, quite rightly, that there was an immediate need for research on the period that begins in 1870, an era for which the records of the Hudson's Bay Company Archives had recently been opened; he thought that the "most notable advances" were likely to take place as a result of the analysis of these records.

The six papers that follow in this volume were originally presented in a symposium at the 1981 annual meeting of the American Society for Ethnohistory. They are concerned in large part with *native* economic history and in part with the late nineteenth- and early twentieth-century trade. The essays are linked in a number of ways, especially in their common interest in Indian economic and social adaptations in the context of the fur trade. The authors, who write from the vantage points of three disciplines—anthropology, geography, and history—are all versed in ethnohistory, that is, in "the use of historical and ethnological methods and materials" (Axtell 1981:5) in order to describe and to analyse, perhaps through time, a particular ethnic group's society and culture, and as a way to make sense of interactions between ethnic groups. Some of the authors are interested in the use of innovative methodological techniques to shed light on native economic adaptations, and they report on these here and elsewhere. This collection of essays, therefore, begins to address the needs identified by Williams. The individual papers represent a range of approaches to native economic and social history current in fur-trade historiography; it is hoped that they will provoke scholars to refine and delve more deeply into the issues which they raise, as well as suggest productive avenues for further research.

Moreover, most of the authors in this volume are concerned with themes which, in the past twenty years or so, have been near the centre of fur-trade scholarship: the identification of Indian motivations in the trade; a determination of the degree to which Indians were discriminating consumers and creative participants in the exchange, not just passive recipients of trade goods; and whether or not Indians were dependent upon the trade. In addressing these issues, the papers dwell necessarily on topics (such as fur-trade dependence) raised initially by Harold Innis and E.E. Rich, whose fur-trade scholarship today stands as classic—indeed, some would say formidable, although Innis's contribution is currently undergoing revisionist interpretations (on this issue, see for example, Eccles 1979 and 1981, Grant 1981, Rotstein 1977, and Ray and Freeman 1978).

The opening essay, "Periodic Shortages, Native Welfare and the Hudson's Bay Company 1670–1930" by Arthur J. Ray, clearly sets the tone for the volume. In an essay ranging far geographically and across two and one-half centuries, Ray forcefully questions the received wisdom that modern native welfare societies are recent, post-World War II phenomena, emerging concurrently with the decline of the fur trade and the development of alternative productive activities. Ray asserts that faunal depletions, scarce resources, the establishment of posts in marginal areas, the existence of low-paying seasonal employment, and the extension of goods on credit combined to produce, by the late nineteenth and early twentieth centuries, dependent, welfare societies. It is incorrect, Ray states, to attribute the modern form of welfare dependence solely to post-World War II governmental involvement; rather, we should recognize that Indians had been "put . . . under an obligation through the extension of credit" for a long time and were even considered by Hudson's Bay Company traders as "assets" to carry during unprofitable years in anticipation of future productivity. Thus, Ray reports that in 1924 a district manager stated following the payment of several tens of thousands of dollars in gratuities, advances, and dole for welfare: "It is true that the natives are our assets, that we must keep them alive for future profits even though we carry them at a loss till such time shall come."

Ray's conclusion that the modern welfare society is deeply rooted in the fur trade presents challenges on several important fronts. One is the exception taken to the chronological framework used by many anthropologists to analyse the historical period throughout much of the Subarctic, a framework that reflects their intuition that significant changes in subarctic Indian life did not begin to take place until recently.

It has become commonplace to assume that the era variously called "government-industrial" (Helm and Leacock 1971), "modern government-commercial" (Helm et al. 1975), or "modern" (Helm, Rogers, and Smith 1981) did not begin throughout most if not all of the Subarctic until after World War II. Ray's essay and the finer-grained empirical studies of Jarvenpa and

Brumbach and others should give pause to those who believe this to be the case and who seek to analyse persistence and change in the twentieth-century Canadian Subarctic.[1] It may be more accurate to trace the beginnings of modern welfare societies to the late nineteenth and early twentieth centuries. At this earlier time, significant changes seem to have begun in many Indian communities, as post-provided goods, including food, became more important. Dependence, as defined in the papers that follow, may have become marked in this period. The origins of significant changes in productive activities and of structural changes in historic subarctic Indian economy and society may perhaps be traced to the turn of the twentieth century, by which time a *welfare-commercial* orientation began to take hold.

Resource depletions and other ecological changes, the advent of new mercantilistic impulses, the relentless though far from inevitable development of dependence—all themes of great concern to Ray—are brought up time and again in other essays in this volume. The three papers that follow immediately, by Charles A. Bishop, Toby Morantz, and Carol Judd, focus on Northern Algonquians in the eastern Subarctic and on the earlier centuries of the trade.

In "The First Century: Adaptive Changes among the Western James Bay Cree between the Early Seventeenth and Early Eighteenth Centuries," Charles A. Bishop rejects the simplistic idea that contact with European fur traders either produced breakdown and discontinuity or resulted in an essential persistence of Indian culture and society. Bishop believes that "behavioural and social structural changes were related to material and ecological causes" and that "ideational modifications both reflected and reinforced these" changes; furthermore, he argues that "post-contact adaptations are . . . the result of a synthesis of the old and the new . . . . What has persisted has become embedded in a new, constantly changing configuration; because of this, it is hazardous to select data for ethnographic reconstruction unless it can be demonstrated that such data logically could have been part of an earlier system." Bishop maintains that we should expect to find shifts in adaptive emphases in Indian societies, not immediate radical departures from old ways, although at one point the shifts—which result in part from decisions made by Indians themselves—become cumulative and lead to fundamental discontinuities with the past.

On the basis of an examination of Fort Albany records, Bishop suggests that Cree Indians living west of James Bay received in the late seventeenth and early eighteenth centuries a "startling" volume of trade goods; that a Cree homeguard, amounting to a substantial force of over one hundred, acted as goose-hunters and providers of other provisions and services and in return received food (oatmeal and fish), guns, tobacco, and brandy; and that other Crees, who became subject to "food stress"—owing to climatic vagaries and faunal depletions that in turn resulted in part from new technology—could (and did) depend on the Fort Albany larder as well. Bishop hypothesizes that the ties which bound male kin became more important because trade goods were used in ways to increase prestige and social inequality; and he proposes that by 1725 these Crees—especially the goose-hunters—were dependent upon guns and ammunition and during some seasons at least on store foods. However, Bishop sees persistence in other aspects of culture.

Although Bishop's argument is too detailed to do justice to adequately here, his major propositions are that changes in Cree Indian adaptations happened in and were in turn produced by man-caused depletions of game, by a new technology, and by specialized economic or subsistence activities; in other words, that changes occurred—first and most significantly—in forces of production rather than in relations of production, where modifications came later and were less extreme.

Assessment (or comparative extension) of Bishop's propositions should await an examination of the paper following his: "Economic and Social Accommodations of the James Bay Inlanders to the Fur Trade" by Toby Morantz. In this essay, Morantz deals with similar questions in an area directly east of Fort Albany, across James Bay, from the mid-eighteenth through the first half of the nineteenth centuries. In her search for statements on economic adaptations and on territorial and social organization, Morantz departs from a sole reliance on the published or archival accounts of traders, explorers, and missionaries—a reliance she regards as "fraught with danger" and one conducive to "find [ing] in the records whatever one is looking for." Instead, Morantz insists upon assessing the fit between propositions on aboriginal patterns derived from the historical record and the archaelogical record and on that historical record being firmly grounded empirically in what are called "profiles" of each hunter constructed from journals and reports (Morantz 1980, 1983). Thus, Morantz's conclusions are based on an innovative methodological technique: an exhaustive compilation and indexing of data on many hunters over as many decades as they continue to show up in post journals (in this case, Eastmain).

Bishop and Morantz differ over the impact of the trade in the two separate (though practically contiguous) regions each knows best. Bishop argues for economic and social changes by 1725; specifically, for the emergence of a goose-hunting homeguard dependent on guns and other trade goods, for the development (or perhaps amplification of existing) concepts of private ownership of beaver lodges, and for a greater emphasis on agnatic ties. Morantz, interested mainly in the more isolated inlanders who came once a year to the coast to trade, describes local groups (in the period from 1815 to 1840) as formed on the basis of both consanguineal and affinal ties, though with a patrilateral skewing because of patrilocal post-marital residence preferences. On the basis of far less evidence, she argues for a similar social configuration in the eighteenth century.

Both Morantz and Bishop are striking at a fairly large debate that is current among ethnohistorian-anthropologists working on subarctic Indians: it is an argument over the effects of the trade, if any, on social as well as economic organization (see Bishop and Krech 1980, Krech 1980). To their credit, neither is willing to speculate loosely about pre-contact social organization. A difference remains, however (though it should again be stressed for different regions on James Bay and different trading populations): Bishop describes dependence of homeguard Indians in productive activities while Morantz finds it difficult to say, for upland or inland Indians, that involvement in the direct fur trade produced significant changes. To understand further the significance of these differences, it may be necessary to examine, if at all possible, through Morantz's indexing technique inlanders who came to Fort Albany. If the adaptations of these Crees are not the same as those of the inland Eastmain Cree, then the differences may be attributable to a combination of historical and ecological factors, including the timing and intensity of the trade, fur-trade competition, and productivity of the region.

The time may have come for ethnohistorians to specify with greater precision exactly what it is they think is changing or persisting in subarctic Indian social and cultural ideas and arrangements. One of the key interests of both Bishop and Morantz (and of most of the other authors in this book) is in economic persistence or change. Bishop suggests changes in productive forces, while Morantz finds it "difficult to conclude" that there was any change in mode of production. Although neither specifies what might have been the aboriginal mode of production of these subarctic Indians, it is probably fair to say that it will prove to be a variant of the more general "foraging" mode described by Richard Lee (1979). After describing in great detail the various productive factors or forces (land and natural resources, capital and technology, and the expenditure of labour) characteristic of the !Kung San, Lee (1979) suggests the following as features of the social relations of production of these and other band-organized foragers: land available to all, with no exclusive individual ownership; no accumulation of surpluses; an insignificant investment in material (or any capital) goods; flexible social arrangements; egalitarian social and political arrangements; and generalized reciprocity. Egalitarianism is especially important, Woodburn (1982:445)—another ethnologist interested in hunting-gathering society economics—remarks, because it "above all . . . disengage [s] people from property, from the potentiality in property rights for creating dependency." For future investigation is the extent to which subarctic Indian fisher-hunters "fit" the general models developed by Lee, Woodburn, and others; essays in this book (and elsewhere) present evidence for the accumulation of surpluses and for living off of stored foods, which suggests certain significant departures from the general models.

At what point during the history of contact with external, sometimes colonial societies do changes in the characteristics of "foraging mode of production" societies take place? (Might some of the characteristics that are documented be the result of such contact?) And what specific changes do occur? Most of the authors in this volume are concerned with changes or persistences in ecology, technology, and social relations that determine access to resources and distribution of goods (with changes or persistences in infrastructure, in other words [Godelier 1980:6]). Certainly, for some (though not all) groups, involvement in the fur trade and in trapping and exchanging, on an individual basis, furs, skins and meat for goods acquired from traders who are agents of an external market, stands in some sense in basic conflict with productive forces and relations characteristic of egalitarian foragers (see Leacock 1982:160, Leacock and Lee 1982:15).

Some time ago, Eleanor Leacock (1954:7), elaborating on distinctions made initially by others and using as a case history the eastern subarctic Montagnais, contrasted production for use (sharing of food, immediate consumption, interdependence of families within the group) with production for exchange (less sharing, delayed consumption, and dependence of individual families on ties outside the group). Leacock proposed that the first was characteristic of aboriginal society and that during the historic fur-trade era there occurred a transformation in this important aspect of mode of production, with production for exchange the result. In his discussion of domestic mode of production, Marshall Sahlins (1972:83) has suggested that what is crucial is the transformation in production for use-value: "primitive peoples remain constant in their pursuit of use values, related always to exchange with an interest in consumption, so to production with an interest in provisioning. And in this respect the historical opposite of *both* is the bourgeois entrepreneur with an interest in exchange value." A main distinction is that between the two systems, use-value and exchange-value.

However, the distinctions drawn by Leacock and Sahlins, while widely known and cited, are not so clear-cut, and the degree to which the results hypothesized by Leacock have actually taken place in the Subarctic is a matter of debate. As Adrian Tanner (1979:6–13, 62–72) points out, fur-trade enterprises, though of a profit-oriented capitalistic nature, were adapted in various ways to ensure a continued flow of furs (see also Ray and Freeman 1978), and instead of a clean-cut transformation from a use-value mode of production to an exchange-value mode, there was in place an intermediate, syncretistic mode until the twentieth century. (Surely, however, it is beside the point to require, as some researchers do, that change somehow does not become "significant" until it is a whole-scale transformation in mode of production?) Moreover, at least one subarctic ethnographer argues that economic dependence on trade goods and/or production for exchange has *not* been the inevitable end: in winter, contemporary (late 1960's) Waswanipi Crees devote approximately 60 per cent of their "harvesting man-days" to hunting beaver (for exchange and food); 30 per cent to moose, fowl, and fish; and only 7 per cent to fine-furs (Feit 1982:380ff). It seems clear that more work is needed in order to clarify whether economic transformations or persistences have occurred.

In "Sakie, Esquawenoe, and the Foundation of a Dual-Native Tradition at Moose Factory," Carol Judd focuses on the same general region and time as Morantz and Bishop: James Bay in the eighteenth century. But Judd's paper is very different, owing to her historian's lenses, interest in biography, and narrative predispositions. Accordingly, Judd contrasts Sakie, a homeguard Cree "Captain" or leader, and Esquawenoe, also called Snuff the Blanket, a leader of the upland or inland Cree. Sakie comes across as a savvy, influential, crafty leader (even though the traders regarded him—in Judd's words—as a "mixed blessing at best and a drunken albatross at worst"), who played off French against English and perhaps one English fort (Albany) against another (Moose Factory). In contrast, Esquawenoe or Snuff the Blanket seems to have been far less dependent on the trade than Sakie, coming to the post only once a year for lavish presents and an exchange. Yet Judd argues that his independence or freedom was "more illusory than real." Snuff the Blanket was also dealing with the French, and because the British suspected him (correctly, Judd says) of collaboration with the French, he was put in jail where he committed suicide.

Biography of Indians participating in the trade is a difficult task; elsewhere, Bishop (1980:191) has pointed out the biases, selectivity, and "incompleteness" in biographical data and the dangers involved in constructing a life from reports "filtered through the eyes of persons of an alien culture" (see also Krech 1982). Still, Judd's essay continues the important task of constructing native biography, of adding to the necessary effort to bring Indians to life as creative, thinking, plotting, active human participants in the trade. It is too seldom done in ethnohistorical accounts.

The two final essays shift the focus of the volume from the trade of Northern Algonquians in the eastern Subarctic to Northern Athapaskans in the western Subarctic. In "The Trade of the Slavey and Dogrib at Fort Simpson in the Early Nineteenth Century," Shepard Krech III turns to a region largely neglected in fur-trade historiography: the early nineteenth-century Mackenzie River. This paper describes and analyses the trade at Fort Simpson, the major post in the area, and assesses its impact on the Northern Athapaskan Dogrib and Slavey. Empirical statements on the economics of the exchange are based in large part on an analysis of over sixteen hundred transactions by roughly two hundred trappers, whose exchanges were recorded in Indian account books in the 1820's. Up to now, data of these sort have been neglected by historians of the trade, although fur-trade historiography based on account books was pioneered by Ray (1974, Ray and

Freeman 1978) and thus is not new. The core of this paper concerns the exchange of furs and skins for various goods, a surprising quantity of which are dry goods of various types; of interest also are diseases and interethnic relations, which, together with the exchange, constituted in part the context in which native adaptations unfolded.

In this paper it is asked, as in a number of the others, whether it is possible to specify the degree to which Indians were dependent on or independent of the trade. The conclusion here is that while dependence (defined primarily by reliance on goods necessary for survival and by other economic indices) was not great at Fort Simpson in the 1820's, it is impossible to understand the adaptations of natives without embedding them firmly and concretely in the context of the exchange itself, of diseases brought by traders, and of interethnic tensions spawned by the desire for middleman profits or for furs. The success of traditional adaptations was contingent upon a smooth accommodation to trade-related factors.

The data presented and analysed in the essays by Bishop, Judd, Krech, and Morantz once again have a bearing on the chronological framework used by most ethnologists in their analyses of the post-contact historic era. For the period following the era of earliest contact with Europeans, labels such as "stabilized fur and mission" (Helm and Leacock 1971) or "contact-traditional" (Helm et al. 1975; Helm, Rogers, and Smith 1981) have been used by ethnologists. These terms evoke a sense of tradition and stability, of undramatic change, which seems clearly at variance with the impact of events in some sections of the Subarctic. It might make far more sense to develop and use a chronological framework consisting of five, not three, eras: (1) *protohistoric era* for the era beginning with the first knowledge of Europeans, with the initial arrival of their goods or impact of their diseases, their economic desires on economic-related hostilities; (2) *early fur-trade era*, initiated by direct trade with Europeans (Euro-Canadians), at a post in or near a group's territory or involving travel to a distant post; (3) *fur and mission era,* starting with missionary contact and involving more lasting links with the major agents of Euro-Canadian society, formal education and the like; and (4) *welfare-commercial era* and (5) *government-industrial era* for, roughly, the first half of the twentieth century and the decades since 1950 respectively (see also Bishop and Ray 1976; Krech 1983, 1984).[2]

The final essay, "The Microeconomics of Southern Chipewyan Fur-Trade History," by Robert Jarvenpa and Hetty Jo Brumbach, continues the focus on Northern Athapaskans and as it happens relates directly to Ray's search for the origins of welfare dependence in the late nineteenth and early twentieth centuries. Jarvenpa and Brumbach explore Chipewyan material adaptations in a broadly conceived ecological context, in much the same way that Bishop, Morantz, and Krech are concerned with Cree, Slavey and Dogrib economic adaptations. This paper is especially valuable because it demonstrates the changes in the adaptations of Upper Churchill Chipewyan in the final decade of the nineteenth century in comparison to the first two-thirds of that century. In the 1890's, gatherings at the post became more frequent, winter hunting took place closer to the post, and operating expenses (goods) rose while fur returns declined. An analysis of Chipewyan accounts (the same type of data used by Krech) reveals that Chipewyans were in debt and spent a large proportion (39 per cent) of their credit on food, but that their diet would have had to have been heavily supplemented by hunting to have been at all sufficient.*

Readers of this collection will become more fully aware both of the issues considered important today by anthropologists, geographers, and historians interested broadly in native economic history and of the methods increasingly being used to arrive at empirically based answers to questions. In addition to furthering our understanding of native adaptations in the trade, I hope the papers will themselves spawn meaningful questions and spur others, through the use of more sophisticated techniques or more refined textual interpretations, to greater advances in fur-trade scholarship.

---

*Weights and measures in these texts are given in imperial units since those are the measurements used in the essential records.

Notes

Acknowledgements: I am grateful for the comments of Charles Bishop, Hetty Jo Brumbach, Toby Morantz, Skip Ray, and Shirlee Anne Smith on this Introduction.

1. Ray's findings receive support also in an empirical study of Naskapi who traded at Fort Nascopie in Quebec by Marc Hammond (1981), who presented his findings at the ASE symposium. Hammond reported that from the mid-nineteenth century on, Fort Nascopie was stocked with food, following game depletions and as a hedge against starvation. By 1890, the Canadian government, through the Hudson's Bay Company, was distributing flour and other relief, and just before the turn of the century, Naskapi began to rush to the post each summer to exchange their labour for goods. Events in the first half of the twentieth century were similar, and by 1953 these Naskapi had been "brought to their knees."
2. Compare Krech (1983), where post-contact chronology distinguishes four stages: protohistoric, early fur trade, fur and mission, and government-industrial. There, the fur and mission era is regarded as lasting from the advent of missionaries until post-1940 or so. In this Introduction, fur and mission is split into two eras: fur and mission and welfare—commercial, in recognition of the notion that "the decades beginning in the 1880s and 1890s were very important from the standpoint of changes in native adaptations" (Krech 1983:139).

References Cited

Axtell, James
  1981   The European and the Indian: Essays in the Ethnohistory of Colonial North
         America. New York: Oxford University Press.
Bishop, Charles A.
  1980   Kwah: A Carrier Chief. *In* Old Trails and New Directions: Papers of the Third North
         American Fur Trade Conference. Carol M. Judd and Arthur J. Ray, eds., pp.
         191–204. Toronto: University of Toronto Press.
Bishop, Charles A., and Shepard Krech III
  1980   Matriorganization: The Basis of Aboriginal Subarctic Social Organization. Arctic
         Anthropology 17 (2):34–45.
Bishop, Charles A., and Arthur J. Ray
  1976   Ethnohistoric Research in the Central Subarctic: Some Conceptual and Methodolog-
         ical Problems. Western Canadian Journal of Anthropology 6 (1):117–44.
Eccles, W.J.
  1979   A Belated Review of Harold Adams Innis, *The Fur Trade in Canada.* Canadian
         Historical Review 60:419–41.
  1981   A Response to Hugh M. Grant on Innis. Canadian Historical Review 62:323–29.
Feit, Harvey A.
  1982   The Future of Hunters within Nation-States: Anthropology and the James Bay Cree.
         In Politics and History in Band Society. Eleanor Leacock and Richard Lee, eds., pp.
         373–412. Cambridge: Cambridge University Press.
Godelier, Maurice
  1980   The Emergence and Development of Marxism in Anthropology in France. *In* Soviet
         and Western Anthropology. Ernest Gellner, ed., pp. 3–17. New York: Columbia
         University Press.
Grant, Hugh M.
  1981   One Step Forward, Two Steps Back: Innis, Eccles and the Canadian Fur Trade.
         Canadian Historical Review 62:304–322.
Hammond, Marc
  1981   Why Did the Naskapis of Quebec Quit Their Life on the Land? Paper presented at
         the 1981 Annual Meeting of the American Society for Ethnohistory.
Helm, June, and Eleanor B. Leacock
  1971   The Hunting Tribes of Subarctic Canada. *In* North American Indians in Historical
         Perspective. Eleanor B. Leacock and Nancie O. Lurie, eds., pp. 343–74. New York:
         Random House.
Helm, June et al.
  1975   The Contact History of the Subarctic Athapaskans: An Overview. *In* Proceedings:
         Northern Athapaskan Conference, 1971. Vol. 1. Annette McFadyen Clark, ed., pp.
         302–46. Ottawa: National Museums of Canada.
Helm, June, Edward S. Rogers, and James G.E. Smith
  1981   Intercultural Relations and Cultural Change in the Shield and Mackenzie Border-
         lands. *In* Handbook of North American Indians. Vol. 6. Subarctic. William C.
         Sturtevant, gen. ed. June Helm, ed., pp. 146–57. Washington, D.C.: Smithsonian
         Institution.
Krech, Shepard III
  1980   Northern Athapaskan Ethnology in the 1970's. Annual Review of Anthropology
         9:83–100.
  1982   The Death of Barbue, A Kutchin Trading Chief. Arctic 35:429–37.
  1983   The Influence of Diseases and the Fur Trade on Arctic Drainage Lowlands Dene,
         1800–1850. Journal of Anthropological Research 39:123–46.
  1984   Ethnohistory and Ethnography in the Subarctic (review article). American Anthro-
         pologist, in press.

Leacock, Eleanor
    1954   The Montagnais "Hunting Territory" and the Fur Trade. American Anthropological Association Memoir 78.
    1982   Relations of Production in Band Society. *In* Politics and History in Band Society. Eleanor Leacock and Richard Lee, eds., pp. 159-70. Cambridge: Cambridge University Press.
Leacock, Eleanor, and Richard B. Lee
    1982   Introduction. *In* Politics and History in Band Society. Eleanor Leacock and Richard Lee, eds., pp. 1-20. Cambridge: Cambridge University Press.
Lee, Richard B.
    1979   The !Kung San: Men, Women, and Work in a Foraging Society. New York and Cambridge: Cambridge University Press.
Morantz, Toby
    1980   The Fur Trade and the Cree of James Bay. *In* Old Trails and New Directions: Papers of the Third North American Fur Trade Conference. Carol M. Judd and Arthur J. Ray, eds., pp. 39-58. Toronto: University of Toronto Press.
    1983   An Ethnohistoric Study of Eastern James Bay Cree Social Organization, 1700-1850. National Museum of Man Mercury Series. Canadian Ethnology Service Paper No. 88. Ottawa: National Museums of Canada.
Ray, Arthur J.
    1974   Indians in the Fur Trade: Their Role as Hunters, Trappers, and Middlemen in the Lands Southwest of Hudson Bay, 1660-1870. Toronto: University of Toronto Press.
Ray, Arthur J., and Donald B. Freeman
    1978   "Give Us Good Measure": An Economic Analysis of Relations between the Indians and the Hudson's Bay Company before 1763. Toronto: University of Toronto Press.
Rotstein, Abraham
    1977   Innis: The Alchemy of Fur and Wheat. Journal of Canadian Studies/Revue d'Etudes Canadiennes 12 (5):6-31.
Sahlins, Marshall
    1972   Stone Age Economics. Chicago: Aldine
Tanner, Adrian
    1979   Bringing Home Animals: Religious Ideology and Mode of Production of the Mistassini Cree Hunters. New York: St. Martin's Press.
Williams, Glyndwr
    1980   Epilogue: Old Trails and New Directions. *In* Old Trails and New Directions: Papers of the Third North American Fur Trade Conference. Carol M. Judd and Arthur J. Ray, eds., pp. 309-18. Toronto: University of Toronto Press.
Woodburn, James
    1982   Egalitarian Societies. Man 17:431-51.

1

Periodic Shortages, Native Welfare, and the Hudson's Bay Company 1670–1930

Arthur J. Ray

Today, various forms of government assistance provide the principal sources of income for many northern Canadian native settlements, thereby supporting a welfare society. It is widely believed that this modern welfare society emerged recently, as the fur trade declined and was no longer able to provide native people with the income they needed to obtain basic necessities. The historical chronologies that have been most widely used by ethnologists reflect this belief. The most recent example is the chronology employed as the framework in the Smithsonian Subarctic Handbook, which dates the end of the "stabilized fur and mission stage," the end of the era of fur-trade society in other words, at 1945. This was the time when the so-called "modern era" began, when, it is thought, "the Canadian government began to assume direct responsibility for native health, education, and welfare needs long neglected" (Helm, Rogers, and Smith 1981:149). When reflecting upon this conceptualization of the economic history of native peoples, one must question whether it is a valid and useful way to view the cultural and economic transformations that have taken place in the north (see also Bishop and Ray 1976, Krech 1983). Does it, for example, give a proper appreciation of the continuities of northern Indian cultures and the roots of contemporary native economic problems? To answer this and related questions it is necessary to examine the problems of resource shortages in the north and the ways in which the native peoples and the incoming European traders dealt with them.

Today, opinions are divided whether hunting, fishing, and gathering societies generally faced a problem of chronic starvation—the more traditional viewpoint—or whether they were the original affluent societies, as Marshall Sahlins has suggested. Sahlins does not deny that occasional starvation plagued hunters and gatherers, but, as he points out, more advanced horticulturalists and farmers faced this problem as well. Of greater importance, Sahlins posits that demand for basic commodities is curtailed in "primitive economies" and brought into line with available resources. He further argues that only a relatively small amount of time is devoted to basic subsistence pursuits (Sahlins 1972:1-100 passim).[1]

In Sahlins's terms it is clear that the parkland-grassland bison hunters, the barren ground caribou hunters, the Ojibwa fishing villagers, the Iroquoian horticulturalists, and the wood bison-moose hunters of the Peace River country could probably be classified as "affluent." All had reasonably stable food resources that normally exceeded the requirements of the local populations. The situation of hunters of the full boreal forest at the time of contact is more uncertain. For this region, references abound concerning food shortages during the early years of contact. The problem with such accounts, however, is that native complaints of privation were part of their bargaining strategy, and therefore Indians not infrequently exaggerated their actual situation. This is not meant to suggest that Indians did not experience real hardships; rather, that it is risky to accept all such accounts at face value without carefully considering the contexts in which they were made.

More to the point, it is clear that native people had developed resource management and redistribution strategies in the pre-contact period which served to minimize the risk of severe privation as a consequence of localized short-term scarcities of basic staples. Traditionally, most native groups had the capability of exploiting a wide range of resources even in areas where hunting activities were highly focused on single species such as the grassland bison, moose, or barren ground caribou. If these primary game were not readily available, secondary ones such as red deer (wapiti), woodland caribou, and beaver were pursued (Ray 1974:27-50). Furthermore, in many areas, such as the flanks of the shield uplands, the parklands, and the northern transitional forests, the seasonal hunting cycle took groups on lengthy migratory routes that exposed them to a wide variety of ecological niches, any one of which could be resorted to in times of need. Furthermore, these cycles of movement lessened the risk of overhunting any single locality. The need for spatial flexibility in pre-contact big-game economies was recognized in the territorial control system that emerged. As E.S. Rogers has shown, in the boreal forest, native groups tended to hunt in the same areas every year—their hunting range. However, if game was scarce in that range, they could temporarily hunt on the lands of their neighbours to obtain basic necessities (Rogers 1963). On the other hand, hunting or trapping for essentially commercial purposes was not permitted under the hunting range system.

While potential scarcity was minimized by exploiting diverse ranges (parkland-grassland, parkland-boreal forest, shield upland-Hudson Bay lowland, and northern transitional forest-tundra) and by having the capability to hunt a number of different species of game, the possibility of serious shortages stemming from unusual weather conditions, forest fires, and faunal epidemics still existed. To deal with these occasional hard times, native economies were structured to reinforce co-operation and sharing. Under such a system, general reciprocity was the dominant mode of internal exchange. Individuals were expected to share whatever surpluses they had with their families, close relatives, and members of their band. Indeed, as European traders learned, aid was often extended to strangers. According to the rules of general reciprocity, one did not expect an immediate return for aid rendered nor was any economic value placed on the obligation. The reciprocal obligation that accrued was generalized. The giver simply expected help in return when he was in need. In this way, general reciprocity served to knit groups together by a series of mutual obligations to render aid. This increased the survival chances of all members of the group. Sharing basic necessities of life with neighbouring groups was accomplished through the hunting-range system described above. To reinforce the co-operative orientation of their cultures, most groups, except perhaps those in the grassland area, negatively sanctioned the hoarding of wealth by individuals.[2] This does not mean that Indians were not interested in gaining access to wealth. Rather, individuals derived prestige from wealth by giving it away. For instance, generosity was a virtue that was expected of all chiefs or "captains," as the Europeans called them. It appears that most Indian trading captains distributed their wealth to their followers, thereby enhancing their social position (Ray and Freeman 1978:63–69).

The fur trade negatively affected Indian economies in two fundamental ways. It served to increase the risk of serious resource shortages for native groups. At the same time, it increasingly undermined their ability to deal with this problem. For example, the fur trade tended to favour economic specialization among all native groups who took part in it. One of the earliest forms of specialization involved commercial trapping. Native people had always taken furs for their own use in making clothing. Probably the best known example was the use of beaver pelts to make beaver robes and coats. Indians began to hunt more selectively when they trapped for commercial purposes, often choosing furs that fetched the best prices. Initially, beaver and marten loomed large in the trade.

Very quickly, another specialty emerged: engaging in the trade as middlemen. Indians who became middlemen devoted little or no time to commercial trapping activities. Instead, they obtained furs from other Indian groups in exchange for trade goods they had acquired from Europeans. Middlemen often travelled great distances to carry on this exchange. It meant that less time could be spent than traditionally had been the case in food-gathering activities in the summer. To compensate, food supplies had to be secured from Europeans, from other Indian groups, or by increasing the role of women and children in food-gathering activities.

Still other groups specialized by becoming commercial hunters who supplied trading posts with provisions or "country produce," as it was called. Probably the most notable early examples of these types of groups were the homeguard Indians of the Hudson Bay lowlands—Cree at Moose Factory, Fort Albany, Fort Severn, York Factory, and Fort Churchill in the early years and Chipewyan at the latter post by the late eighteenth century; Ojibwa in the region between Lake Superior and Lake of the Woods, who supplied wild rice and, later, corn; and plains-dwelling Assiniboine, Blackfoot, and Cree, who supplied pemmican in the Parkland area (Ray 1974:51–57; Ray and Freeman 1978:39–51; Moodie 1980). Indeed, by the early nineteenth century, the number of Indians who specialized as commercial hunters was probably very large, given the proliferation of trading posts that took place during the period of intensive competition and considering that each post received a sizeable portion of its foods from local natives.

The commercialization of native economies and the concomitant specialization of resource orientation began to favour a shift in traditional attitudes toward sharing among unrelated groups. Though it appears that bands continued to be willing to share basic survival resources with their neighbours, to define survival needs clearly became increasingly difficult. For instance, in the precommercial era it was easy to determine how much hunting of any given species was necessary for a group to meet its immediate requirements for food, clothing, and shelter. But with the advent of the fur trade and the growing dependence on imported technologies, it was no longer a simple task to define need. Rather than directly applying an aboriginal technology to the local environment to obtain food, clothing, and shelter, the Indians, through the process of technological replacement, were increasingly caught in the trap of having to buy the tools that they needed to hunt, fish, and trap, to say nothing of utensils, blankets, and cloth. Native groups thus faced a problem whose impact on resource use was circular and cumulative. Items of European origin that originally were basically novel or luxury articles—firearms, hatchets, knives, and kettles, to name a few—became essentials. Partly for this reason, despite a traditional conservational attitude—in the sense that animals were hunted only to the degree that they were needed for food or clothing—once they began to trade, Indians overexploited many of their environments in response to the demands of an open-ended market.

The implications of this development for interband relations, resource use, and group survival can perhaps best be illustrated by examining the situation of the Blackfoot and their neighbours. In the 1750's, Anthony Henday accompanied a group of the Assiniboine and Cree who travelled from York Factory to the lands of the Blackfoot. Henday learned from his companions that the Blackfoot would allow them to hunt bison freely. The situation with regard to beaver was more complex, however. Henday tried to persuade the Assiniboine and Cree accompanying him to trap beaver. They refused. Not only was trapping unnecessary, since trading in the spring would give them more furs than they could carry in their canoes, but they indicated that the Blackfoot would kill them if they trapped beaver in Blackfoot territory (Burpee 1907:91–122). Curiously, perhaps, subsequent entries in Henday's journal indicate that his Indian companions were trapping beaver. However, the women were using the pelts to make winter clothing (ibid.). In short, the Blackfoot prohibition related only to commercial trapping. The prohibition caused no hardship for the Assiniboine and Cree at this time because the Blackfoot provided more furs for trade than the former middlemen needed to satisfy their trade good requirements and allowed them to collect the furs they needed to survive the winter.

A century later the situation had changed drastically. Many former luxuries had become necessities. Growing trapping pressures led to the serious depletion of many fur-bearing animals in the area. Fortunately, while animal populations were under growing stress, the fur trade offered Indians of the parkland-grassland area an alternative economic opportunity. Bison could be commercially hunted to meet the burgeoning provision requirements of the fur trade. This was a significant development for the Blackfoot and their confederates as well as for their former trading partners, the Assiniboine and Cree. The expansion of the fur-trade operations of the Hudson's Bay and the North West Companies had displaced the Assiniboine and Cree from their middleman positions and provided the Blackfoot with direct access to European trading posts. For this reason, the Assiniboine and Cree who lived in the parkland became suppliers of provisions. By selling pemmican and grease to the traders, they could still obtain the European articles that they formerly obtained through their prairie trading networks (Ray 1974:131–35).

The commercialization of the buffalo hunt had several unfortunate results. Hunting pressures began to deplete this once abundant food resource. By the 1850's, bison ranges were beginning to contract. Increasingly, Assiniboine and Cree groups were forced to encroach on Blackfoot lands in pursuit of the dwindling herds. As the bison diminished in numbers, they became more valuable. Also, bison were absolutely essential for the highly specialized economies that had developed among the plains Assiniboine, Blackfoot, and Cree. Not surprisingly, the Blackfoot were no longer willing to share this resource with their neighbours (Ray 1974:223–26). They now competed with the Assiniboine and Cree for control over a valuable commercial subsistence resource that was in rapid decline. Consequently, persistent hostility developed between the Assiniboine-Plains Cree and the Blackfoot.[3]

The growing unwillingness of the Blackfoot to share their territory occurred in many other areas of Rupert's Land as an outgrowth of resource depletion. For instance, by 1821 beaver and other valuable fur-bearing animals were becoming scarce throughout the woodlands between James Bay and the Churchill River. Hudson's Bay Company traders and Indians alike began to see the need for conservation. However, the traditional tenure system was not well suited to a situation in which scarcity had become a chronic and widespread problem instead of an occasional and localized one. When certain Indian bands attempted to husband the fur resources in their hunting and trapping ranges by curtailing trapping activities, their neighbours frequently moved in and collected the furs (Ray 1975:61–62; Bishop 1970:10–11; Krech, this volume). While this might have been appropriate according to old customs, it meant that conservation schemes were virtually impossible to implement when the need for them arose. Local Indian bands apparently grew resentful of the incursions of their neighbours for trapping, but the band organization of the Subarctic offered no effective means of rationalizing access to or use of resources that were being depleted at an accelerating rate. The situation was particularly complicated with respect to beaver. This animal had always been a secondary source of food after moose and woodland caribou. With the destruction of these two big-game animal populations because of overhunting, beaver took on added significance in the provision quest of groups living in the boreal forest. Thus, beaver was not purely the commercial resource that some other fur bearers, such as marten, mink, and otter, were (Ray 1975:65).

Under the direction of Sir George Simpson, the Hudson's Bay Company attempted to use its considerable economic power to introduce a conservation programme. In areas where it held a monopoly, it began to exert pressures on local bands to restrict their trapping activities to assigned territories. The company's efforts were effective only in those areas where caribou populations had already declined sharply, forcing the Indians to shift to food sources that were less mobile, usually fish and hare (Ray 1975:61; Bishop 1970:10–14). In other places, particularly in districts where competition persisted, such as along the American border, encroachment of bands on each other's territories continued to be a vexing problem and the subject of considerable commentary in Hudson's Bay Company correspondence.[4]

Thus, as resources became valuable commercially and in turn more scarce as a result of heavy hunting and trapping, more rigid and spatially restrictive land-tenure systems began to emerge. The hunting range was supplanted by the system of band territories in many areas by the middle of the nineteenth century. During the late nineteenth century and the early part of this century, the trap line replaced this system in most of the woodland areas. In this way the mobility of the native peoples was increasingly curtailed.

Resource depletions depressed native economies in another important way. By the early nineteenth century, reduction of game had forced many woodland groups living south and east of the Churchill River to rely more intensively on less valuable fur-bearing animals, such as muskrat, and on alternative sources of food, such as hare and fish. This trend increased the hardships that several groups experienced because many of these less valuable species, fish excepted, exhibited more erratic fluctuations in their population cycles. For example, beaver and marten populations vary less from high point to low point, enjoy greater population wave lengths, and endure less erratic cycles than do muskrat and hare. Because of resource depletion, Indians were forced to spend more time hunting and trapping species of lesser value and more uncertain yield. In the 1820's Governor Simpson remarked, not surprisingly, that the Ojibwa living in the muskrat country of the lower Saskatchewan River area had a feast-and-famine economy, owing to oscillations in the population of this aquatic animal.[5]

Similarly, in areas where hare had become the dominant food source in the late nineteenth and early twentieth centuries, native economies were on a very precarious footing. This was especially true of the Hudson Bay-James Bay lowlands. When hare populations dropped sharply, Indians were forced to divert their attentions from trapping to the food quest.[6] Consequently, fur returns from posts like Moose Factory and Fort Albany exhibit great fluctuations. These variations are often more a consequence of the changing availability of hare than a reflection of the population cycles of the principal fur bearers (various fox) in the area.[7] Only those Indians who had access to a good fishery, usually sturgeon or whitefish, escaped the hardships that resulted from overdependence on hare.

The plight of Indians who took up residence in the Hudson Bay-James Bay lowland area was not brought about solely by overhunting. It was also in part the consequence of a major alteration that they made in their pre-contact ecological cycle. As noted earlier, prior to European penetration into the region, Indians apparently did not inhabit the lowlands throughout the year. There simply was not enough game. Therefore, they only visited the region during the summer to hunt geese and to fish, retreating to the Shield uplands in winter. Nevertheless, the arrival of the Hudson's Bay Company and the establishment of trading posts on the shores of Hudson and James Bays meant that a need developed for post hunters. These hunters were particularly important for the spring and autumn goose hunts, and geese became one of the principal ingredients in the men's diet at the posts.[8] But to obtain a maximum return on the fall hunt, Indians often had to remain in the lowlands near the posts long after they normally would have returned inland to hunt and trap. In this way, specialization as post hunters favoured the permanent occupation of the Hudson Bay-James Bay lowlands and curtailed the spatial mobility of the Cree and Chipewyan who were involved. In essence, they discontinued the aboriginal practice of moving through their hunting range to seasonal surpluses, and instead developed a symbiotic relationship with the Hudson's Bay Company post where regional surpluses were stockpiled (see

Fig. 1). When the Indians faced privation, usually in the winter, they turned to the company for relief, which was always provided.

Even when Indian groups did not attach themselves to trading posts as provision suppliers, involvement in the fur trade often curtailed the exploitation of a diverse environment in favour of a new scheme that was more narrowly focused and riskier in terms of the food quest. For example, as noted above, the Chipewyan originally occupied the food-rich northern transitional forest-tundra zone, where they subsisted principally on moose and barren ground caribou (Gillespie 1975). This was not prime fur country, however. As

FIGURE 1

CHANGING SPATIAL ECOLOGY OF THE NORTH

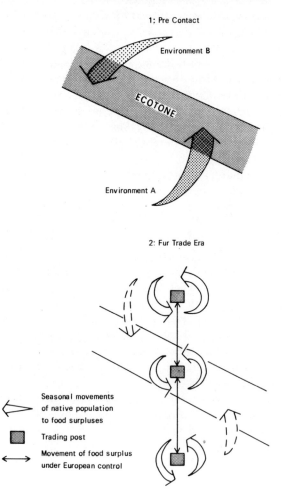

the Chipewyan were drawn into the fur trade in the eighteenth century, bands responded in three ways. Some drew near to Fort Churchill and became post hunters, with results that have already been described. Others became middlemen. Still others began to trap. Both of the latter two groups were drawn southwestward into the boreal forest where furs were more plentiful. These forests were located northeast of Great Slave, Athabasca, and Reindeer Lakes. However, while this ecozone was a better trapping environment, it was not as well stocked with game as their aboriginal homeland had been.[9] The increased population pressure on local resources that would have been the consequence of this historical migration must have further undermined the ability of these micro-environments to support a sound big-game economy.

When these developments are considered together, it is clear that one of the most far-reaching aspects of European expansion into the north involved overturning basic aboriginal ecological strategies. While pre-contact Indian bands often followed extensive migration circuits to take advantage of seasonal food surpluses, Europeans were unable to adopt this approach. Trade required the maintenance of large, spatially fixed settlements, together with rigid time schedules for cargo shipments along set routeways. This meant that the European companies had to devise sophisticated logistical systems that could move food from surplus areas to their posts for storage and redistribution. Needless to say, this was a revolutionary ecological strategy for northern Canada.

Generally, the significance of this revolution has been overlooked. Surely it was as important as the technological innovations that were introduced to the native economies, but most attention has been addressed to this latter issue. By being able to move large stocks of food from surplus areas (the grasslands, the Peace River country, the fisheries on the edge of the Shield, and wild rice areas) and by importing it from eastern North America and Europe, the traders not only managed to maintain their posts, but also increasingly were able to sustain native populations in many areas that were either initially marginal in terms of provisions or became so because of overhunting. Indeed, as the late nineteenth century progressed, country provisions became more unreliable in most areas of historic Rupert's Land, and foodstuffs imported from eastern Canada and Europe or purchased from the developing prairie farming community of Red River had to be counted on more and more. Throughout the old area of Rupert's Land native peoples grew to depend on the trading posts for food. This dependence emerged partly out of necessity and partly out of the deliberate policy of the Hudson Bay Company. As noted, when country food stocks declined, native people had to spend more time searching for food; therefore, they had less time to devote to trapping activities. To combat this trend, in many areas the Hudson's Bay Company imported flour and sold it well below cost to the Indians.[10] It was hoped that this subsidy would encourage trapping. The policy was generally effective, although it served to further reduce native self-sufficiency in subsistence and to orient their diet toward a much higher starch intake than had been the case traditionally.

As native vulnerability to shortages of basic staples increased, the European traders were better able to manipulate them to serve their own interests. After 1821, one of the principal concerns of the Hudson's Bay Company involved maintaining a sufficiently large and low-cost labour force in the regions south and east of the Churchill River to assure that a profitable fur trade would continue. This meant that large scale emigration of native people from seriously depleted areas, such as the Nelson and Hay Rivers territories, to non-fur-producing regions, such as the Red River Colony, was strongly discouraged (Ray 1974:218). Furthermore, company hiring policies largely excluded Indians from occupations that involved work during the winter trapping season (Judd 1980:307). Instead, Indians were generally employed during the summer when they were hired to man boat brigades and carry on unskilled maintenance work around posts or to serve as hunters and fishermen. Significantly, there never were enough of these low-paying seasonal jobs to hire all who might have wished to be employed. Therefore, the practice developed of awarding summer jobs only to the most reliable hunters and trappers, mainly those who had paid their debts. Housing was also often provided for them at the post.[11] In this way, the employment practices of the Hudson's Bay Company were specifically designed to encourage Indians to remain in the traditional hunting and trapping sector of the economy well beyond the time that many were finding it difficult to do so.

Additional support for, and control of, native people was achieved by the extension of credit as well as by the distribution of gratuities. The former was made available to able-bodied adult males; the latter to widows, orphans, the aged, and the infirm. The use of credit in the fur trade can be traced back to the earliest days of the Hudson's Bay Company's operations. By advancing to Indians outfits of goods, the company, and other traders as well, hoped to secure the future returns of hunts; credit, as well as gratuities, served to tide Indians over during times of poor hunting and trapping. Thus, from the beginning, debt and gratuities became essential to the fur trade. When European competition for Indians' furs was modest and the fur market steady or rising, the system was not too costly, and it gave Europeans greater control over the Indians.[12]

The debt-gratuity system became increasingly troublesome for the fur traders as time passed. When Indians specialized economically, and as resource depletion became an ever more serious problem, Indians grew more vulnerable to shortages of food and low fur returns. Hard times occurred with increasing frequency, and in some areas, such as the Hudson Bay-James Bay lowlands, inadequate supplies of food had become a chronic problem by the turn of this century.[13] While traditional sharing practices continued to operate within Indian bands, deprivation could only be alleviated by increasingly resorting to the Hudson's Bay Company posts for gratuities and credit. At the same time, the ability, and perhaps willingness, of Indians to repay their debts seems to have diminished.

Reflecting these changing conditions, by the late nineteenth century the Hudson's Bay Company adopted a policy of discounting the face value of all Indian debts by 25 per cent at the time they were issued. Thus, for every 100 Made Beaver (MB) of credit issued to an Indian only 75 MB was entered into the account books. Furthermore, any credit outstanding after one year was written off as a bad debt.[14]

The company could well afford to write off debts in this fashion. The standards of trade that it used to value goods and furs allowed for a very considerable gross profit margin.[15] Indeed, it could be argued that the standards not only served to underwrite the credit/gratuity system, but that they increasingly made it necessary. For instance, the resource base continued to decline to the point that in some areas native purchasing power was no longer adequate to serve basic Indian consumer requirements. The Hudson's Bay Company could have relieved the plight of the Indians by lowering the prices it charged for staple items or by advancing the prices it paid for furs. James Ray, the district manager for James Bay, considered this option as a solution to the problems that native people at Great Whale River faced in the early 1920's. He rejected this course of action as others had done before him. In explaining his decision, he wrote: "Beyond the slight reductions mentioned (for ammunition which has been selling at 100 per cent of cost landed price) I am not in favour of reducing our selling prices for it would be difficult to raise them again when better times shall come to the natives. So it seems the only solution, if it can be called a solution, to the problem is for us to go on advancing to these peoples as if for debt, though they have little hope of ever paying it . . . . If we continue as I proposed, the debt system as a means of keeping the natives alive during the lean years, the Company may in some small measure—be reimbursed by the amounts the natives may be persuaded to pay when the fat years shall come again and in the main, I imagine it will be more easily handled than any system of gratuity we may devise."[16] Thus, Ray preferred the large scale use of credit instead of resorting to a system of more flexible prices or to straight-forward welfare.

Indians living in the southern James Bay area and the Montreal Department had been aware for some time that the Hudson's Bay Company's practice of issuing credit in the form of relatively high priced merchandise was aggravating their economic hardships. Therefore, when the Canadian Pacific Railroad was built, opening the southern portions of Rupert's Land to renewed competition in the late nineteenth century, Indians began to pressure the Hudson's Bay Company traders to give them credit in the form of cash advances, that is, consumer loans. The Indians intended to take this money to the "line" where they could buy their outfits at reduced prices. Indeed, some were said to be prepared to go as far as Montreal and Trois Rivières to get cheaper goods.[17] Not surprisingly, the company traders did not willingly comply with this request. Non-payment of credit in goods represented a potential loss of something less than 50 per cent of face value of the loan. Furthermore, as Inspecting Officer P. McKenzie noted in 1890, "There is no profit to be made in cash advances to Indians in large amounts even supposing they . . . pay up their accounts in full every year."[18]

Of fundamental importance, the extensive use of credit under near monopoly conditions favoured the persistence of a credit/barter economy, using the Made Beaver standards. It was not simply the result of Indian conservatism or an inability on their part to operate in a monetized economy. It served the company's interest to conduct the trade in this fashion until the late nineteenth century. Holding a near monopoly, the Hudson's Bay Company was able to maintain high prices, pay low seasonal wages, and put the Indians under an obligation to it through the extension of credit.

By the final quarter of the nineteenth century the old order was, however, coming under increasing stress. The construction of the Canadian Pacific Railroad along the southern periphery of Rupert's Land not only increased competition, but it also brought a new kind of competitor. Rather than bartering furs for goods as in the past, increasingly, company opponents paid cash for the Indians' returns.[19] The Indians were able to take the money and search out the best prices for the commodities they needed. Traditionally, the prices of trade goods had been relatively constant and most bargaining was focused on the values assigned to furs and country provisions. Direct competition in trade good prices began in most areas of southern and southwestern Rupert's Land in the 1870's with the signing of treaties. Treaty payments injected cash into the local economies and encouraged small travelling pedlars to compete with the Hudson's Bay Company for the treaty money. The building of the Canadian Pacific Railroad thus served to accelerate a new trend by offering small fur buyers and merchants relatively cheap access to the north. The Indians benefited by being able to seek out the best prices for furs and goods rather than having to continue to deal with a single company which largely monopolized fur purchases and goods sales in most areas of the north.

Reflecting this new development, by 1899 the Hudson's Bay Company employed cash and barter standards in all districts except Mackenzie River, and Fur Trade Commissioner C.C. Chipman recommended that steps be taken immediately to introduce it to that district.[20] As Figure 2 shows, by 1922–23 a significant portion (6–35 per cent) of the merchandise transactions of the fur-trade division of the Hudson's Bay Company consisted of cash sales. In the

Lake Huron, Lake Superior, and Athabasca areas, competition was strong and major inroads were being made into the old credit/barter system of trade.

As competition escalated, the issuing of credit became risky once again as it had been in the days of sharp rivalry between the Hudson's Bay and North West Companies in the period from 1790 to 1821. A significant number of

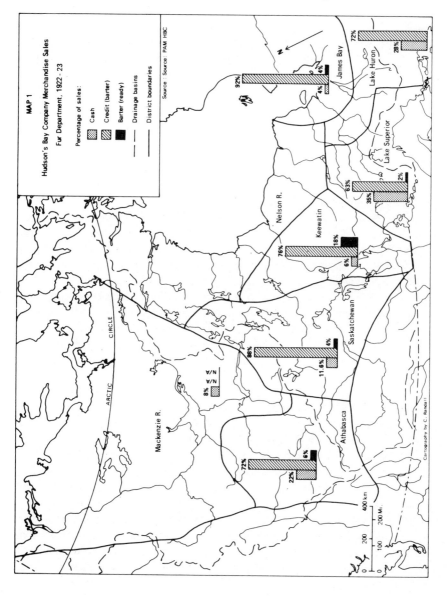

Indians simply preferred to deal with whoever offered the best prices for furs in the spring, regardless of whether or not they owed debts to someone else. Consequently, to offset the growing number of bad debts, in the 1890's the Hudson's Bay Company began a concerted effort to curtail the use of credit in the hope of eventually operating the business on a basis of ready barter or cash. This objective was given the highest priority in so called "frontier districts," or areas open to intensive competition. Such districts included all areas lying within fifty miles of a railway line. Indeed, Indians adjacent to the line were regarded as unreliable because they roamed up and down it looking for the best prices.[21]

Other pressures were also mounting that encouraged the Hudson's Bay Company to curtail the credit/barter trade and to seek relief from the escalating expenses it was incurring giving gratuities to sick and destitute Indians. When fur returns were at a sufficiently high volume, the rate of advance built into the standard of trade provided the company with a gross profit margin that was sufficient to cover overhead costs and assure it an ample net return. By the late nineteenth century, however, the turnover at many posts had declined to the point where this was no longer the case. As Figure 3 shows, by the early 1920's, the Hudson's Bay Company registered net losses in three of its more southerly trading districts. Furthermore, the net gains made in the Moose River and Athabasca districts were relatively small and were based largely on the operations of a few posts that did not experience strong competition.

In the late 1870's and early 1880's, York Factory, one of the company's oldest posts, had so taxed its local environment during its heyday that the trading returns of the local Indians were no longer sufficient to cover the post's operating expenses. W.J. Fortescue, who was in charge of the post at that time, thought the Indians there should be encouraged to enter into treaty negotiations with the government. Fortescue believed this arrangement desirable because the Indian's welfare would then become a government responsibility (Ray 1982). In addition, the annuity payments would constitute a new source of revenue for the company.[22] Thus, by the late nineteenth century, some interest in having the government assume the growing burden of Indian welfare needs was beginning to develop within the company.

While Fortescue was somewhat ahead of his time in making this suggestion, by the early part of this century the government was beginning to underwrite these expenses even outside treaty areas. For example, in the James Bay district, where company gratuity expenses were particularly large compared to other regions, the Hudson's Bay Company frequently submitted bills for this cost to the government. The government usually paid them.[23] In this way, the process of transferring responsibility for a welfare system that was an integral part of the fur trade from the company to the government began in the late nineteenth century. It happened slowly because the government was not eager to assume this burden. And, for humanitarian as well as practical business reasons, the Hudson's Bay Company could not simply abolish the practice of providing gratuities to needy Indians before alternative arrangements had been made. The company's predicament in this regard was

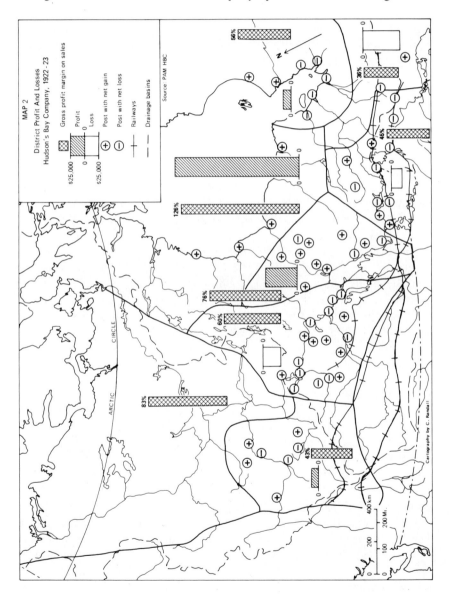

illustrated by the problems that it faced in the Richmond Gulf area in 1924. In that year the Hudson's Bay Company provided over $31,000 in assistance in the form of gratuities, unpaid advances, and sick and destitute accounts. In discussing what should be done about the problem, District Manager James Ray noted: "it is true that the natives are our assets, that we must keep them alive for future profits even though we carry them at a loss till such time shall come. On occasion we have taken large profits out of the post as the following figures will show; Outfit 249 (1919) profit $51,724, Outfit 250 profit $250,497. (year of high realizations) Outfit 251 profits $1,017. (Year when slump in prices occurred) Outfit 252 profit $46,141. Outfit 253 profit $99,430. But the question arises, is it consistent with good business to go on assisting these people to the sum of $25,000 a year till such times as good tax years return to us? There are limits to what the Company may consider generous and judicious treatment" (HBCA DFTR/19).

Clearly the company faced a dilemma. Resources were seriously depleted in the Richmond Gulf area and the natives were reduced to a heavy dependence on two species: hare to serve as food; fox as fur. When either failed, the Indians were destitute. When hare and fox were plentiful, the Indians lived well and the company reaped handsome profits. Similar circumstances prevailed elsewhere.

From the company's economic position, the ideal solution would have the government assume the financial burden of carrying the Indians through lean years. Then, despite deteriorating conditions, the company would be free to continue to prosecute the fur trade on a highly profitable basis. This eventually transpired, and by the 1940's the government was heavily involved in a wide variety of welfare programmes for native people. From the point of view of the traders, one of the negative aspects of this development—a problem apparently not foreseen by Fortesue—was the loss of their control over the local Indian populations. Unlike the company's scheme, government assistance did not carry any obligation to hunt and trap.

From this discussion it is clear that the modern welfare society of the north is not a post-World War II phenomenon. It is deeply rooted in the fur trade. The welfare system was a necessary by-product of several processes: economic specialization by native peoples, a concomitant decreasing spatial mobility, European control of food surpluses and the depletion of resources. Reinforcing these were the labour policies, wage schedules, and standards of trade that assured the Hudson's Bay Company large gross profit margins in good years under near monopoly conditions, but that also allowed native peoples only a marginal return. Some scheme for the additional redistribution of excess profits to the Indians in the form of gratuities and "debt" to supplement their meagre returns from hunting and trapping was absolutely essential. Otherwise, the company could not have stemmed a migration of Indians from the boreal woodlands, and the loss of this labour force would have seriously undermined the prosecution of the trade in many districts south and east of the Churchill River.

Finally, it is clear that we must reconsider the stereotype of the Indian as essentially conservative economically. By holding a virtual monopoly on most aspects of the northern economy until the last quarter of the nineteenth century, the Hudson's Bay Company was the key determinant for development and change. In many areas of the north, it was in the company's interest and ability to perpetuate the use of a credit/barter or truck system until the late nineteenth century. The arrangement discouraged, and often prevented, Indians from leaving this part of the primary resource sector of the economy, even in regions where resources were so depleted that only marginal livelihoods could be sustained. The system failed to encourage the spread of the cash economy through cash buying of furs, partly to insure a higher gross profit margin and partly to minimize losses from bad debts. In summary, the Hudson's Bay Company was partly responsible for limiting the ability of Indians to adjust to the new economic circumstances at the beginning of this century. Debt-ridden, repeatedly blocked from alternative opportunities for over a century, and accustomed to various forms of relief over two centuries, Indians became so evidently demoralized in this century, but the groundwork for this was laid in the more distant past.

Notes

Acknowledgements: The author would like to thank the Social Sciences and Humanities Research Council of Canada and the Faculty Grants Committee of the University of British Columbia for financial assistance they provided to help defray research expenses. I would like to thank the Hudson's Bay Company for permission to consult and quote from their archives. Finally, I would like to express my appreciation to Mrs. Shirlee Anne Smith, Hudson's Bay Company Archivist, and Professor I.M. Spry for commenting on earlier drafts of this paper. The author, of course, is responsible for its contents.

1. Some ethnologists question whether even big-game hunters like the Caribou Eater Chipewyan could be said to have had an aboriginal affluent society (Smith 1978:66–68).
2. After the horse was adopted into the northern plains culture in the early eighteenth century (for Canada), it became a symbol of wealth and Indians did try to accumulate as many as possible. However, it is uncertain whether or not this was simply a post-contact development or was built on earlier traditions.
3. This situation had apparently developed sometime after 1774, judging from the account of M. Cocking, who visited the Blackfoot territory in 1772–73. Trade between the Assiniboine-Cree was still going on. However, shortly thereafter, the inland expansion by the Nor'Westers and the Hudson's Bay Company upset this arrangement.

4. Many comments of this nature can be found in Governor Simpson's correspondence in the Hudson's Bay Company Archives (HBCA A.12) (Dr. Irene M. Spy personal communication 3 March 1981).

5. For discussion of animal population cycles, see Hewitt (1921). Simpson's observation is cited in Ray (1974:121).

6. According to the various documents dealing with the James Bay district between 1880 and 1920, one of the most common causes of poor fur returns was the failure of hare. See, for example, letters from Moose Factory to the Hudson's Bay Company Secretary, 1871-1889, Public Archives of Manitoba, Hudson's Bay Company Archives (hereinafter HBCA), A.11/47. In particular, the letter of 15 September 1890 noted the very poor return and claimed: "The causes of . . . falling off is attributed to scarcity of rabbit, the principal food of the Indians thus preventing them from hunting being occupied all of their time in procuring food. This is most apparent in Rupert River where the decline in these skins is no less than 900 percent. As you are probably aware this scarcity arises from disease, and is periodical running in a cycle of ten to eleven years, with 3 years of maximum and 3 years of minimum" (HBCA A.11/47).

7. This was also true inland on the Shield uplands of northern Ontario (Winterhalder 1980:873-74).

8. Reflecting the importance of these hunts, the correspondence between the posts on the bay almost always commented on the success or failure of the local hunts. The record pertaining to York Factory indicates that geese were one of the cheapest provisions that could be obtained before 1880 (Fortescue to Armit, York Factory, 1 Dec. 1880 [HBCA A/119a, fo. 149].

9. C. Yerbury, personal communication.

10. For example, the Inspection Report for Cumberland District in 1886, recommended using cheap flour in the northern portion of district to discourage Chipewyans from hunting deer (HBCA D.25/1/1). Similar recommendations were made for other parts of the district.

11. William Anderson, Fort Albany, May, 1980 (personal communication). Mr. Anderson served as a company clerk in James Bay.

12. In the early years credit even may have been used to increase Indian fur outputs beyond the level that could have been achieved otherwise. In offering an historical overview of the fur trade, the Fur Trade Department Annual Report for 1929 included the following observation: "It was found then [after natives adopted European goods] that only sufficient game would be killed to meet the natives' own requirements, and so a plan was adopted to overcome that. Advances were given through the chief. These Chiefs and clans were a proud lot. . . . The clan with the largest advance was the most influential, and in order to remain influential all debt had to be paid" (HBCA A.74/43). Regarding the declining ability of the environment in some areas to cover these costs, see Fortescue (HBCA A.11/119a).

13. Beaver were said to be in steady decline as of the early 1890's. Other furs showed the normal cyclical variations. The problem was that the principal food was rabbit, which was said to run in ten- to twelve-year cycles with three years maxima and three years minima. The low points in the cycle frequently caused starvation. (See footnote 6 above.) Many other examples of the adverse effects of food shortages on trapping activities in this area betwen 1880 and 1930 could be cited. For example, Inspection Reports, 1888-90 (HBCA S 54/4-10); Annual Reports, 1890-94 (HBCA A.74/1-3); Fur Trade Reports 1912-24 (HBCA DFTR/1-19).

14. Rules and Regulations, London, 1887, rules 72-76 (HBCA D.26/3). These rules specified further that "doubtful" debts, those beyond current outfit but less than a year old, were to be entered in the accounts at 50 per cent of original value.

15. On several occasions traders pointed out that the indebtedness of the Indians shown in their accounts did not represent the money actually owed the company, given that the debt was in terms of goods advanced and valued as per the standard of trade. The debts thus represented a loss of potential profit. As the inspection report for Bersimi in 1890 indicated, "the profit on goods (supposing the hunter or hunters been paying up pretty regularly for a few years previous) ought to be sufficient to prevent actual loss to the Company" (HBCA D.25/4).

16. Throughout the company's records, suggestions to lower prices are always turned down with the same explanation—that is, Indians would not allow them to be raised again (HBCA DFTR/19).
17. Indians dealt with C.P.R. employees. Also, the railroad had a store car. In the Bersimis and Saguenay Districts cash advances had to be given to combat competition despite company opposition (HBCA D.25/4).
18. Of course, the profit margin would be reduced, given that it became a fur-cash transaction rather than fur and goods in which the company extracted profit both ways (Inspection Report for Bersimis, 1890 [HBCA D.25/4]).
19. By 1898 cash tariffs and barter standards (MB) were in use in the southern portion of the Montreal, Southern, and Northern Departments. Hudson's Bay Company Commisioner C.C. Chipman indicated that the company would soon have to introduce it to the Mackenzie Department before opponents did, as had been the case elsewhere (HBCA A.12/FT 229/3).
20. Evidence for this can be obtained from a variety of sources. In 1880 W.J. Fortescue indicated that the MB tariff for goods was inelastic but that of furs was not (HBCA A.11/119a).
21. From the earliest years of the company's history there were efforts to curtail credit when competition was strong. The efforts usually were unsuccessful, and this was true in the 1880's also. (Report for 1890 [HBCA D.25/4]).
22. A concerted effort was made in treaty areas to obtain as much of this money as was possible. Also credit was extended against Treaty payments (HBCA A.11/119a).
23. See HBCA A.12/FT 243/1 dealing with Destitute Indians and Treaties.

References Cited

Bishop, Charles A.
    1970   The Emergence of Hunting Territories among the Northern Ojibwa. Ethnology 9:1-15.
Bishop, Charles A. and Arthur J. Ray
    1970   Ethnohistoric Research in the Central Subarctic: Some Conceptual and Methodological Problems. Western Canadian Journal of Anthropology 4:116-44.
Burpee, L.J., ed.
    1907   Journal of Journey Performed by Anthony Hendry: to Explore the Country Inland and to Endeavor to Increase the Hudson's Bay Company's Trade, A.D. 1754-1755. Transactions. Royal Society of Canada. Series 3, vol. 1, section 2:91-122.
Gillespie, Beryl G.
    1975   Territorial Expansion of the Chipewyan in the Eighteenth Century. In A.M. Clark, ed., Proceedings: Northern Athapaskan Conference, 1971, vol. 2, pp. 350-88. National Museum of Man Mercury Series. Canadian Ethnology Service Paper No. 27. Ottawa: National Museums of Canada.
Helm, June, Edward S. Rogers, and James G.E. Smith
    1981   Intercultural Relations and Cultural Change in the Shield and Mackenzie Borderlands. In Handbook of North American Indians. Vol. 6, Subarctic. W.C. Sturtevant, gen. ed. June Helm, ed. pp. 145-57. Washington, D.C.: Smithsonian Institution.
Hewitt, C.G.
    1921   The Conservation of Wild Life in Canada. New York: Charles Scribner and Sons.

Hudson's Bay Company Archives (HBCA)
        HBCA A.11/47, 119a. Moose Factory Correspondence Outward 1871-1889
        HBCA A.12/FT. Fur Trade Commissioners Correspondence
        HBCA A.74/1-3, 43. Fur Trade Department Annual Reports 1890-94, 1929
        HBCA D.25/1,4. Inspection Report for Cumberland District 1886, 1890
        HBCA D.26/3. Rules and Regulations, London 1887
        HBCA S.54/4-10. Inspection Reports 1889-90
        HBCA DTFR/1-19. Fur Trade Annual Reports, 1912-24
Judd, Carol M.
    1980   Native Labour and Social Stratification in the Hudson's Bay Company's Northern Department, 1770-1870. Canadian Review of Sociology and Anthropology 17:305-314.
Krech, Shepard III
    1983   The Influence of Disease and the Fur Trade on Arctic Drainage Lowlands Dene, 1800-1850. Journal of Anthropological Research 39:123-146.
Moodie, D. Wayne
    1980   Agriculture and the Fur Trade. *In* C. Judd and A. J. Ray, eds., Old Trails and New Directions, pp. 272-90. Toronto: University of Toronto Press.
Ray, Arthur J.
    1974   Indians in the Fur Trade. Toronto: University of Toronto Press.
    1975   Some Conservation Schemes of the Hudson's Bay Company, 1821-50: An Examination of the Problems of Resource Management in the Fur Trade. Journal of Historical Geography 1 (1):61-62.
    1982   York Factory: The Crises of Transition, 1870-1880. The Beaver (Autumn):26-31.
Ray, Arthur J., and Donald B. Freeman
    1978   Give Us Good Measure. Toronto: University of Toronto Press.
Rogers, Edward S.
    1963   The Hunting Group—Hunting Territory Complex Among the Mistassini. Ottawa: National Museum of Canada Bulletin 195.
Sahlins, Marshall
    1972   Stone Age Economics. Chicago: Aldine.
Smith, James G.E.
    1978   Economic Uncertainty in an "Original Affluent Society": Caribou and Caribou-Eater Chipewyan Adaptive Strategies. Arctic Anthropology 15 (1):68-88.
Winterhalder, B.P.
    1980   Canadian Fur Bearer Cycles and Cree-Ojibwa Hunting and Trapping Practices. American Naturalist 115 (6):870-79.

2

The First Century: Adaptive Changes among the Western James Bay Cree between the Early Seventeenth and Early Eighteenth Centuries

Charles A. Bishop

> While most foraging societies have ideologies which value "tradition" and may seem to manifest resistance to change at the intellectual level . . . this cannot be taken as evidence that nothing ever happened. . . . [T]he assumption that what exists in the present can be equated precisely with what existed in the past can hardly be sustained (Hamilton 1982:231).

> What aspects of hunting-gathering lifestyles as we now find them are relatively autonomous from the colonial setting? How? What does that say about their adaptation to the colonial setting? Answers to these questions require examination of the colonial encounter itself, not just analysis of the hunters and gatherers (Collmann 1982:347-48).

A major difficulty in studies of Northern Algonquians is determining which cultural patterns prevailed at the time of earliest European influence.[1] It is necessary to determine baseline sociocultural conditions in different regions in order both to evaluate post-contact changes and to understand better hunter-gatherer ways of life prior to the changes caused by interaction with representatives of state-type societies. It is usually assumed that processes of change generated by this type of contact differed significantly in magnitude and velocity from those arising from contact with egalitarian or even so-called ranked societies, an assumption based on the fact that most contemporary hunter-gatherer societies are politically dominated by and economically dependent upon the state-organized political systems in which they are embedded.

It is easiest to reconstruct aboriginal culture and its subsequent modifications in those regions where historical records are earliest and most complete. With respect to the Cree Indians, the western James Bay area provides the greatest advantages because this region was mentioned by French traders in the mid-seventeenth century and settled by the Hudson's Bay Company in the 1670's, when posts were established. In this paper, both French accounts and evidence preserved in the Hudson's Bay Company Archives will be used in order to determine baseline conditions in the western James Bay region and to isolate the factors that best explain adaptive modifications among western James Bay Cree between the early seventeenth and early eighteenth centuries.

METHODOLOGICAL AND THEORETICAL ISSUES

Although the origins of present conditions are of considerable interest to anthropologists, the reconstruction of lifeways at the moment of external influence is no easy task. Both archival and archaeological data are very incomplete; and there has been little collaboration between prehistoric archaeologists and historically-minded ethnologists in the Northern Algonquian area, partly because intensive archaeology and ethnohistory both began only in the 1960's (Bishop 1982:254–257). Research strategies that might aid in reconstruction have been either poorly formulated or not at all, and so one may legitimately question the extent to which the evidence used actually reflects prehistoric conditions.[2] Granted, the earliest written materials are often so sketchy that they can be interpreted, and have been, in more than one way. With respect to socioterritorial organization, comparative data from other hunter-gatherers may be of little aid or may create confusion, since these may be the result of prehistoric or historic processes as yet poorly understood.

A deficiency of data is not the only reason for many current problems in reconstruction. Aboriginal reconstruction is to a large degree a function of one's understanding of how cultural systems function and how they change. Since the data themselves do not always provide ready answers, they require interpretation, and interpretation may involve the selection of evidence supporting a priori assumptions. What survived among Northern Algonquians from aboriginal times and how it survived, what changed and how it changed are issues that have over the years created heated debates. At the heart of the matter has been the epistemological question of cultural continuity. To oversimplify, some scholars such as E.S. Rogers (1963) and J.G.E. Smith (1973) have argued for persistence in certain traits, especially features of social organization, often in the face of recognized and documented changes in other areas or aspects of society and culture. Most recently, in an essay purporting to reconstruct aboriginal conditions in the vast Shield and Mackenzie borderlands region of the Subarctic, Rogers and Smith (1981:144) state that "kinship systems were bilateral in type and egobased . . . the flexibility of which has remained evident in the modern context." However, no evidence is given to indicate that aboriginal groupings were flexible, bilateral, egobased kindreds.

It is assumed that because this form of social organization exists today and because it seems to be the most ecologically viable form under present or recent conditions, then similar social adjustments existed in the past. The failure to consider alternative cultural arrangements during prehistoric times when conditions may have differed gives unwarranted emphasis to persistence and directs attention away from processes of change. Indeed, Rogers and Smith (1981:151) assume that little change occurred among interior Northern Algonquians during the first part of what they define as the "early contact" period (1670 to 1763), when they say: "aboriginal subsistence patterns were largely unaltered. To them were simply added the occasional taking of furs, which were exchanged for a limited variety and quantity of trade goods." Others (Bishop 1974:308–27, 1976; Bishop and Smith 1975; Ray 1974), however, provide data indicating that the search for new fur resources in combination with attempts to retain and extend middleman relationships had significantly altered the spatial distribution and hence subsistence patterns of Indians southwest of Hudson Bay by 1763. Also, Hudson's Bay Company fur returns record that large quantities of furs were traded from hinterland Indians during the first half of the eighteenth century, contradicting the idea that Indians only occasionally took fur bearers. In the Mackenzie borderlands region, similar processes, coupled with the impact of disease, were at work (Krech 1983). Thus, the bilateral kindred of later times, here and elsewhere, could have been a consequence of new adaptive strategies rather than simply a "survival" from the prehistoric past.

Some recent field workers among Cree Indians acknowledge that the fur trade produced changes; nevertheless, they describe the Cree ideological system as one in which much has remained the same (Preston 1975; Tanner 1979). These scholars document, in basically contemporary groups, beliefs and practices which are qualitatively distinct from those of Euro-Canadians. The issue, however, is not whether these features are distinctly Indian adaptations; that, few would debate. Rather, the issue is the extent to which they were also aboriginal. Can one say that because certain behavioural practices and beliefs are Ojibwa or Cree practices and beliefs, they have undergone no modification or that the systems of which they are a part have also remained unchanged? Can one say that, because more recent adaptive modes are functionally and systemically efficient under present conditions, they must also represent more ancient adaptive modes under conditions where other systemically linked variables were either absent or different, or where they are unknown? To make such assumptions is extremely risky.

Caution is also required when employing historical materials lest discontinuity with the past in one particular subsystem of culture be extended to the entire cultural system. The use of such loaded terms as "breakup" or "breakdown," implying cultural genocide, erroneously suggests that Indians were mere pawns of mercantile diplomacy, having no say in their own destiny. While the range of options open to Indians may have been narrowed at certain times by circumstances that required adaptive shifts in behaviour, beliefs and practices that remained viable appear to have been retained within the new matrix, but in slightly different form or with slightly altered meaning. In the same way, new beliefs and practices were incorporated which in time came to be considered "traditional" ones.[3]

Reconstruction of baseline culture is facilitated if certain assumptions about prehistoric adaptive strategies are made. One assumption is that Indians, in aboriginal times, did not engage in fur-trapping to the degree that they did by the late seventeenth century, because the satisfaction of physical needs usually took priority over exchange wants. Adaptive strategies, therefore, were temporally geared to maximize subsistence efficiency, and they did not compete or interfere with strategies designed to acquire aboriginal trade materials. Likewise, the historical evidence on Northern Algonquians indicates that stability is more evident in what Marxists refer to as "relations of production" that involve sociopolitical and ideological variables than in technoeconomic "forces of production." While together these define the particular "mode of production" at a given moment in time (see, for example, Lee 1981), abrupt changes more often occur in forces of production, with relations of production tending to be more stable. But since the forces and relations articulate with each other, a transformation will ultimately occur. Stability in relations of production doesn't mean persistence; it means simply that it is through the relations that continuity with the past is maintained.

What creates difficulties of interpretation for the ethnohistorian is that shortly after European trade goods became available, Indian behavioural changes involving a greater emphasis on obtaining pelts seem to have been incorporated in such a way that, given the sketchy evidence, it is difficult to distinguish prehistoric from historic patterns. That is, what may be altered strategies may be regarded as prehistoric, since they may be perceived to differ only slightly from the latter. Consequently, scholars can easily be lulled into the false security of relying upon later historical data, or even field-obtained data, to reconstruct pre-contact conditions. In no sense does this deny the importance of field studies, nor does it imply that nothing can be learned about aboriginal Indians from them. However, until baseline sociocultural patterns—including subsistence strategies, sociopolitical organizations, ideologies, and the distribution and size of various groups—and subsequent historic changes can be determined with reasonable certainty, there is simply no way of knowing whether what is being described is a prehistoric or a post-contact configuration. This paper is an attempt to deal directly with this problem in one area of the Subartic, the western James Bay region.

Exactly when Cree living west of James Bay first were influenced by events farther to the southeast is uncertain, although an early seventeenth century date is suggested. Discounting possible Norse contacts, Henry Hudson was probably the first European to meet a Cree. On his 1610–11 voyage to James Bay, he met and traded with only one Indian (Morton 1973:27–28). More important influences must have occurred through trade networks. One trade route followed the Saguenay River inland to probably include within its sphere Indians southeast of James Bay. The other route was well established, used by the Nipissing to visit the Cree, and was noted by Samuel de Champlain when he visited the Nipissing in 1613. Both trade routes probably pre-dated the arrival of Europeans (Trigger 1976:283, 352). Prehistoric Cree living south of James Bay seem to have been involved in an exchange of moose hides and precious stones (Adams 1961:147) for wampum (Willson 1900:75) and ceramics produced by more southerly Algonquians. The burgeoning fur trade along the St. Lawrence during the first half of the seventeenth century surely augmented exchange relations.

French knowledge of the Cree was probably first obtained from Algonquin middlemen, perhaps during the 1620's and 1630's. The *Jesuit Relations* for 1640 stated that the "Kilistinons" (Cree) "dwell on the rivers of the north sea where the Nipissings go to trade with them" (Thwaites 1896–1901, 18:229). These may have been the Moose River Cree (see Honigmann 1981:229). The Iroquois wars of the 1640's may temporarily have severed trade relations with the Cree and even driven some Algonquin groups to the shores of James Bay (see below). Nevertheless, trade with Cree through Algonquian middlemen via the Saguenay route probably resumed quickly, and the ability of the Jesuits to distinguish four divisions of "Kilistinons," one of which was located just west of James Bay, by the 1650's (Thwaites 1896–1901, 44:325), indicates that their knowledge was growing more precise. The Jesuits knew that upon James Bay "are found, at certain seasons of the year, many surrounding Nations embraced under the general name of Kilistinon" (Thwaites 1896–1901, 46:249).

By at least the 1650's, the French were contacting the Cree directly. The two *coureurs de bois,* Pierre Esprit Radisson and Médard des Groseilliers, on their Mississippi voyage from 1658–1660, learned from the Mascoutens of a nation whose "dwelling was on the side of the salt water in summertime, and in the land in the wintertime. . . . They call themselves Christinos" (Adams 1961:89). Shortly after, Radisson and Groseilliers met Cree on the south shore of Lake Superior: "Here comes a company of Christinos from the Bay of the North Sea" who intended to winter in this area (Adams 1961:95). "The Bay of the North Sea" probably refers to James Bay, a likely summer locale for these Cree. Radisson said that the Cree clothed themselves in beaver skins in winter and that "they are the best huntsmen of all American and scorns to catch a castor in a trap. . . . They kill not the young castors, but leave them in the water, being that they are sure that they will take him again, which no other nation doth" (Adams 1961:147). The practice of not killing young beaver could exist only if different groups of Indians respected each other's rights to certain lodges. If so, it implies that an aboriginal socioterritorial organization was still functioning largely intact, unlike that of their southern neighbours who had either been dislodged by the Iroquois or who were competing for furs for exchange or periodic distribution, or both, at lavish Feasts of the Dead (Hickerson 1960).

During the 1660's, Father Claude-Jean Allouez established a mission among the Cree near Lake Superior (Thwaites 1896–1901, 51:57). While he had little success, he did confirm Radisson's statement that some Cree travelled regularly between James Bay (the "North Sea") and Lake Superior. The fur trader Nicolas Perrot (Blair 1911, 1:107–8) added that the Cree "often frequent the region along the shores of Lake Superior, and the great rivers, where moose are commonly found." No doubt these rivers included the Missinaibi, Moose, Ogoki, and Albany, all of which flowed into James Bay. Perrot also described the Cree method of moose-hunting.

It is unlikely that Radisson and Groseilliers actually travelled to James Bay as they claimed; still, their conversations with Cree indicated that trading posts on the bay could service a vast hinterland. Others were also aware of this. Radisson's subsequent assurances of a profitable trade at the "Bottom of the Bay" convinced the English that the Cree would be eager customers.

The Early Trade on James Bay

The events leading to the founding of the Hudson's Bay Company are well known (see MacKay 1949, Rich 1960 for details). Financed by the English aristocracy, Groseilliers, Captain Zachary Gillam, Thomas Gorst, the accountant, and the ship's crew settled in September 1668 at the mouth of Rupert's River at what became known as Charles Fort. Four days after their arrival, a band of Nodway Indians who had been hunting nearby arrived and promised to return with furs and to spread the word that traders were on the bay. Groseilliers made several excursions inland during the fall and winter visiting camps of Nodways, Kilistinons, Ottawas, and others (Willson 1900:48). In April 1669, Indians arrived to trade their pelts, and by June, Gillam's party had traded 3,000 pounds of beaver from three hundred Indians. Gillam described these Indians as "using bows and arrows, living in tents, wch they remove from one place to another, according to the seasons of hunting, fowling, fishing. As for their meat, they live on venison, wild foule, as geese, partridges, and rabbats . . . of wch there is great abundance, the Captain affirming, to have kill'd above 700 such white partridges. Their fish are Sturgeon, brave pikes, Salmon-troutes taken by ym with nets" (Nute 1978:118).

The traders of the newly founded (2 May 1670) Hudson's Bay Company returned to Rupert's River in 1670, and over the next four years provided accounts of Indians. For example, on 25 March 1673, "6 Men, as Ambassadors, came from King *Cuscudidah,* to notify his Approach. . . . He brought a Retinue with him, but little Beaver, the Indians having sent the best to *Canada*" (Tyrrell 1931:386). The term "king" was applied at the time to band leaders. Again, on 12 May 1674, twelve Indians belonging to Cuscudidah's group held a feast at the post. Among the participants was Cuscudidah's brother. On 22 May, a shaking tent ceremony, which appears to have differed little from one at York Factory thirty years later, was held (Tyrrell 1931:228-9, 389). On 27 May, "about 50 Men, Women and Children, came in 22 Canoes, to trade, but brought little or no Beaver with them. They were of the Nation call'd *Pishhapocanoes"* (ibid.:390). They seem to have come from the east side of James Bay (see Preston 1981:205), and it was reported that the French had acquired most of their furs.

Partly because Charles Fort was capturing some of the trade that previously had gone to Quebec, Father Charles Albanel in 1671-72 made the first authenticated overland journey to James Bay. En route he met Indians on their way to visit the English (Morton 1973:70-71). At the mouth of Rupert's River, he noted the distribution of various Indian peoples. The concern here is with the groups to the west of Rupert's River: "Upon the point to the Westward the Kinistinons are settled; and, upon the bay, the Mataouakiri-nouek and Monsounik" (Thwaites 1896-1901, 56:203). The Kinistinons were Cree. The Monsounik are usually equated with the Monsoni, a Cree-like group, who appear to have wintered in the area northwest of Lake Superior (Tyrrell 1931:263). If they were the same, then they must have travelled a considerable distance, as of course had the Cree with whom Radisson wintered. They may have reached James Bay via the Moose River, apparently named after them, in order to trade with the English. The Mataouakirinouek may have been the same as the Mataouchkarini, an Algonquian group who in 1640 lived on the Madawaska River some three hundred miles south of James Bay (Thwaites 1896-1901, 18:229). At the time of the Iroquois wars, the Mataouchkarini are reported to have fled north. If so, then it is possible that the composition of peoples near James Bay in 1670 differed from that of 1640, an interpretation reinforced by Thomas Gorst's remark that "the Indians at the Bottom of the Bay is like the rest distinguished by several Dialects" (Tyrrell 1931:396). If these peoples had been closely related or had lived in close proximity to each other, then these apparent dialectical differences probably would not have obtained. Today, the Moose Cree speak a dialect distinct from that spoken by Fort Albany Cree (Honigmann 1981:217, 227), suggesting southern influences (see also McNulty and Gilbert 1981:215).

During the summer of 1674, Thomas Bayly, the governor, Groseilliers, Gorst, and several others made a trip along the west coast of the bay. At the mouth of the Moose River, they encountered a group of "Tabittee" (probably Abitibi from further south) from whom they traded 250 skins. The Tabittee captain "blam'd the English for trading with such pitiful Nations, as *Cuscudidahs* and *Pishhapocanoes,* advising them to settle at *Moose Sebee,* and the *Upland* Indians would come down and trade with them." While at Moose River they obtained "1500 skins" from the "Shechittawams, 50 Leagues from that River, having come to trade with him." From Moose River the traders travelled north to the "Schettawam" (Albany) River (Honigmann 1981:229), and Bayly "treated with the King, and his Son made them a Promise to come with a Ship and trade with them the next Year. In return, they assur'd him, they would provide Store of Beaver, and bring the *Upland* Indians down" (Tyrrell 1931:390–91).

These are the first explicit references to the Albany River Indians. A short distance north of the mouth of the Albany River the party encountered seven "distress'd Indians" and also found the bodies of several dead persons: "There had been a great Mortality among them, and several were starv'd to Death for want of Food; this Country being such a miserable Wilderness, that it affords not sufficient Sustenance for the wretched Inhabitants" (1931:392). While mention of starvation and death reflects the poverty of the coastal area, starvation during the summer even along the coast does not seem likely. Had these people attempted to winter along the coast? Or might starvation have been the result of some epidemic introduced by Europeans? Then again, perhaps these people had only recently moved to this area from winter quarters in more favourable settings inland. The traders continued their voyage to the mouth of either the Severn or the Winisk River, where they met "Washahoe" Indians; they then returned to Charles Fort.

Among other Indians mentioned were the *Nodways* (the term literally means enemy or snake), who were then threatening the Indians who traded at Rupert's River. From the limited evidence, it appears that they wintered inland south of James Bay. It is possible that they were an Algonquin group related to the Abitibi. The Abitibi, as mentioned before, seem to have had little respect for the peoples near Rupert's River, and so may have been considered enemies by the latter. More likely, however, they were Iroquois. Iroquois had penetrated to Lake Kesagami as early as 1651 (Thwaites 1896–1901, 37:69), and were at Lake Nemiscau, a mere 80 miles east of Charles Fort, in 1671–72 (Thwaites 1896–1901, 56:171).

An opaque picture of the socioterritorial organization of James Bay Indians is given during these early years—both from brief accounts of particular groups and from more explicit statements. For instance, John Oldmixon, citing Thomas Gorst's 1671 journal, said "The *Indians* of certain Districhs, which are bounded by such and such Rivers, have each an *Okimah,* as they call him, or Captain over them, who is an Old Man, Consider'd only for his Prudence and Experience. He has no Authority but what they think fit to give him upon certain Occasions. He is their Speech-maker to the *English*; as also in their own grave Debates, when they meet every Spring and Fall, to settle the Disposition of their Quarters for Hunting, Fowling, and Fishing. Every Family have their Boundaries adjusted, which they seldom quit, unless they have not Success there in Hunting, and then they join in with some Family who have succeeded" (Tyrrell 1931:382).

It would appear from these remarks that the Indians of certain regions constituted the various "nations" mentioned in these early records. Questions remain: did each nation (band?) exploit a district (band territory?)? What size were these districts? How many Indians exploited them: was the *Pishhapocanoe* group of fifty persons typical? And what does Gorst mean when he speaks of a "family"? Data from a slightly later period suggest that winter co-residential groups numbered about a dozen persons. But larger groups are in evidence at other times. The length of time when smaller units remained apart and the size of co-residential units were probably functions of the amount of time devoted to the exploitation of certain resources, as well as of seasonal and regional fluctuations in resource biomass. For example, beaver, which were hunted for meat and for their pelts, which were used as coats, and other small game can best be hunted by small, dispersed family-like groups. In contrast, caribou, when abundant, can more effectively be exploited by multi-family groups whose male members co-operate in the chase. Thus, multi-family groupings may have existed more frequently farther inland on the Canadian Shield, where the total resource biomass was greater. Nevertheless, the number of caribou in the region west of James Bay appears to have been considerably greater before than after 1700.

Gorst's remark that the *okimah,* probably in consultation with other adult hunters, determined where different families would hunt, provides support for Radisson's earlier comment that the Cree were able to leave young beaver for a future date. However, given regional and temporal variability in resources, it is unlikely that co-residential groups exploited exactly the same area each year; otherwise, there would have been no need for the Indians to, as Gorst put it, "have their Boundaries adjusted."

What was the structure of social relations among families within and between districts? We can surmise that Northern Algonquians practised the levirate, sororate, polygyny, and cross-cousin marriage (Honigmann 1981:221), but nothing is known of their system of kinship nomenclature. Honigmann (1981:221), however, states that in 1947, Attawapiskat Cree cousin terminology was Iroquois. If it be accepted that rules of kin classification can persist or change independently of social structure, then it is possible that an Iroquois system "persisted" *after*, and in spite of, earlier structural changes. While any reconstruction of aboriginal Cree social organization must remain somewhat conjectural, a few data pertaining to late seventeenth and early eighteenth–century York Factory Cree suggest that post-marital residence was matrilocal (Bishop and Krech 1980). There is no direct evidence for similar customs among western James Bay Indians. It is possible that there were differences among Cree from different regions. Extensive trade networks between Indians of the James Bay area and groups to the south, networks that by at least the 1640's involved the exchange of beaver skins for trade items, may have created a patrilocal emphasis by the time that the first Hudson's Bay Company establishments were built in the 1670's. By this it is meant that if men were the primary traders, then male agnates might have preferred to form trading (and also beaver-hunting) units rather than share the benefits of trade with male affines. During early contact times, trade goods, unlike foodstuffs, were likely luxuries, albeit useful ones; unlike foodstuffs, the distribution of trade items could bestow prestige on the donors, and thus they were a political source of social, not material, inequality, and may have reinforced agnatic relationships at the expense of affinal obligations. If so, then temporary rather than permanent post-marital matrilocality might have become common. While this argument for an organizational change is conjectural, nevertheless, a few data suggest it may be correct: as mentioned earlier, Cuscudidah and his brother belonged to the same group, and at the mouth of the Albany River, traders met the chief and his son. There are similar data from a slightly later period. There is no question about the importance of trade. Father Albanel (Thwaites 1896–1901, 56:203) remarked of the area twenty leagues (about twenty-five miles; probably Point Comfort) northeast of Charles Fort: "it is a long rocky point at the fifty-first degree of latitude, where from time immemorial the Savages have been wont to gather for purposes of trade." There is also evidence that some Indian groups were enemies of others; for example, the Nodways, who tried to discourage the traders from trading with people further east. Cuscudidah's band, for instance, feared the Nodways (Morton 1973:68). Hostility, perhaps generated by competition over trade rights, provides the conditions for patrilocality (Ember and Ember 1971). In contrast, explicit references to matrilocality among the York Factory Cree may have been more a function of their later involvement in regularized exchange relationships, rather than simply a lacuna in the more easterly data (see Innis 1962:47–48 for a discussion of the problems encountered by the more westerly Cree in obtaining trade goods before the 1670's).

In the early historical records, glimpses are provided of what may have been the aboriginal seasonal cycle among the James Bay Cree. In May, Indians came to the coast to kill geese, and afterwards they went a short distance inland to hunt moose or caribou. In late August, they returned to coastal waters to fish with nets and hooks for pike, trout, and sturgeon (Nute 1978:288). At some point in the summer, groups gathered at a predetermined locale to trade with upland Cree middlemen. By mid-September, Indians had retreated inland; some went a considerable distance. It does not seem that Indians wintered on the coast: Henry Hudson, at the mouth of Rupert's River in the winter of 1610-11, met only one Indian (Morton 1973:28); Thomas Button, at the mouth of the Nelson River during the winter of 1612-13, did not contact a single Indian; and the Jesuits said that Indians lived on James Bay only "at certain seasons of the year."

It is unlikely that Indians exploited geese either early in the spring or late in the fall; goose-hunting during the late April and early May break-up would have been hazardous; and after late August, full-feathered birds unencumbered by flightless offspring would have been difficult quarry. Furthermore, and probably more important, Indians who remained near the coast after mid-September would have been exposed to an unpredictable existence in an area where travel was difficult. Perhaps this is why the Indians that Bayly encountered in 1674 had starved. Support, albeit indirect, for Indians quitting the coast for inland regions in fall is provided in Thomas Gorst's statement of late September 1670, that although Indians brought fish to Charles Fort, "They themselves feast cheifly on dryed moose and Beaver" (Nute 1978:288). Moose do not inhabit the coast, and Indians probably had been hunting inland and had come down to the coast to visit the traders. Gorst added that when the weather got colder, Indians moved several leagues into the woods in order to kill deer, wild fowl (grouse and ptarmigan), and hare. How far inland Indians wintered is uncertain, although the Canadian Shield with its somewhat richer habitat lies only about 75 miles from the south end of James Bay. West of the bay, however, the Shield lies nearly 200 miles inland. Thus, it is possible that the seasonal movements of people who lived nearer Moose and Rupert's Rivers were somewhat shorter than the movements of Indians who exploited the Albany River drainage area. It will be remembered that Radisson met Cree who may have summered on James Bay some 600 miles from the coast. Geographic variability along with differential involvement in exchange networks may account for differences among the various Cree groups.

Even before the first trading post was built on James Bay in 1668, it seems that Indian adaptive strategies were altering. During the 1660's, Cree were either trading furs through Indian middlemen or were travelling to French encampments near the Upper Great Lakes to trade directly. After 1670, while Cree continued to deal with the French, English goods appear to have induced them to trap more. It thus seems certain that more time and energy were being expended to acquire Euro-Canadian goods, whether French or English, than had been the case when prehistoric exchange goods were involved. Also, many more Indians were drawn directly into the trade with Europeans after new Hudson's Bay Company posts were opened at the mouths of the Moose River in 1673 and Albany River in 1675.

The first three decades of Hudson's Bay Company trade saw the formulation of policies designed to protect company interests and to attract and maintain an Indian clientele (Ray and Freeman 1978:12–18). At this time gift-giving and ritualized friendship alliances with band captains were established in attempts to exclude the French. That Hudson's Bay Company efforts were moderately successful is attested by Antoine Silvy, who wrote in 1684–85 that "the Indians along the sea coast like the English better than the French" (Tyrrell 1931:68). In 1686, the De Troyes expedition from New France captured the English James Bay posts and held them until Governor James Knight retook them in the summer of 1693. We learn little about the James Bay Cree during the French interval except that they were dissatisfied with their treatment (Rich 1957:206). Between 1686 and 1693, the French, because of their monopoly on the trade between James Bay and the Great Lakes, would have been able to drive a hard bargain with Indians. As well, it was reported that their coastal posts were poorly outfitted. Thus, when the English regained Fort Albany in 1693, Indians arrived that summer, "Overjoyed to see us" (HBCA B.3/d/1). To welcome the captains and reaffirm their allegiance, lavish presents were given according to company policy. At Fort Albany, "Tick-a-tuickoy ye great Leading Indian of this River" was given some ninety pounds of shot, nineteen pounds of powder, and seven pounds of Brazil tobacco as well as a new gun and a copper kettle. Other leaders also received large gifts.

Other policies already in effect at Port Nelson were instituted immediately. In 1689, Port Nelson Indians had been encouraged to "gett Fresh Provisions by Hunting Fowleing and Fishing at all Seasons when they Can" (Rich 1957:78). Within a few weeks after Fort Albany was recaptured, Indians traded 3,500 fish (HBCA B.3/d/1). After 1690, Indians were encouraged "to weare more of our Cloth; &c their beavor Coates Lesse, that wee may have the more Returnes of Skin Beavor" (Rich 1957:98); and in 1694, Fort Albany was sent lamb skins "for a tryall hopeing you may Induce the Indians to use them for Lineing of their Coates &ca. which wee apprehend may be as warme & Convenient for them as Beavr Skins" (Rich 1957:234). Attempts to persuade Indians to trade beaver skins instead of making clothing out of them met with little success since Indians needed winter clothing. Although Cree leaders were treated with respect and gift-giving became an established pattern, Fort Albany frequently suffered shortages of certain materials or lacked materials of good quality, including guns, kettles, and tobacco (HBCA B. 3/d/2). This disgusted Indians, who by the 1690's would refuse what they considered trash. Not only had they come to recognize the value of different items, but they also had developed definite trade preferences.

FORT ALBANY INDIANS, 1693-1725

The year 1693 marked a turning point for the Indians who came to trade at Fort Albany. Within a few years, trade goods became more abundant and Indians were attracted to the post from near and far. The trade of Indians who wintered several hundred miles to the west and southwest was the most coveted, since the bulk of furs, especially beaver, usually came from that direction inland. However, because they were near the French traders, these "uplanders," as they were designated by the Fort Albany traders (or "French Indians" if they had been in the habit of trading with *coureurs de bois*), were less predictable in their visits than were Indians who wintered nearer the post. Nevertheless, it is possible to piece together a general picture of the various groups of Indians that visited the post, especially those in the more immediate area.

The captain of the Albany River Indians was Tick-aw-tucky, who came to the post regularly with his son, Na-peen-aw-tas. During the summer of 1696, the son "and his gang at their going to ye warrs" received gifts from the post (HBCA B.3/d/4 fo.14). It is not known with whom they were warring. When Tick-aw-tucky died in early 1700, the son became the captain of the "gang" (HBCA B.3/d/11 fo.17). He died in 1702, at which point his brother, Moos-a-chest, became leader. While the wintering area of the group is not noted, it may have been several day's travel up the Albany River, since in 1701, Na-peen-aw-tas was given presents "to prevent his going to new Severn to trade wth the French" (HBCA B.3/d/13 fo.13). This temptation may not have existed had his group hunted closer to Fort Albany. The French who then occupied York Factory (Fort Bourbon) had reopened an outpost near the former location of Fort Severn, and this threatened to lure the more westerly Indians. The special treatment accorded this group reflects the pivotal position that they held with respect to their contacts with more distant groups.

The Indians from the Moose River area also traded regularly at Fort Albany, but being somewhat nearer to the French, they were often harder to please. They also were in the habit of spreading rumours that the French or their Indian allies were on their way to capture the post. The leader of the Moose River Indians during the 1690's was named Noah. Noah apparently traded at Charles Fort in 1668-69, and he and his brother are mentioned by Thomas Gorst on 31 August 1670 (Nute 1978:286). When Noah visited Fort

Albany in 1695, he was given presents "to feast ye Southern Indians wth all to Invite them down here—" (HBCA B.3/d/5 fo.16). He was clearly the most important Indian from the Moose River region, and the account book for 1695–96 refers to him as "Old Noah Capt. of Moose river" (HBCA B.3/d/7). That same year another "Moose river Leading Indian call'd Mis-qua-mot" received presents. "Mis-qua-mot" or Miscamot is said to have been Noah's son (HBCA B.3/d/5 fo.16). He hunted for the post during the 1690's and early 1700's, and as he grew older, lingered near the post to be fed by the traders. In 1707–1708, Miscamot is called "Captain of the Home Indians" (HBCA B.3/d/17 fo.11), which suggests that he and some Moose River Indians had shifted their winter residence to be closer to Fort Albany. Perhaps he wintered just to the north of the Albany River, since on 26 January 1706, Anthony Beale reported the arrival of "Sward Indians from the Northward" (Williams 1975:334). Miscamot's decision to hunt geese for the post may have led him to hunt nearby; he never appears to have gone far from Fort Albany.

There seem to have been two closely related groups of Moose River Indians trading at Fort Albany. One group was the Sagomies (or Salkemys) (HBCA B.3/d/13 fo.13). In spring and summer of 1706, twelve canoes of "Salkemy Indians" arrived (HBCA B.3/a/1). The Salkemys are distinguished from another group, the "Shaggomies" (or "Shashioggames"). In 1702, the "Sagomy Capt call'd Scatch-a-mis" received gifts (HBCA B.3/d/13 fo. 13). In 1707–1708, "Scotchamoss" (or "Scatchamisey") is referred to as a "Sowthoaugomy Captain" (HBCA B.3/d/17/ fo.11). Whether the trader erred or was unable to distinguish the two groups, or whether these were in fact the same group is not clear. Additional evidence suggests that there were two groups. For instance, in 1707–1708, the account books mention "Wat-tang" (or "Wattaine"), who is also called "another Sowthoaugomy Captain" (HBCA B.3/d/17 fo.11). He may have headed another group, or he may have been junior to Scatchamis. In 1708, presents were "Given ye Capt of the Susaugmis, his Wife, who brought downe hither A great Gang of Inds wth a Great Deal of Beaver" (HBCA B.3/d/18). Clearly Scatchamis was the leader, since in 1727, Joseph Myatt reminisced, "in the year 1712 when Old Scratchemisse, the great leading Indian of Moose River, came here to trade with eighteen or twenty canoes," they were so hungry that they were forced to eat their beaver skins (Davies 1965:124). As early as 1694, the account books mention "ye young Capt of Moose River" (HBCA B.3/d/4). This may have been Scatchamis, who also may have been another of Noah's sons, but of this there is no evidence. Wattang might have been still another son who headed another division. Wattang brought sixteen canoes to Fort Albany on 2 May 1707. By 1715–16, however, it was reported that the captain of the "Susagamis" is "young AcchimySee ye Leading Indian of Moose river" (HBCA B.3/a/2 fo.24). That same year the records mention "ould Flagg Merchant of

Moose river." Was he Scatchamis, and was Acchimysee his son? We cannot tell, but it is evident that the Salkemy Indians exploited the hinterland southwest of the Moose River estuary. In 1727, Myatt (Davies 1965:124) said that a factory at Moose River would attract "the Sockemy Indians which border near the mouth of Moose River" and who brought most of the "small furs" to Fort Albany. Moose River Indians usually reached the post by travelling along the sea coast. It is impossible to know how many Indians may have lived along or near the Moose River, but references to a "Great gang" and twenty canoes indicate that perhaps fifty or more persons were involved.

There were other groups that appear to have wintered within 150 miles of Fort Albany and who were regular visitors there. On 8 July 1693, gifts were presented to a "very Leading Ind. Capt of a distinct tribe Called Mottaw-war-ish-tha." Again in 1694–95, presents were given to "the Metla-warith Capt at several times." The leader was probably Metuass-cum (or Mete wa es cam) (HBCA B.3/d/1,5,11,12). On 9 May 1707, "6 Canoes of Mathawarenes Indians came down the River" (HBCA B.3/a/2 fo.4). Again, it is impossible to determine precisely from where these Indians were coming, but their relatively early arrival after break-up and their annual visit suggest that they may have wintered northwest of the post. For instance, in 1707, some came down the Albany while others "came from the Northd" (HBCA B.3/a/2 fo.30). Perhaps they were the same people mentioned by Thomas McCleish on 16 July 1716: "It is certain I have traded 1500 martens with the northward Indians this spring, they have used this place almost twenty years, and most of their wives are this country Indians. The women in general stomachs their going to leave friends and relations" (Davies 1965:44–45,50). Whether or not they were the Metlawarith, this remark indicates close kin ties among certain groups trading at Fort Albany and suggests patrilocality as well. Might the reference to women *tolerating* leaving their own kin reflect a relatively recent change in post-marital residence?

These were the main groups who traded regularly at Fort Albany in the 1600's and early 1700's. There appear to have been a few other small scattered settlements or splinter groups. Information concerning both their group affiliation and their territory is usually lacking. The Indians who after the early 1700's became known as the "homeguards" or "home Indians" were probably, in the main, drawn from these nearby groups.

The post was frequented less regularly by Indians living farther inland. One such group was the Rabbit Indians. On 29 May 1720, "15 Cunnous of Rabbit Inds came here to trade down this Rir" (HBCA B.3/a/9 fo.56). It is of interest that in the summer of 1696 "a Northern Indian called Mistapa (alias) Politi-cian . . . brought us the news of Port Nelson being taken by the french" (HBCA B.3/d/7). The name *Mistapa* appears to be cognate with *mista poos,* meaning jack rabbit in Plains Cree (Anderson 1975:187), and suggests that the

Rabbit Indians may have been named after their leader of the 1690's. The knowledge of the above Indian of events far to the northwest might mean that he and his group wintered in the region part way to Fort Severn.

Other groups who visited Fort Albany included the "PakanaShes" perhaps from south or southeast of Moose River (HBCA B.3/a/9 fo.56d). From far to the south in 1694–95 came "a Capt of a tribe of Indians up Moose River Very near half way to Canada Called Ta-mish-ka-mein" (HBCA B.3/d/5 fo.17), perhaps Timiskaming who originally inhabited the Lake Timiskaming area. On 12 July 1717, from perhaps the Lake Abitibi area, five canoes of "Tibitiby Indians" came to trade and reported four more canoes on their way (HBCA B.3/a/9 fo.22d). Again in 1694–95, "Strange Indians Called Ka-chi-ga-mein [alias] the great Lake Indians" arrived. Another upland group mentioned that year was the "Ryga-ga-mees." Were these groups Ojibwa? During 1700–1701, presents were "Sent to ye Capt of the Ottaways to invite him hither" (HBCA B.3/d/12 fo.13). From the region north and northwest of Lake Superior came the "Cristeen" (e.g., HBCA B.3/d/17 fo.11). The Cristeens were distinguished by the traders from Cree living nearer to the post. The main Cristeen captains of the 1710's and 1720's were the Marten and Shemenycoat. The former appears to have come from the region west of Lake Superior. Occasionally, a few canoes of woodland Assiniboine from the Lake of the Woods region accompanied the Cristeens to Fort Albany. All groups were in the extreme outer orbit of trade at Fort Albany, but their visits were no less coveted.

THE FUR TRADE AT FORT ALBANY, 1700–1710

Although all of the Indians west of James Bay were involved in the fur trade, those who wintered nearer to Fort Albany arrived more frequently. During the spring months these latter brought in their furs. The reports indicate that they obtained proportionally more "small" furs, especially martens, but unfortunately no breakdown of the quantities and species of pelts by group is given during this period. Only the totals are provided, and these tended to fluctuate with the number of uplanders that arrived, as well as with ecological conditions. Between 1700 and 1710, the high figure calculated in Made Beaver (MB), the standard of value, was 25,118 MB for the period from 1 July 1708–30 June 1709, while the low figure was 8,907 MB for 1704–05 (HBCA B.3/d/14). (See Ray and Freeman 1978:168–170, Table 18, for a breakdown of the beaver and marten returns by year between 1701 and 1727.) Perhaps from 4,000 to 6,000 MB were obtained by roughly seventy-five Indians who traded regularly each year, but these are only estimates; if approximately correct, then the average was 65 MB per hunter. But as will be shown, there may have been considerable annual and areal variation in fur returns related primarily to ecological factors.

The Cree as Provisioners

Country provisions, most importantly geese, largely procured by the Cree, helped to feed the more than twenty people employed at the post. Attempts to involve Cree in the goose hunt began immediately after Fort Albany was recaptured in 1693 (HBCA B.3/d/4 fo.58). In 1693–94, the governor "Gave away and traded" 20 flints, 40 pounds of powder, and 390 pounds of shot for a "Considerable quantity of Geese" (HBCA B.3/d/1). In 1706, a pound of powder was given for every fifteen geese killed, suggesting that six hundred geese were killed in 1693–94. Few Indians hunted geese for the post until after the winter of 1701. By 1706, however, several families amounting to a dozen or more hunters and a total of fifty or sixty Indians were participating. Usually Indians congregated at the post in late August and again in April. In the early spring, Indians often arrived in a starving condition and had to be maintained on post food until the geese arrived. By 4 May 1706, the families that hunted geese were being called "home Indians" and were distinguished from "upland-ers," those who came from farther inland and did not participate in the hunt (Williams 1975:51). During these early years, however, the distinction between homeguards and uplanders was not so clear-cut as it became in later years (Judd, this volume), and the limited evidence suggests that the number of families that participated in the spring goose-hunt varied somewhat from year to year. The reasons for annual variations will be discussed shortly. Nevertheless, the number of families participating gradually grew. After 1710, from fifty to ninety Indians were usually involved annually; on 15 April 1717, it was reported that "here is 109 home Inds" at the post awaiting the arrival of geese. Before the hunt, Indians were fed oatmeal and fish, and for their effort received tobacco and brandy as well as guns, powder, shot, knives, flints and gunworms, all of which were needed in the marshes. As geese were killed, Indians brought them to the post in their canoes. Usually, they hunted from stages erected in the marsh to protect them from spring floods. Hunters used duck shot to kill the flying birds and were said sometimes to be able to kill as many as four birds with a single shot. Women appear to have plucked the feathers from geese, which were also traded, and may have kept the guns in ready order. The leader of the goose-hunt during the 1690's and early 1700's was Miscamote, formerly from Moose River. Later in the eighteenth century, the term "captain" was applied to the goose-hunt leader.

The amount of powder and shot expended varied considerably from season to season depending upon the availability of geese, the number of hunters involved, and post needs. For example, only 50 pounds of powder and 250 pounds of shot were used in the spring of 1710, compared with 276 pounds of powder and 1,384 pounds of shot in the fall of 1722. Although a portion of the ammunition was employed in hunting species other than geese, and some was used by the Europeans, the largest quantity, perhaps 90 per cent, was used by Indians to kill geese.

Other foods provided to the HBC traders by Indians included fish and ducks in the summer, and venison, grouse, ptarmigan, hare, and beaver in winter and at other times. Venison was the most important. During 1694–95, presents were given to Indians for "deer" (caribou) and moose meat (HBCA B.3/d/6 fo.16); on one occasion, 25 pounds of shot and 7.5 pounds of powder were given for "200 deer tongues." While this figure represents what might seem to be a large number of animals, it should be noted that on several other occasions over the next decade substantial amounts of venison were supplied. For example, in 1699–1700, one Indian presented the governor "wth 80 Deers Tongues"; and in 1703, presents were given to an Indian who brought 105 caribou tongues (HBCA B.3/d/11 fo.13, B.3/d/13). Lesser quantities were brought at other times.

At Fort Albany, the Cree were relied upon for certain goods and services. Each year, birchbark canoes had to be obtained. In 1695 a canoe was exchanged for a 4½ foot gun, four skeins of twine, two net lines, sixteen knives, and two pounds of tobacco, "it being impossible to Procure one at a Cheaper rate" (HBCA B.3/d/5 fo.15). Between 1695 and 1710, Indians received tobacco for bringing intelligence about French activities. The Fort Albany traders were constantly on the alert against a French attack and so made efforts to gain the support of Indians. For example, in 1696, tobacco was given to Indians who held "a great Councill for whom they should be if the french come, wither for us or them, and haveing found them divided gave this present to draw them unanimously (if possible to Our side)" (HBCA B.3/d/7). Indeed, during the summer of 1704 a party of French and Indian allies threatened to take the post and might have had John Fullartine not opened fire, killing many and discouraging the others (Willson 1900:193–94). Again in 1709 a contingent of French and their Mohawk allies descended on Albany, but thanks to Cree intelligence, the traders were prepared. Two French commanders and sixteen others were killed in the fracas (Davies 1965:xxxviii–xxix).

Trade Goods

While tobacco of three types (Brazil, English roll, and Virginia leaf) and brandy were the main "presents" given to Indians in exchange for goods and services, most trade items were procured by trapping fur bearers. But, while the quantities of furs and goods traded were substantial, there is no way of determining the proportion brought and received by the homeguards. Table 1 lists the quantities of what probably were the most important goods traded between 1 July 1694 and 30 June 1695. Goods that appear to have been less "practical" or which were traded in smaller quantities have been omitted from the table.

TABLE 1: GOODS TRADED AT FORT ALBANY, 1694-95.

11,653	lbs. of shot	634	lbs. of twine
4,956	lbs. of powder	30	net lines
5,555	flints	74	scrapers
396	guns (4½, 4, 3½ foot)	118	arrow heads
272	gun worms	430	coats (several types)
201	powder horns	287	blankets
5,329	knives	98	shirts
1,146	hatchets	66	men's caps
495	steels	756	yds. broad cloth
1,384	awls	150	yds. duffle cloth
348	kettles (brass or copper)	78	yds. bayse cloth
288	ice chisels	26	yds. kersey cloth

Figures have been rounded off to the nearest digit.
Source: HBCA B.3/d/5

In addition, 2,308 pounds of tobacco (mostly Brazil), 192 pounds of beads, 205 combs, 54 painted boxes, 1,546 hawks bells, as well as a wide range of lesser items in smaller quantities were traded. The value of these trade goods was 21,301 MB, while the value of furs received amounted to 23,446 MB. (See Ray and Freeman 1978:125-62 for a discussion of the terms of trade.)

Presents were also given to trade captains with whom gift exchange ceremonies had been established (see Ray and Freeman 1978:55-59, 66-75 for a discussion of the trade ceremony). For example, the Moose River captain, Scatchamisey, in the early fall of 1708 received a "Fine Scarlet Coat Laced with St. Martins Lace," a gun, four pounds of powder, sixteen pounds of shot, and five pounds of tobacco. These gifts were typical of those received by other leaders.

SUBSISTENCE STRESS: ECOLOGY AND TRADE

While Indians supplied Fort Albany with furs and food, the early records indicate that, at times, they themselves experienced severe food privations. Did aboriginal Indians experience similar hardships, or were they relatively more capable of obtaining provisions? Before attempting an answer to this, let us examine the evidence for food stress (for a comparable approach in the Subarctic, see Krech [1980, 1983] on Northern Athapaskans).

The first reference to death by starvation among the western James Bay Cree is in 1674. The next account of starvation comes in 1701, an extreme winter and the first detailed account for pervasive starvation in the Fort Albany region. That winter, according to John Fullartine, "I had abundance of starved Indians lying upon me, and had I not a good store of fish afore hand I had shrunk my pease and oatmeal that an hundred bushels had not excused me; for they eat me at least 16,000 fish, besides peas, oatmeal and geese that I gave them every now and then. It was a very hard winter (for provisions) all over the country, for abundance of the poor Indians perished and were so hard put to it that whole families of them were killed and eaten by one another: the young men killed and eat their parents and the women were so put to it for hunger that they spared not the poor sucking infants at their breasts but devoured them. The reason of this famine amongst them was the little snow that fell so that they could not hunt beasts" (Davies 1965:8–9). During the late 1690's, Fort Albany established the practice of laying up a larder of several thousand fish, specifically to feed starving Indians.

While Indians did not experience food stress every year and often appear to have lived comfortably, starvation was a recurrent phenomenon during the early historic period. Traders often attributed food stress to a variety of ecological factors. The winter of 1705–1706 was especially severe, and since it is the earliest for which daily post journal records exist, it will be examined closely (see Williams 1975:10–73).

Unfavourable climatic conditions caused hardships as early as 28 October 1705, when four Indians reported that "'tis very hard with them by reason the Snow fell on the Ground before there was any frost, which kept the Ground still open so that they are not able to travell the Woods and Swamps to get their livelyhood." On 13 January 1706, an Indian arrived from the southward reporting that two families of Southward Indians were "so very poore that they Eate all there Doggs." They were sent oatmeal and fish to enable them to reach the post. On 21 January one of the Indians left to hunt and saw two deer "but could not come nigh them the Snow makeing so much Noise, with a person Walking on it by reason of the Thaw" of the 15th. Some of the Indians were given food and sent away on 4 February, but being unable to kill anything, they returned nine days later. On their arrival they were given ninety fish and three quarts of oatmeal. Another Indian who had lived at the post since 17 January left five weeks later with seventy fish and four quarts of oatmeal to enable him to hunt. When an Indian killed some caribou on 25 February, two Indians were sent away to live on the flesh. However, after the meat was consumed, they all returned starving in early March. By 10 March, twenty Indians were living on post food. Other Indians, however, appear to have done well, since on 23 March, three Moose River hunters arrived with "a good quantity of furs" and "40 deers tongues." Again, on 29 March, some Indians came with "4 Sides of Dears flesh and 19 Dears Tongues and 9 Deares Heads." But the venison that they retained for themselves was rapidly consumed by the other Indians at the post so that by 4 April, fifty Indians "Great and Small" had to be given 150 fish. On 2 May, Indians said that several persons who wintered to the north had starved to death during the winter (Williams 1975:50 passim).

While the winter of 1705–1706 has been singled out for intensive scrutiny, other years prior to 1720 prove to have been equally severe; this seemed true of 1714, 1716, 1718, 1719, and 1720. Between 4 December 1715 and 18 January 1716, some fifteen gallons of oatmeal, four gallons of peas, and 130 fish were supplied to hungry Indians (HBCA B.3/a/9). Greater quantities appear to have been given after 18 January.

As the above data indicate, stress was attributed to snow conditions. There are other examples suggesting a direct link between precipitation (snow) and hardship. In 1718, Indians suffered greatly "by Reason little Snow on the ground and Exceeding cold winter." In contrast, on 11 February 1720, "here is more Snow on the ground then the oldest Indian does Remember." Nevertheless, six Indians died of starvation and two more froze to death. On 8 April 1719, ninety-five Indians huddled at the post to receive food, although the reasons for their hardships are not provided (HBCA B.3/a/9). On 4 March 1720, there were forty-seven Indians living at the post.

Regional variability in resources could create abundance for some and starvation for others. For instance, on 26 March 1707, it was said that the Indians who wintered to the north were in poor shape, "3 or four familys of Indians that ways has perrished this Winter by Reason there was but Fuew Beasts . . . though it has been a plentifull a Year to the South as ever I heard" (HBCA B.3/a/2 fo. 25).

It is unlikely that ecological factors, as important as they were, were the sole reasons for Indian misfortunes (see Krech 1980, 1983). A number of variables related to the fur trade, operating in conjunction with environmental ones, were, I suggest, sufficient at times to create severe stress. More specifically, I argue that many, if not most, hardships were either directly or indirectly the result of: (1) the introduction of a new productive technology for acquiring food and fur bearers, themselves obtained to gain access to that technology; (2) changes in labour patterns involving an intensification and specialization of efforts to acquire pelts and foods for the trading post; and (3) a reduction in the total resource biomass, especially beaver and caribou.

The sheer volume of trade goods listed in the early account books as having been traded or given to Indians is startling. While some items appear to have had no known practical value, furs still had to be produced to get them. Many other items were probably employed directly or indirectly to acquire both furs and food. Over the years, Indians who became accustomed to receiving these goods would have grown dependent upon them, especially if they were used in hunting. The most frequently mentioned item suggestive of dependency is the gun. For instance, in 1697, four old guns were given to Indians "who stood in great need of guns to preserve their Lives" (HBCA B.3/d/8 fo.6) Again in 1703, the Fort Albany post was forced to trade coat beaver from Indians "or else some of them would have perished . . . so that before the last ship came they had not goods to kill beasts" (Davies 1965:16). On 9 January 1724, an Indian arrived, starving, having left his family behind. Although he encountered deer en route, "he was forced to lave them his Gun being broke and Sayes the other Inds Gunn is alsoe broke wch is the cause of theire being Starved" (HBCA B.3/a/12 fo.14). These statements run counter to the evidence that guns were inefficient and that bows and arrows continued in use for many years. (Indeed, steel arrowheads were traded well into the eighteenth century.) Either these remarks reflect a European bias about hunting requirements, or the Indians actually had developed a physical dependency on guns. I suggest that an examination of the conditions under which hunting took place provides the answer. Where Indians were separated into family trapping camps, caribou-hunting with bow and arrow by one or two persons might have been ineffectual. Retreating animals might soon have outdistanced the bow hunter, but two hunters with guns perhaps could at least have wounded an animal, even at a considerable distance. In contrast, a band of hunters co-operating in the chase could apply tactics that made use of the aboriginal technology. Also, trapping activities may have functioned to inhibit collective hunts, thereby transforming the gun, ammunition, and other associated items into necessities in the space of a few decades. Reliance upon guns, then, does not mean that Indians "forgot" either how to produce their old technology or how best to employ it.

The production of furs for the HBC and French markets as well as animal skins and flesh for local consumption must have altered Indian labour patterns. These may have changed in two related ways. First, Indians would have had to have expended more energy to produce both pelts and provisions. Because beaver, valued both for their flesh and skins, were scarcer in the lowlands than farther inland, Indians in the lowlands probably would have focused their attention more on such small furs as marten, mink, and fisher. Moose River Indians, as stated earlier, were the chief suppliers of "small furs." But these animals provide little meat and are often found in areas where there are few other foods. It is possible that some families wintered in areas where they expected to obtain such animals but which were devoid of these as well as animals suitable for subsistence. The following example suggests this. On 26 January 1706, Anthony Beale remarked: "Here came a southward Indian from the northward and brought nothing at all . . . but nine small Skins" (Williams 1975:34). His polygynous extended family of three women and four children had eaten nothing for three days before he left them to get help from the post.

The second change in productive activities may have involved a tendency for family groups to remain separated for longer periods of time in winter than had been the case in pre-contact times. This would have been related to efficiency in fur-hunting and also to a possible decline in the number of food animals. Although data are fragmentary, there is some evidence that when Indians did come to the post in winter, they often arrived in family groups. For example, on 15 December 1715, "A Indian man & his wife came here almost starved"; on 5 March 1716, "the Indn Doctor & his Family came here, being 9 in number," and on 21 March 1717, "12 Inds came her from y Nord which belongs to y Indian that came last night" (HBCA B.3/a/9 passim). Finally, on 4 February 1717, seven Indians came to the post together. In all these (and other) examples, the Indians were reported to have been starving. In contrast, when food was easier to obtain or when Indians were able to hunt caribou, winter settlements appear to have been slightly larger. On 24 February 1707, three families arrived together with "many of furs as well as Victuals." These families left together and returned within two weeks with the meat from seventeen caribou. Again, on 14 March that year, three other families arrived together from the westward with thirty-six caribou tongues and other meat (HBCA B.3/a/2 passim). When caribou were present in large numbers, winter co-residential units exploiting them appear to have been larger. These animals could be exploited more efficiently by several co-operating hunters than by one or two persons. In turn, they provide a greater amount of meat in bulk form. This does not imply that big-game hunters will not trap fur bearers, although this sometimes was the case. Rather, a windfall in caribou often provided the subsistence needed in order to conduct trapping activities, as witness instances when Indians arrived with both venison and excellent fur hunts.

The resource biomass available to Indians probably declined in the area west of James Bay between 1670 and 1725. The two species most affected were beaver and caribou. Apparently never numerous in the lowlands, beaver may have been overhunted if the techniques for obtaining them were similar to those employed by the early eighteenth-century Cree near York Factory. According to La Potherie, when Indians hunted beaver in rivers, "they find out as nearly as possible the number of outlets they have . . . [and] cut the ice so as to let the water run off, hemming the house in with poles and stakes to prevent the beavers from escaping, and leave in the middle a net made of deer skin. . . . [I]n the lakes, they srround their ordinary houses with nets . . . and then destroy their country houses. . . . [I]n the smaller streams they destroy their dams so as to dry them out" (Tyrrell 1931:235–36).

While it is not certain that Fort Albany Indians employed the same methods, it is nevertheless evident that these practices would have led to the death of all the beaver in a lodge. Either they would have been killed immediately or, if they escaped would have frozen or starved to death. Contrast these techniques with those noted four decades earlier by Pierre Radisson! Such practices, if widespread and regularized, soon would deplete a beaver population. Indeed, this is suggested by the gradual increase in the number of marten traded at Fort Albany, assuming that the lowland Cree produced most of these. In 1702, a mere 123 marten were traded, whereas in 1719, 1,790 were traded. Also, relatively large numbers were traded during years when starvation was prevalent, suggesting that beaver, which may formerly have been an important food source during stressful times, had been significantly reduced (Ray and Freeman 1978:168–69).

Fort Albany Indians also appear to have been killing large numbers of caribou when they had the opportunity. The herds near Fort Albany may have been considerably larger in the seventeenth century than the limited evidence suggests was the case after 1710. As noted, the account books for the 1690's and early 1700's make frequent references to Indians receiving presents of tobacco in return for venison. At different times during this period Indians made presents of 36, 40, 80, 105, and even 200 deer tongues, as well as smaller quantities on other occasions. A reading of the archives, pertaining to the period after about 1705, indicates that the quantity of venison given to traders gradually diminished. This meant that Indians either were consuming the venison themselves, were spending less time hunting caribou, or, most likely, that there were fewer animals available to kill.

There were moose to be found a short distance south of James Bay during the 1670's. Although it is uncertain, a few moose may also have once inhabited the lowlands west of James Bay except for the coastal plain: in 1694–95 presents were given "to Severall Ind that brought us in Moose flesh & deer tongues" (HBCA B.3/d/6 fo.16). That same year ten pounds of shot was given for forty pounds of "Moose Marrow fatt." Moose hooves and hides were traded annually at Fort Albany. In 1702–1703, 186 pairs of moose hooves were traded, and the following year, 240 pairs were traded (HBCA B.3/d/13 fo.63; B.3/d/14 fo.9). Whether these animals had been killed in the lowlands or further inland is impossible to determine. There are no known references to moose being taken by the Cree who wintered nearer the post in later times, but references to venison do not distinguish moose from caribou. Thus, if there had once been moose in the lowlands, they must soon have been exterminated.

Through the practice of supplying the post with venison during the early years, the number of large animals may have been sufficiently reduced so as to make hunting them less predictable and thus less reliable. For example, Indians who went caribou-hunting in the winter of 1720 returned to the post starving on 16 February, "having Seen no Dear nor Beavr" (HBCA B.3/a/9 fo.49d). Under these conditions, Indians may have come to devote more time to obtaining such highly variable quarry as snowshoe hares, as did some people in 1707. On 17 February that winter, two women came to beg food "for some Indians that Lies a Rabbit Catching" (HBCA B.3/a/2 fo.22d). Or, as already discussed, Indians may have ignored certain subsistence options in favour of concentrating on fur bearers. In either case, they would have been forced to live on what was available. They would have been much more vulnerable to the effects of climatic factors and to regional and seasonal variations in resource productivity. Consequently, in bad times they would have starved, as the evidence clearly indicates.

The relative rapidity with which some families became involved in the goose-hunt on a regular basis can, in part, be explained by the increasingly frequent and intensive stresses that they began to experience after the 1690's. The presence of store foods proved to be a godsend for many, and may even have inhibited some families from going any great distance from the post in winter. Old Miscamot and his family appear never to have gone more than a few miles from the post after the mid 1710's. For example, on 26 January 1716, Thomas McCleish stated: "Miscamot & his Family hath lain here ever Since my Arrival. He is to Decripled & Ancient y he cannot hunt, for if I did not maintain him and his family, which are 4 in number: they would perish" (HBCA B.3/a/9 fo.6d). By March and April the post was often crowded with starving Indians. For instance, there were 50 Indians living at the post on 1 April 1706, 109 Indians on 15 April 1717, 45 on 25 February 1718, 95 on 8 April 1719, and 47 on 4 March 1720 (HBCA B.3/a/1,9 passim). Indians who relied upon post food in March and April were available and willing to kill geese for the traders. By goose-hunting they could obtain the trade goods they wanted that during unfavourable years they couldn't get by trapping. As well, they could eat fat geese relatively early in the spring, at a time when the break-up made travel in search for other foods difficult.

While some Cree appear to have been willing participants in both the spring and the autumn goose-hunts, they preferred to curtail hunting by mid-September. They did not wish to remain near the coast too late when, traditionally, they should be preparing for the winter at their inland camps. For instance, on 9 September 1721, the home Indians asked to be discharged from goose-hunting in order to hunt marten and beaver (HBCA B.3/a/10 fo.3d). Again, on 24 September 1723, the goose-hunters refused to return to the marsh unless Joseph Myatt promised "them to keep in the winter if in case they should be starved soe that I shall let them goe and provide for theire families" (HBCA B.3/a/12 fos. 5d–6). Nevertheless, the fall hunt came to be considered more important by the traders, since it provided a source of winter food.

The willingness of traders to tide destitute Indians over, and a correspond-ing awareness on the part of the homeguard Cree that help was available to those who could reach the post, created a recurrent dependence on post assistance. Granted, Indians supplied the post with far more food than they received from it, and, except for a few persons like Miscamot, most Indians produced most of the food they consumed. Nevertheless, it would be misleading to mask periodic stresses and their behavioural consequences with long-term mean conditions. There can be no doubt that some Indians would have died had they not received store foods. Such knowledge may have encouraged hunters to trap when they otherwise might have concentrated on food-hunting. Altered adaptive strategies combined with an apparent decline in such key food resources as beaver and caribou were sufficient to tip the balance and produce the numerous cases of starvation recorded in the journals. In consequence of actual or potential catastrophes, Indians came to rely on certain trade items and periodic donations of food that would counterbalance the adverse conditions with which they had to cope. Thus, although starvation may have occurred in prehistoric times, it must have been far less frequent and severe.

Ecological degradation along with weakening social bonds among families periodically created severe physical and psychological stress for many Indians. Elsewhere, I (Bishop 1975b) have argued that these conditions generated what in later times can be called the Windigo complex. In view of Marano's (1982) recent assessment, I now refrain from using "Windigo psychosis," since we cannot determine whether individuals reported to have been windigos were psychotic. Clearly, however, abnormal behaviour could come to be associated with the Windigo, and the collective witch-fear response could be grounded in violent reality. For example, Joseph Myatt reported what possibly is the earliest example of an Indian reaction to, and possibly interpretation of, a murder at Fort Albany on 17 April 1723: "one of our home Ind Lyes about 20 mils to the Southward, Distracted or Lunatick, and hath Murder'd one of his wifes and would the other had she not . . . made an Escape to our hunters . . . wch hath soe terrified them tt th'y will not tarry there Longer, but intend to Pitch under Gunn Shott of the Factory" (HBCA B.3/a/11 fo.21). On 24 April the above Indian came to the post and admitted that he had murdered his wife. While Myatt provides no information about his mental state, suggesting that he was not "possessed," the earlier reaction by the goose-hunters to the murder fits Marano's witch-fear argument well.

Involutionary processes operated to intensify a reliance upon trapping and/or other post-related activities. They also established preconditions for changes in property relations, particularly those pertaining to fur bearers. About the early eighteenth-century York Factory Cree La Potherie wrote: "[W]hen an Indian has discovered the lodge of a beaver, he may be sure that no one else will be so unfair as to hunt it. They put marks in the neighbourhood, so that people may know it has already been discovered. But if, by chance, an Indian passing that way is hard-pressed by hunger, he is allowed to kill the beaver, provided that he leaves the skin, and the tail which is the most delicate morsel" (Tyrrell 1931:233). Morantz (1978:233) provides a similar example from the Eastmain Cree in 1745. Given these examples from widely separated Indians, it is not likely that the western James Bay Cree differed markedly. It is, of course, possible that family rights to beaver lodges were aboriginal, as Frank Speck and other early twentieth-century scholars argued. Beaver pelts were sewn into robes and apparel that were possessed by individuals—until they were traded. And Radisson's remark that young beaver in a lodge were left for future use suggests that the same families may have intended to return to kill them. But if this was the case, and if an allotment system existed similar to that described by Thomas Gorst in the 1670's, then there would have been no need to leave "marks" near the lodge. It is only when Indians were moving about in search of beaver lodges that such marks would have been necessary. And, in turn, it is unlikely that Indians would have been deliberately searching for beaver unless the demand for them was great—much greater than would have been required to meet aboriginal food and clothing requirements. In sum, the rudiments of a family hunting territory system may have been present among those Cree who became known as homeguards by the early eighteenth century at York Factory, Eastmain (Morantz 1978), and, more than likely, Fort Albany. The factors that may account for these supposed changes in property relations were, I suggest, an apparent decline in the beaver population in the vicinity of Hudson's Bay Company posts combined with a growing importance of all fur bearers as means of obtaining trade items. At a minimum these changes would have amplified the importance of whatever property concepts pertaining to beaver may have existed prior to the late seventeenth century.

That the western James Bay Cree had developed a relationship of dependency upon the Fort Albany post by the early 1700's in no way contradicts the evidence that they still were free to engage in a wide range of activities of their own choosing. Dependency does not necessarily mean that Hudson's Bay Company traders were able to control the behaviour of Indians. Indeed, the traders were frequently concerned that the intruding *coureurs de bois* would lure Indians away, and at times these fears were well founded. However, by opting to hunt furs and provisions for the post, the Fort Albany Cree created the very conditions that led to dependency. Though traders encouraged them in these activities, the Cree were willing participants. For instance, in 1706, John Fullartine "was continually bidding the Indians Kill martens, foxes, quickhatch [wolverines] etc. and for which they wanted no encouragement to induce them to the same" (Davies 1965:15). Thus, while the effects of the fur trade "were neither monolithic nor total" (Morantz 1980:39), and Indians indeed influenced trade policies, the Western James Bay Cree, nevertheless, required post goods. Although disasters only occurred periodically, an awareness that they might or would happen created, I suggest, both a psychological and a physical dependence upon the post and certain trade materials. However, a tool such as a gun was more than just a psychological crutch despite disadvantages associated with its use. Rather, it became a means of averting a potential catastrophe under conditions where the range of options had been narrowed by a decision to hunt fur bearers or by a decline in subsistence resources or both. The only alternative, and one that many Indians opted for often, was to take refuge at the post. It matters not that Indians expended much of their hard earned pelts on tobacco, brandy and other "trifles". They had, in fact, grown dependent upon certain goods or services by the early eighteenth century, even though most of their food was obtained from the environment and much of their material culture continued unaltered. Company policy of tiding Indians over bad times and supplying them with certain items functioned to keep them alive to trap and simultaneously to establish a bond that made it easier to obtain their assistance in other activities. This bond, which was reinforced by ritual gift-giving, together with Indian involvement in the welfare of the post which came to benefit them as well, led to the coalescence of a core of nearby Indians. These Indians usually remained loyal to the Hudson's Bay Company, visited the post more often than those at a distance, and within the space of three decades after Fort Albany's construction in 1675 formed the nucleus of the trading post band commonly called "homeguard Indians." The strength of this bond is reflected in the death wish of old Miscamote, who died on 12 September 1721: "he being desireous when living that he might be buried nigh the English" (HBCA B.3/a/10 fo.4). The symbolism of Miscamote's wish seems clear.

CONCLUSIONS

This paper has attempted to document social and cultural changes among the western James Bay Cree during the first century that they were influenced by Europeans. It has been argued that behavioural shifts, albeit small initially, ultimately—after the late seventeenth century—came to have a direct impact upon survival, creating new needs as well as wants, and through these, new structural alignments and relationships. Because the evidence for change is often sketchy, many interpretations must necessarily remain conjectural. Nevertheless, the absence of the kind of detailed data obtainable through fieldwork is insufficient reason to reject these data, provided that certain assumptions about aboriginal Indian behaviour hold true. Likewise, if the basic anthropological premises that cultures must be viewed as wholes and that change is a given are accepted, then it follows that dynamic structural and functional relationships exist among different aspects of sociocultural systems. In the case of the Cree, behavioural and social structural changes were related to material and ecological causes. Ideational modifications both reflected and reinforced these.

More specifically, it has been argued that the prime movers of change were three systemically linked and interdependent variables: (1) a new and usually superior technology; (2) an intensification of and specialization in productive activities designed to acquire the raw materials by which the new technology could be obtained; and (3) a corresponding reduction in the human/animal biomass ratio that amplified the significance of the first two variables. These three variables constitute the "forces of production," and, together with sociopolitical and ideational factors, define the mode of production. The forces of production, through positive feedback mechanisms, in time came to alter the relations of production. The apparent emergence of private owner-ship of beaver lodges during the early eighteenth century provides an example. Novelty is more evident in forces than in relations of production, however, primarily because sociopolitical relationships involve rules of conduct and beliefs the perpetuation of which guarantees the degree of predictability necessary to the survival of a society. Thus, while abrupt changes could occur in the productive forces, and sometimes did, sociopolitical and ideological changes were less perceptible, both to the outside observers and probably to the people among whom they were occurring. It is for this reason that those scholars who have argued for persistence have usually focused upon either social organization or the ideological system, since these often give the appearance of remaining unchanged. In contrast, those who have argued for rapid change have given heavy emphasis to the forces of production. In the case of subarctic Indians, the fur-trade records, by providing a relative wealth of data bearing on these, have led some scholars to ignore what appear to be more stable elements, especially those pertaining to ideological systems. But as is the case in any logically consistent theory of change, different parts of the total system articulate with each other. Post-contact adaptations, then, are seen to have been the result of a synthesis of the old and the new (Smith 1982). What has persisted has become embedded in a new, constantly changing, configuration; because of this, it is hazardous to select data for ethnographic reconstruction unless it can be demonstrated that such data logically could have been part of an earlier system.

Although these ideas can be transferred to other Algonquian groups, or for that matter to any other group of hunter-gatherers for which there is an adequate corpus of historical data, it should not be expected that such processes were identical to those outlined for the western James Bay Cree. Much of the cultural diversity revealed in the anthropological literature on subarctic Indians and on other hunter-gatherers may, in fact, be the result of such variable change. This remains to be tested.

Notes

Acknowledgements: I wish to thank the Social Sciences and Humanities Research Council of Canada for financial support under research grant 410-77-01520-R2 to investigate the archival records required to produce this study. I am also grateful to the Governor and Committee of the Hudson's Bay Company for their continued permission to view their rich Archives. This paper was originally presented in a symposium chaired by Shepard Krech III at the American Society for Ethnohistory Meetings, Colorado Springs, October 29-November 1, 1981. Special thanks are due my wife, M. Estellie Smith, and Toby Morantz, Lou Marano, and Shepard Krech for their helpful suggestions in revising the manuscript.

1. The term "influence" is used here rather than "contact" since Indians living a considerable distance from European centres often experienced the effects of contact indirectly through other Indians long before they themselves had face-to-face contact (see Bishop and Ray 1976; Krech 1983).

2. When attempting to bridge the gap between the prehistoric and historic periods, scholars have been tempted to rely on later ethnographic accounts. Not only does this assume cultural persistence, it also assumes ethnic continuity. This paper illustrates the hazards of the former, while Trigger (1982:12) warns archaeologists against such "facile interpretation of the archaeological record in ethnic terms and, in particular, to the assumption that the absence of obvious continuities in a vaguely understood cultural sequence necessarily indicates ethnic continuity."

3. M.E. Smith (1982) also provides a model that attempts to circumvent the theoretical dilemma that pits those who argue for persistence against those who stress change by introducing the concept of sociocultural continuity. At first glance, continuity might appear to be synonymous with persistence or tradition, but this is not the case. Rather, continuity "manifests both tradition and change at all times. . . . Continuity is the process whereby societies and individual members of these societies persist by deliberately or unwittingly altering and adapting in matters major or minor. . . . Continuity . . . is a synthesis of events and elements that are variously perceived as replicative or innovative, and it is the synthesis that is critical. We cannot isolate its components and define their stable properties as if "tradition" and "change" were the protons, neutrons, and electrons of atoms" (1982:127-29). Continuity, then, means that the synthesis itself is constantly undergoing modification. Smith's model focuses upon how insiders view sociocultural elements, that is, emic matters, rather than etic explanations as such. While the latter should take the former into account, they must be kept analytically separate—otherwise it is possible to fall into the trap of assuming that the memory history of living informants is "real" history. In this case, "[T]he past will always seem more stable than the present because humans are cognizant of a multitude of events in the present while the past is blurred into long stretches of "nonoccurrence" only occasionally punctuated by memory" (Smith 1982:128). Similarly, the relative scarcity of early historical documents can erroneously be interpreted to imply that the fewer events recorded meant that Indian systems were largerly uninfluenced. This does not mean that many time-honoured customs that continued to be viable were not retained. Rather it means that the total milieu in which they existed had altered so as perhaps to distort their meaning and/or function. From the emic perspective, it was this very distortion that reflected continuity—not persistence—and continuity is a major aim of all sociocultural systems.

References Cited

Adams, Arthur T., ed.
  1961   The Explorations of Pierre Esprit Radisson. Minneapolis: Ross and Haines.
Anderson, Anne
  1975   Plains Cree Dictionary in the "y" Dialect. Edmonton.
Bishop, Charles A.
  1970   The Emergence of Hunting Territories among the Northern Ojibwa. Ethnology
          9:1–15.
  1972   Demography, Ecology and Trade among the Northern Ojibwa and Swampy Cree.
          Western Canadian Journal of Anthropology 3:58–71.
  1974   The Northern Ojibwa and the Fur Trade: An Historical and Ecological Study.
          Toronto: Holt, Rinehart and Winston of Canada.
  1975a Ojibwa, Cree and the Hudson's Bay Company in Northern Ontario: Culture and
          Conflict in the Eighteenth Century. *In* Western Canada Past and Present. A.W.
          Rasporich, ed., pp. 150–62. Calgary: McClelland and Stewart West.
  1975b Northern Algonkian Cannibalism and Windigo Psychosis. *In* Psychological
          Anthropology. Thomas R. Williams, ed., pp. 237–48. The Hague: Mouton.
  1978   Cultural and Biological Adaptations to Deprivation: The Northern Ojibwa Case. *In*
          Extinction and Survival in Human Populations. Charles Laughlin, Jr., and Ivan
          Brady, eds., pp. 208–30. New York: Columbia University Press.
  1981   Territorial Groups Before 1821: Cree and Ojibwa. *In* Handbook of North American
          Indians. Vol. 6: Subarctic. W.C. Sturtevant, gen. ed. June Helm, ed., pp. 158–60.
          Washington, D.C.: Smithsonian Institution.
  1982   The Indian Inhabitants of Northern Ontario at the Time of Contact: Socio-territorial
          Considerations. *In* Approaches to Algonquian Archaeology. Margaret Hanna and
          Brian Kooyman, eds., pp. 253–73. The Archaeological Association of the University
          of Calgary.
  1983   Limiting Access to Limited Goods: The Origins of Stratification in Interior British
          Columbia. *In* 1979 Proceedings of the American Ethnological Society. Elisabeth
          Tooker, ed., pp. 148–161. The American Ethnological Society.
Bishop, Charles A., and Shepard Krech, III
  1980   Matriorganization: The Basis of Aboriginal Subarctic Social Organization. Arctic
          Anthropology 17 (2):34–45.
Bishop, Charles A., and Arthur J. Ray
  1976   Ethnohistoric Research in the Central Subarctic: Some Conceptual and Methodo-
          logical Problems. Western Canadian Journal of Anthropology 4:116–44.
Bishop, Charles A., and M. Estellie Smith
  1975   Early Historic Populations in Northwestern Ontario: Archaeological and Ethno-
          historical Interpretations. American Antiquity 40:54–63.
Blair, Emma Helen, ed.
  1911   The Indian Tribes of the Upper Mississippi Valley and Region of the Great Lakes. 2
          vols. Cleveland: Arthur H. Clark Company.
Collman, Jeff
  1982   New Thoughts on Perennial Issues. Reviews in Anthropology 9 (4): 339–48.
Davies, K.G., ed.
  1965   Letters From Hudson Bay: 1703–40. London: Hudson's Bay Record Society.
Dawson, K.C.A.
  1976   Albany River Survey, Patricia District, Ontario. Archaeological Survey of Canada
          Paper No. 51, National Museum of Man Mercury Series. Ottawa: National Museum
          of Canada.
Ember, Melvin, and Carol R. Ember
  1971   The Conditions Favoring Matrilocal versus Patrilocal Residence. American
          Anthropologist 73:571–94.

Hamilton, Annette
 1982   The Unity of Hunting-Gathering Societies. Reflections on Economic Forms and Resource Management. *In* Resource Managers: North American and Australian Hunter Gatherers. Nancy M. Williams and Eugene S. Hunn, eds., pp. 229–47. Boulder: Westview Press.
Helm, June, Edward S. Rogers, and J.G.E. Smith
 1981   Intercultural Relations and Cultural Change in the Shield and Mackenzie Borderlands. *In* Handbook of North American Indians. Vol. 6. Subarctic. W.C. Sturtevant, gen. ed. June Helm, ed., pp. 146–57. Washington, D.C.: Smithsonian Institution.
Hickerson, Harold
 1960   The Feast of the Dead among the Seventeenth Century Algonkians of the Upper Great Lakes. American Anthropologist 62:81–107.
Hongimann, John J.
 1981   West Main Cree. *In* Handbook of North American Indians. Vol. 6. Subarctic W.C. Sturtevant, gen. ed. June Helm, ed., pp. 217–30. Washington, D.C.: Smithsonian Institution.
Hudson's Bay Company Archives (HBCA)
 HBCA B.3/a/1–150. Fort Albany Post Journals, 1705–1845
 HBCA B.3/d/1–78. Fort Albany Account Books, 1692–1770
 HBCA B.3/e/1–19. Fort Albany District Reports, 1815–1837
 HBCA B.3/z/1–3. Fort Albany Miscellaneous Items, 1694–1871
Innis, Harold A.
 1962   The Fur Trade in Canada. New Haven: Yale University Press.
Krech, Shepard III
 1978   Disease, Starvation and Northern Athapaskan Social Organization. American Ethnologist 5:710–732.
 1980   Introduction: "Reconsiderations" and Ethnohistorical Research. Arctic Anthropology 17 (2):1–11.
 1983   The Influence of Disease and the Fur Trade on Arctic Drainage Lowlands Dene, 1800–1850. Journal of Anthropological Research 39:123–146.
Lee, Richard B.
 1981   Is There a Foraging Mode of Production? Canadian Journal of Anthropology 2:13–19.
MacKay, Douglas
 1949   The Honourable Company: A History of the Hudson's Bay Company. Toronto: McClelland and Stewart.
Marano, Lou
 1982   Windigo Psychosis: The Anatomy of an Emic-Etic Confusion. Current Anthropology 23 (4):385–412.
McNulty, Gerard E., and Louis Gilbert
 1981   Attikamek (Tête de Boule). *In* Handbook of North American Indians. Vol. 6. Subarctic. W.C. Sturtevant, gen. ed. June Helm, ed., pp. 208–16. Washington, D.C.: Smithsonian Institution.
Morantz, Toby
 1978   The Probability of Family Hunting Territories in Eighteenth Century James Bay: Old Evidence Newly Presented. *In* Papers of the Ninth Algonquian Conference. William Cowan, ed., pp. 224–36. Ottawa: Carleton University.
 1980   The Fur Trade and the Cree of James Bay. *In* Old Trails and New Directions. Carol M. Judd and Arthur J. Ray, eds., pp. 39–58. Toronto: University of Toronto Press.
 1982   Northern Algonquian Concepts of Status and Leadership Reviewed: A Case Study of the Eighteenth-Century Trading Captain System. Canadian Review of Sociology and Anthropology 19 (4):482–501.
Morton, Arthur S.
 1973   A History of the Canadian West to 1870–71. 2nd ed. Edited by Lewis G. Thomas. Toronto: University of Toronto Press.

Nute, Grace Lee
1978   Caesars of the Wilderness: Médard Chouart, Sieur Des Groseilliers and Pierre Esprit Radisson, 1618–1710. St. Paul: Minnesota Historical Society Press.
Preston, Richard J.
1975   Cree Narrative: Expressing the Personal Meanings of Events. Canadian Ethnological Service Paper No. 30. National Museum of Man Mercury Series. Ottawa: National Museum of Canada.
1981   East Main Cree. *In* Handbook of North American Indians. Vol. 6. Subarctic. W.C. Sturtevant, gen. ed. June Helm, ed., pp. 196–207. Washington, D.C.: Smithsonian Institution.
Ray, Arthur J.
1974   Indians in the Fur Trade: Their Role as Hunters, Trappers and Middlemen in the Lands Southwest of Hudson Bay, 1660–1870. Toronto: University of Toronto Press.
Ray, Arthur J., and Donald Freeman
1978   "Give Us Good Measure": An Economic Analysis of Relations between the Indians and the Hudson's Bay Company before 1763. Toronto: University of Toronto Press.
Rich, E.E., ed.
1960   The Hudson's Bay Company, 1670–1870. 3 vols. Toronto: McClelland and Stewart.
1967   The Fur Trade and the Northwest to 1857. Toronto: McClelland and Stewart.
1957   Hudson's Bay Copy Booke of Letters Commissions Instructions Outward 1688–1696. London: Hudson's Bay Record Society.
Rogers, Edward S.
1963   Changing Settlement Patterns of the Cree-Ojibwa of Northern Ontario. Southwestern Journal of Anthropology 19:64–88.
Rogers, Edward S., and James G.E. Smith
1981   Environment and Culture in the Shield and Mackenzie Borderlands. *In* Handbook of North American Indians. Vol. 6. Subarctic. W.C. Sturtevant, gen. ed. June Helm, ed., pp. 130–45. Washington, D.C.: Smithsonian Institution.
Smith, James G.E.
1973   Leadership Among the Southwestern Ojibwa. Publications in Ethnology, No. 7. Ottawa: National Museums of Canada.
Smith, M. Estellie
1982   The Process of Sociocultural Continuity. Current Anthropology 23:127–42.
Tanner, Adrian
1979   Bringing Home Animals: Religious Ideology and Mode of Production of the Mistassini Cree Hunters. New York: St. Martin's Press.
Thwaites, Reuben Gold, ed.
1896–   The Jesuit Relations and Allied Documents. 73 vols. Cleveland: Burrows Brothers.
1901
Trigger, Bruce G.
1976   The Children of Aataentsic: A History of the Huron People to 1660. 2 vols. Montreal and London: McGill-Queen's University Press.
1982   Concluding Remarks on the 1982 McMaster Symposium—The Ontario Iroquois Tradition Revisited. Arch Notes. Newsletter of the Ontario Archaeological Society. September/October 5:9–13.
Tyrrell, J.B., ed.
1931   Documents Relating to the Early History of Hudson Bay. Toronto: Champlain Society.
Williams, Glyndwr, ed.
1975   Hudson's Bay Miscellany: 1670–1870. Winnipeg: Hudson's Bay Record Society.
Willson, Beckles
1900   The Great Company. New York: Dodd, Mead and Company.
Wright, James V.
1972   Ontario Prehistory: An Eleven-Thousand-Year Archaeological Outline. Archaeological Survey of Canada, National Museum of Man. Ottawa: National Museums of Canada.

3

Economic and Social Accommodations of the James Bay Inlanders to the Fur Trade

Toby Morantz

In the study of the fur trade and its impact on native populations, it has come to be unequivocally accepted that native responses to the fur trade were almost as varied as the number of social groups and regions involved. Thus, when the geographical area of research I have concentrated upon seems to show developments at variance with those found for contiguous Northern Algonquian areas, I am not surprised. However, several anthropologists have attributed dramatic changes in early nineteenth-century native populations to their involvement in the fur trade. They make such claims on the basis of having reconstructed an aboriginal culture and describe as *changes* the differing social patterns to be found in later historical and ethnographic writings.

I would argue that unless archaeological evidence is utilized, we have little basis for establishing pre-contact social configurations. Although regional archaeological studies of the boreal forest have been carried out for the past twenty years or so, ethnohistorians have chosen to ignore this fundamental source. They have chosen instead, as evidence of earlier times, traders' or missionaries' accounts in the post-contact era. Moreover, while systematic archival records begin in the early eighteenth century, this source also has not been fully exploited. One of the aims of this paper is to present the kind of data that can be extracted from these sources and to show how these data can be regarded as valid in building models of pre-contact society.

Another aim is to present an in-depth analysis of eighteenth-century archival records in order to determine the lifestyle, that is, the economic bases and overall social patterning, of natives in one region. The two principal discussions in the paper focus on the exploitation of a particular ecosystem and on the organization and structure of the group that provided an economic base.

The region of focus is the eastern James Bay area of Northern Quebec, from roughly 50° to 54°N latitude encompassing the present day coastal settlements of Rupert House, Eastmain, Wemindji, Chisasibi (formerly Fort

LOCATION OF FUR TRADE POSTS & PRINCIPAL TOPOGRAPHIC
FEATURES IN EASTERN JAMES BAY

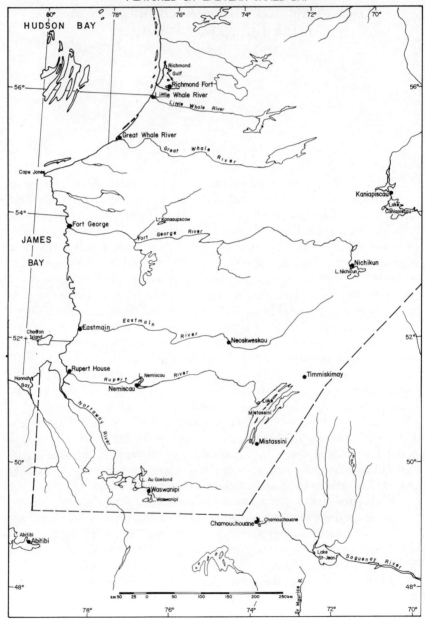

George), and those of inland regions, Nemaska, Mistassini and Waswanipi. In the eighteenth century, the principal post at which the people of this area traded their furs was Eastmain House. Today, these people call themselves Cree; in the early historic period the English traders designated them only by the direction from which they came: north, south, upland or inland, or coast. Jesuits writing in the 1670's, on the other hand, do refer to specific group names, such as "Pitchiboutounibuek" (Thwaites 1896, 56:203). Why the English did not continue this practice of using Algonquian names as they did in western James Bay, remains a mystery. Linguists today identify the Cree of eastern James Bay as Eastern Cree (or sometimes Montagnais) speakers.

The principal source of data used in this paper is the voluminous Hudson's Bay Company Archives (hereafter HBCA). Continuous daily records begin in 1737 at Eastmain, though earlier references to this region can be found sprinkled throughout the Albany Post (western James Bay) records. In contrast to the chatty journal entries and district reports of the nineteenth century, these eighteenth-century records usually consist of cryptic comments on Indians who, except for leading personalities, usually remain anonymous. It is for this reason that I and others working on local histories have chosen in the past to focus attention on the nineteenth century. It is now time to turn our attention to the earlier, less well-documented period. The approach followed here, however, is the same as has been used for the nineteenth century. It involves a complete indexing of all information relevant to the lives of Indians, including profiles of each hunter named. The analyses of the economic base of native adaptations and of group organization are constructed from this index. Wherever possible, the analysis proceeds from these basic archival data, rather than from judgments in the narratives of European traders.

LITERATURE IN ADJACENT AREAS

The focus, analysis, and conclusions in this paper might be placed in the broader context of research on eighteenth-century northern Algonquian social organization. Most important here has been the work of Charles Bishop on Northern Ojibwa living in northwestern Ontario, Eleanor Leacock on the Montagnais of central Quebec, and Edward Rogers on the Mistassini Cree of the eastern part of the James Bay region. Briefly stated, Bishop's (1974:308; 1978:222) finding that fur bearers, and in fact all game, were plentiful in the 1700's led him to propose that a big-game hunting economy was then in effect, that groups numbered from twenty to thirty-five individuals who remained together throughout the year, that in the early contact time these were patrilineal descent groups, and that by the late 1700's, bilateral bonds had become common owing to Ojibwa involvement in the fur trade.

To the east of the James Bay Cree were the Montagnais, whose culture and history have been investigated by Eleanor Leacock. Relying almost totally on the Jesuit Relations, Leacock considers the eighteenth-century Montagnais to have been principally caribou-hunters (Leacock 1954:21). Accordingly, winter hunting groups typically consisted of several lodge groups, numbering thirty-five to seventy-five people (1969:9; 1981:190). Though Montagnais hunted co-operatively throughout most of the winter, Leacock views this winter hunting group as basically unstable. Necessity might force them to separate into what in reality were the basic socioeconomic units: lodge groups, each consisting of several families numbering ten to twenty people. Leacock (1955) later revised her patrilateral orientation for the early historic Montagnais to one reflecting a slight emphasis on matrilocality.

As for the eighteenth-century Mistassini people, Rogers (1963:74), using published historical sources, has suggested a varied diet depending on the season (beaver and porcupine in early winter, caribou in late winter) and as a result, a range in winter hunting group size from five to twenty individuals, with twenty being exceptional. Rogers suggests that in this century, group size was limited by both ecological factors and by such cultural factors as an informal meat distribution system and the habit of moving camp to the site where animals were killed. In his scheme, early historic social organization was ideally patrilineal but in practice bilateral (Rogers 1969:46).

In addition to these directly related ethnographic and ethnohistorical sutdies, there is a significant body of comparative data discussing subarctic social organization in an historic context. Much of the latest thinking has been assembled by Krech (ed., 1980). An aim of this paper is not so much to restate the thinking of others as to illustrate certain of the suppositions with data from one specific area.

ENVIRONMENTAL SETTING

As in so much of the vast region of the Canadian Shield, the James Bay area is low and flat and lacks a well-developed drainage system, leaving the land for the most part marsh or muskeg. Its climate is severe, with average January temperatures of –23 degrees celsius. The area is free of ice for only roughly sixty consecutive days (Lehoux and Rosa 1973:8; Thompson 1968:285). Since plant growth is dictated largely by the length of the growing season and nutrient availability, the productivity of the forest decreases as one moves northward (Dunbar 1968:92). This diminution in productivity can be quantified: for the Fort George area, which is on the northern fringes of the region under study, a productivity value of 250 g/m^2/yr has been assigned, compared to 1200 g/m^2/yr for the temperate deciduous forest in southern Canada

(Berkes and Farkas 1978:157).[1] The presence of big fish in lakes and large populations of migratory game such as caribou and Canada geese may give a superficial impression of abundance; in fact, biological productivity seems to be generally low. Thus, we find Governor George Simpson in 1828 describing this region as "very thinly inhabited and its resources in respect to the means of living by no means plentiful" (HBCA D.4/91 fo.15d).

HISTORY

In this vast boreal-forested region of northern Quebec, archaeological investigations have been carried out primarily in the northern and southern sections. Southward, Martijn (1969:62) doubts that the Lake Mistassini region was permanently occupied until a diversified boreal forest took root, approximately 6,500 years ago. The oldest site uncovered at present is from the Lake Caniapiscau region, several hundred miles inland from Fort George, dated at 3485±95 B.P. (Denton 1981a:293). The archaeological picture emerging from investigations inland from Fort George and in the northern parts of the area under study is one of small groups of "nomadic" hunters annually journeying over a vast territory in search of a variety of animal resources (Laliberté 1978a:96).

Aside from the Inuit, the first non-Algonquian-speaking people to arrive in eastern James Bay were probably the English, under the command of Henry Hudson in 1611. Nevertheless, well before the English firmly established a fur trade in eastern James Bay with the arrival of the Hudson's Bay Company some sixty years later, the natives of eastern James Bay surely participated indirectly in the European trade off the eastern coast of Canada. This participation was probably through a series of Algonquian-speaking middlemen living on the Saguenay River and Lake St. Jean, one of the trade routes listed by Champlain in 1603 (Biggar 1922, 1:124). In fact, small quantities of metal trade goods are showing up in archaeological sites in the region. It is, however, too early to determine how extensive this early, indirect trade was or its characteristics or the nature of its acceptance by the local hunters; this applies not only to this isolated area but to regions better documented. Researchers are just beginning to explore the significance for native populations of early European fur-trade goods (Hamell 1982).

The period leading up to the Hudson's Bay Company's intrusion in eastern James Bay in 1670 may have been a turbulent one for the local inhabitants. A large number of people were said to have been killed by the Iroquois, as at Nemiscau and Mistassini (Thwaites 1896, 68:45), although oral histories (Cree Way 1975) depict the Cree as the victorious ones. Not only were the James Bay Cree victims; so were other Montagnais-speaking people to the south of them.

In 1657–58 Iroquois raiders had attacked, defeated, and dispersed Abitibi and Montagnais Indians of the Lake St. Jean region (Thwaites 1896, 45:223). In his Relation of 1660, Father Lalement suggested that the territory verging on James Bay had become a refuge "where various Algonquin Nations have sought a retreat, fleeing from the Iroquois" (ibid:219). This suggests that the James Bay region might also have become a refugee zone. Later, in the early 1700's, the region may also have received the Montagnais fleeing from a smallpox epidemic and from declining food resources (Angers 1971:24–25). This has yet to be confirmed archaeologically or linguistically. It does suggest, however, that this region probably was not immune to episodes of turmoil; although in the later historic period it was spared such devastating events as occurred west of Hudson Bay and which took the form of wars and feuds between Indian groups, epidemics, and violent clashes between competitive fur trade companies.

DIVERSITY OF ADAPTATION TO THE FUR TRADE

The European fur trade occurred over such a vast area in North America that there is an understandable tendency to view as uniform the adaptations of native people within single culture areas, ecological areas, or historical eras. The eastern James Bay region, where there were at least three distinctive forms of adaptation or accommodation to the trade, indicates otherwise.

At the start of record keeping in the 1670's (Oldmixon 1931), there was already in place a coastal population serving both its own and the Company's needs. Since the coastal lowlands are less productive than inland regions (HBCA B.59/a/12 fo.20), there is some question whether the lowlands were inhabited on other than a seasonal basis before the fur trade (Wright 1972:33). However, aided by European foodstuffs in the scarce seasons, just as Europeans were aided by them, coastal lowlands people seemingly "prospered" in their adaptation to both the coast and the company. This is the homeguard population and homeguard adaptation described elsewhere (Morantz 1983) for this region, and is the same in type as described in this volume by both Bishop and Judd.

Inland from the homeguard were the "trading Indians," or "inlanders," as the traders called them. For almost the entire eighteenth century, there were no HBC posts inland. Those hunters who were too far removed from the competition's seasonal, interior posts of Chamouchouane, Mistassini, and Nemiscau, or who simply chose to trade with the HBC, were unable to descend to the coastal posts more often than once each year in the early summer. It is these trading Indians, who were physically distant from the influence of European posts, who are the subject of this essay.

Another form of accommodation was made by hunters of barren ground caribou. The analysis of records pertaining to these people, who eventually traded on the coast of eastern Hudson Bay, has only recently been undertaken. However, it is apparent that in the eighteenth century they trapped fur animals only minimally, enough to secure from other Indians or the post the most basic trade items. Caribou hunting on the barren grounds was still their primary occupation. However, by the early nineteenth century, their response to a number of changed conditions was to alternate winters of caribou-hunting and fur-trapping farther south in the forested regions (Morantz 1984).

In eastern James Bay, then, lived the range of populations discussed in this volume by Ray, Judd, and Bishop. Some changed ecological zones in their adaptations; some incorporated HBC resources into their survival techniques. One type of adaptation not represented in James Bay is the "entrepreneurial class," the middlemen described by Ray (1978). Although men served in this capacity (HBCA A.11/–/57 fo.38, B.133/a/11 fo.6), it was an informal, intermittent arrangement. No specialized middleman class arose in James Bay. However, the focus of this study is not these specialized adaptations, but rather those people whose lives were not dramatically transformed by the fur trade. Being so far removed from the post, their main preoccupation was subsistence hunting. They did not shift ecological zones but continued to live a lifestyle the antecedents of which are visible in the archaeological record.

ANIMAL RESOURCES UTILIZED

Hudson's Bay Company post records are very informative about the state of James Bay coastal resources, for the simple reason that the Europeans were always concerned with their own food supply. Though the inland region is comparatively neglected, there is information on it because of the connection between the abundance or scarcity of food and fur-trapping.

Throughout the entire James Bay area, caribou were unquestionably the preferred food, with beaver clearly second (HBCA B.59/a/12 fo.22d; B.182/a/1 fo.25; A.11/57 fo.98). A frequent lament of eighteenth-century post masters is the following, randomly selected comment on "northward" Indians in 1765: "Though I have heard there is Beaver to be caught they do not or will not hunt them there being Deer plenty" (HBCA B.59/a/34 fo.30d). That in some years the Indians did trade beaver pelts indicated either that caribou were not always plentiful, that the Indians had all the caribou they needed, or that trade goods were valued.

The caribou hunted in the eastern James Bay area were the woodland, not barren ground, variety and so aggregated not in immense herds of thousands but in groups of only ten to fifteen individuals in winter when these groups were at their largest size (Fitzhugh 1972:172). Periodically the records refer to groups of forty caribou as at Timmiskimay in 1829 (HBCA B.133/a/15 fo.34d). Little is known about the habits of the woodland caribou (Trudel and Huot 1979:6), in part because it is difficult to inventory them (Audet 1979:18); they seem to be highly nomadic, with food and snow conditions being important factors in their movements (Dumais 1979:154). One wonders how easy it was to hunt them. Records from the 1830's indicate that it was difficult: there are reports of woodland caribou being sighted but too wary to approach for a shot (HBCA B.98/a/1 fo.15d); wounded animals eluded hunters (HBCA B.133/a/17 fo.12d); most often, caribou simply could not be found (HBCA B.133/a/22 fo.2d).

Climatic conditions greatly influenced success in hunting woodland caribou. Towards the end of winter, when snow was at its deepest and crusted, was the time when caribou were most successfully hunted (HBCA B.133/e/2 fo.3) and when meat was brought to the post (for example, HBCA B.59/a/18 fos.12d, 16d, 18). However, not all winters produced such optimum conditions. When the snow was shallow (HBCA B.133/a/4 fo.12) or packed hard (HBCA B.133/a/22 fo.18d), the Indians seemed unable to kill any "deer." In areas where caribou seem to have been more plentiful, as in the Nemiscau region, caribou were also hunted in the fall (HBCA B.142/a/1).

Aside from men, wolves are natural predators of caribou. The fact that wolves were not plentiful in eastern James Bay (HBCA A.11/57 fo.87), and in fact were rarely traded, suggests that caribou were not easy prey for them because of their low population density or elusiveness, or both. Forest fires also reduced the caribou populations (HBCA B.186/a/62 fo.16), and forest fires were not isolated occurrences throughout the 150 years of records examined. Some fires were started by Indians themselves, as in 1841, when a group at Hannah Bay made a signal fire to invite their friends to a caribou feast (HBCA B.186/a/64 fo.7), but most were attributed to lightning during summer droughts.

A thorough reading of post journals makes it impossible to regard eighteenth-century James Bay inlanders as exclusively hunters of big game (caribou). They may have thought of themselves as such, but the archival evidence indicates their diet was more varied, by necessity rather than choice. They also subsisted on beaver, ptarmigan, hare, and, of course, fish. This archival evidence on resource exploitation is supported by other data. For example, in the early eighteenth century the French surveyor Normandin (1732:95) commented that the Indians he found in the Chamouchouane River-Lake St. Jean region (southeast of the James Bay area) were "lazy." Rather than trap, they were said to prefer to remain at lake shores fishing for trout and waiting for caribou. In addition to fish and caribou, their food came from bear, lynx, porcupine, and hare.

Becoming fur hunters part-time need not have involved a significant re-orientation in hunting strategies. For instance, the trade of two inland canoes in 1742 consisted of "42 whole, 27 half, 10 coat beavers, 120 martins, 12 otters, 1 black bear, 4 deer skins" (HBCA B.59/a/6 fo.16), which represents a not inconsiderable amount of meat. All these fur animals are food animals today (see Rogers 1973), and they surely were in historic times as well. There are a total of seventy-nine beaver alone represented here. Also, numbers of skins or pelts were not traded at the HBC but were retained for personal use.

Even with a varied diet, the James Bay people of two hundred years ago were not assured of a consistent food supply. Starvation, it seems, was known to each generation. In his study of the Northern Ojibwa, Bishop (1974:277) dismisses starvation (before 1813) as having had an influence on eighteenth-century social organization, although starvation does figure in his analysis of the lowland Cree, or homeguard (1975:157). Among eighteenth-century inland Ojibwa, starvation accounted for comparatively few deaths, whereas in later centuries it was more common and brought about significant changes. However, in eastern James Bay there were no abrupt changes in subsistence resources in the early 1800's from the preceding century, and incidents of starvation throughout the records seem to be of similar consequence. For example, in 1703, starvation was reported to be very severe on the east coast of James Bay and widespread; it extended to Albany Post on the west coast (Davies 1965:8). The earliest Eastmain journals contain reports of starvation: in 1736–37, there is a report of a whole family of northward Indians having died (HBCA B.59/a/1 fo.24); in 1739, "There came in one canno from ye Southard . . . & allso gave me account of severall of his relations being starvd to death this later winter" (HBCA B.59/a/3 fo.26d); in 1747, inland Indians told of several having died for want of food (HBCA B.59/a/14 fo.24); and in 1749 the northern captain reported "a great many Indens was Dead for hungor a hard Winter among ym" (HBCA B.59/a/17 fo.22d). And so the accounts of starvation continue throughout the 1700's and 1800's.

Just how vulnerable the Indians were to hunting factors beyond their control is eloquently depicted in George Gladman's report of 1817. He wrote:

but on the 5th of November it began to thaw and continued until the 12th with very heavy Rain on that day, the Water rose in the River Rapidly, the River Ice was torn up, a heavy Gale and Change of Weather immediately following choaked the Creeks and Rivers with rough Ice and Snow, filled the Marshes also and destroyed alike the fishery and hunting, and a winter of Hunger and Misery commenced that has been seldom equlled; before the end of the year Indians began to arrive with distressing accounts of want. The creeks by the sudden Change of Weather were filled with Ice to an uncommon thickness, making the taking of Beaver Houses in some places impracticable, difficult in all, this was the universal account given by all the Indians who arrived, they also say that many young Beaver perished by the sudden inundation—the same scarcity continued all the Winter, neither Fox nor Marten tracks were to be seen and few indeed were the Rabbits or Partridges procured and even fish did not afford much assistance, the snow was uncommonly shallow and hard, so that when a few Birds were found, the Snow shoes made so much noise in walking that no Hunter could approach them (HBCA B.59/e/5 fo.1d).

This is a description of one type of climatic event which caused widespread hardship. In addition, there were those years when the low peak in the fluctuations of small food animals tended to coincide, creating a general scarcity of food (see also Waisberg 1975). Sickness in a family, forest fires, and a man's lack of skill in hunting also contributed to hardship. These threats to existence, together with the peculiarities of the woodland caribou, explain why the eastern James Bay Cree could not afford to depend on a single resource. In the eighteenth century, they were generalists, not specialized big-game hunters.

SOCIAL ORGANIZATION

The social organization of eastern James Bay Cree displayed a similar tendency toward maximizing options. Elsewhere (Morantz 1983:60–107), I have described in detail and analysed the various levels of social groupings—the family or commensal unit, the co-residential or winter-hunting group, the local group or micro-band, and the regional band or macro-group—for the period from 1815 to 1840. The norm was the co-residential group, which consisted of two or three nuclear or extended families, each of which averaged four to five individuals. When resources were scarce, each co-residential group separated into its component familial or commensal units. A local group or band was composed of from two to nine co-residential groups, averaged six hunters, and was both a migrating and, occasionally, economically co-operating group. As far as the HBC traders were concerned, the members of the local group acknowledged a "principal Indian." A larger regional or macro-grouping is discernible in the records but did not function on an economic basis. The composition of co-residential and local groups was patrilateral. In almost all cases a group of patrilaterally-related kin was at its core, but this was not an exclusive principle of affiliation. Other consanguineal and affinal kin were also incorporated. For example, one man's group consisted of his four sons, his brother, his brother's dependent and his brother's son-in-law (ibid.:94). Residence was usually patrilocal, often with a bride service arrangement.

The earlier records for the 1700's are less explicit. Nevertheless, the evidence that does exist strongly indicates a similar social configuration. In his Northern Ojibwa study, Bishop (1974:268–69, 329; 1978:212) assumes that the late eighteenth-century trading gangs accompanying each captain annually to the post were identical in composition to winter-hunting groups. Each gang numbered from twenty to thirty-five individuals in the late 1700's but was larger earlier in the century. Trading captains and gangs were also an eighteenth-century phenomenon in eastern James Bay and, as elsewhere, were products of the competition with first the French and then the North West Company. However, a detailed analysis, documented elsewhere (Morantz 1982, 1983), shows that for the eastern region this identity did not occur: trading gangs were not necessarily co-residential groups.

There are a number of indications of this. A captain was not regularly guaranteed the support of the same men each year. While the average (modal group) number of canoes of men accompanying a captain was two to three, the number of canoes each brought, in some cases over a twenty-year period, fluctuated greatly from two to fifteen canoes (Morantz 1983:149). This fluctuation was not affected by the size of the trade: in good years fewer men might come and vice versa. As well, men termed "strangers," from far-off locations, sometimes were said to be part of these gangs.

Not all inland hunters chose to trade with the HBC as part of a gang led by a trading captain. A statistical analysis of the use of the trading captain system (ibid.:146) shows that more men were drawn into it as the competition with the North West Company increased and luxury items, such as alcohol and tobacco, flowed. However, never was there 100 per cent participation in the system; some men continued to come to trade on their own or in groups of two and three but without reference to captains or leaders. For instance, of hunters coming from the south, 62 per cent traded in captain-led gangs in the period 1760–74, 98 per cent in 1775–86, and 79 per cent in 1787–1805.[2] Over the eighty-year period when the trading-captain system was in place, men led by captains made up 74 per cent of all arrivals at Eastmain Post from the southern region. For the upland and northern regions, the corresponding figures are much the same, although the upland region shows significantly less participation in the trading-captain system. There never was universal participation. There were always those who remained outside the system.

It is the combination of these factors (fluctuating size of trading gangs and the less-than-total participation in the trading-captain system) that has led me to conclude that in James Bay, trading gangs were task-oriented groups, not co-residential or winter-hunting groups. Trading gangs that consisted of three canoes probably were local groups, but a larger size indicated a temporary, adventure-seeking gang of men. This conclusion is supported by the comments of traders, as this from Moose Fort (western James Bay) in 1761: "the reason of his staying so long before he came down was in order to have collected more Indians together (as I promised him last summer that if he brot a good trade . . . I would make him a Captain) but that several who promised him in the Winter . . . had traded their goods up the country" (HBCA B.135/a/33 fo.32d). In the Eastmain journals are similar statements. For example, Lieutenant Canushirthew arrived in June 1774 with three canoes, but it was reported that "6 men not comd in that came with him Last Year he having not seen them this winter" (HBCA B.59/a/46 fo.31); and Captain Nebbittiabinow, who arrived at Eastmain in May 1790, claimed he could not find any of his gang (HBCA B.59/a/66 fo.31d).

In addition to the evidence from the trading-captain system, there are other indices of the social organization of the inlanders in the eighteenth-century records. As previously cited, before and during the height of the trading-gang period, some Indians arrived to trade without the auspices of a trading captain. These arrivals are recorded at Eastmain either by the number of canoes or by noting the number of men and the direction from which they came. In the years 1737–1753, years in which there were not upland captains, one finds cited, for example, the following: one canoe with a small quantity of goods; two canoes with a small quantity of goods; three Indians with goods; three canoes and 160 made beaver (MB); and four canoes, seven men, and 250 MB (HBCA B.59/a/1 fo.23, B.59/a/2 fo.25d, B.59/a/5 fo.16, B.59/a/12 fo.25d, B.59/a/15 fo.30d).[3] The last two parties are larger than usual; most of the entries are of one or two canoes; that is, of two to four men. Similarly, in 1799–1800 when no captain-led trading gangs arrived, the uplanders who arrived are listed as: two Indians with 60 MB; two canoes and 40 MB; one canoe;[4] two canoes and a few furs; two canoes, a few furs, and a little venison (HBCA B.59/a/77 passim). Even under trading captains, the average number of canoes from inland parties was 3.5 (Morantz 1983:149).

As for the furs traded, the values in MB are much less than Graham gives for York Factory in the 1760's where the European articles obtained in trade usually amounted to 70 MB per hunter each year (Williams 1969:277 and Ray 1978:30). At Eastmain, the comparative figures are in terms of the furs brought to exchange for European goods which are more in the range of 30 MB per hunter. In the few examples provided above of furs traded, the average per hunter is 25 MB in furs. A random selection of another thirteen transactions for the years 1772–1785 shows an average of 27.8 MB as the trade of each hunter. Some debt or credit might have been extended, but it is rarely mentioned in these years of competition with the North West Company. Instead of giving debt, both companies were handing out presents. The point is, though, that the small number of furs traded indicates that trading parties of inlanders were bringing only their *own* hunts and not also those of other members of their social group. Thus, all the above evidence points to small-scale winter-hunting or co-residential groups.

As for the composition of eighteenth-century local and co-residential groups, there are only a few comments from late in the century regarding the inheritance of the title and status of "captain." In one case a brother inherited (HBCA B.59/a/46 fo.30); in another it was a son (HBCA B.59/a/79 fo.25). In yet another a son did not, it was said, because his father's gang was merging with another one (HBCA B.59/a/69 fo.56; B.59/a/70 fo.35). In a fourth case the eldest son was passed over in favour of another person whose relationship was unknown (HBCA B.59/a/54 fo.26d).

There are few other mid-eighteenth-century comments on group composition. At times, trading Indians are reported to come with their sons (HBCA B.59/a/26 fo.14). Sons-in-law are mentioned less frequently and then usually in the context of the homeguard population, as for example in 1775, when a son-in-law was at a summer fishing camp with his father-in-law (HBCA A.11/-/44 fo.17). In 1756, one inland captain was said to be a son-in-law to a homeguard captain (HBCA B.59/a/24 fo.16). In this case they obviously did not reside together. The evidence here is not strong, but it does show that the HBC traders could distinguish sons from sons-in-law and that there was tendency toward or favouring patrilocality in the eighteenth century; the latter is definitely a trait of the early nineteenth century, where matrilocality appears as a bride service arrangement in most, but not all cases.

Drawing together the ecological and social information for the eighteenth century, it is apparent that these Cree inlanders were not large-game hunters, and, accordingly, their social organization was on a smaller scale than that of the Montagnais or Northern Ojibwa of the same period. Furthermore, the patterns of resource exploitation and of social behaviour of eastern James Bay inlanders are continuous, from the earliest records in the 1730's through the 1850's (see Morantz 1983:105–07), at which time new agents of social change, the missionaries, arrived.

OTHER APPROACHES: HISTORICAL NARRATIVES AND ARCHAEOLOGY

Demonstrated in the above analysis of the eighteenth century is the kind of very specific vital information that can be extracted from fur-trade records. Although nineteenth-century records provide far more particulars on individuals, permitting the construction of profiles of each hunter, the details of the eighteenth century are sufficient to allow some commentary on social organization. The analyses of food resources and social organization in this paper demonstrate how one can bypass a dependence on Europeans' impressions of Indian adaptations and, using what I call the "raw data" (such as number of canoes per gang), draw specific pictures of their lifestyle and particular profiles of individuals.

In contrast, the use of early published accounts by traders, priests, and adventurers is fraught with danger in terms of trying to reconstruct the early contact period. Several examples of the hazards of relying on the published records spring to mind. Drawing on the Jesuit Relations, Leacock (1955:32-33) uses Father LeJeune's belief that the Montagnais prefer the children of their sisters as heirs with another priest's statement on residence to conclude that a matrilineal and matrilocal pattern was characteristic among seventeenth-century Montagnais. But LeJeune never really comments on residence patterns! He does, however, write of having wintered in 1633-34 with two *brothers* and their families, nineteen individuals in all, who occupied one "cabin." Travelling with them were two other groups whose relationship is not given (Thwaites 1896, 7:97).

In two separate papers, Leacock (1955:33) and Bishop and Krech (1980:35) quote La Potherie. He visited York Fort when it was in French hands and left a memoire dated 1697 (Tyrrell 1931:229-30). He wrote, in part, that parents favoured daughters over sons because they (the daughters) supported them in their old age. But William Falconer (1768:56), writing of both Forts York and Severn some seventy years later, suggests a different bias: if a woman bore multiple children, all but one child—a male—were destroyed.

In their article on matriorganization, Bishop and Krech (1980:35) quote from Andrew Graham's observation that upon marriage a man lives with his father-in-law. However, in discussing divorce, Graham notes that the woman "returns to her own relations with her children" (Williams 1969:176), demonstrating that an initial bride service arrangement had been transformed into patrilocal or virilocal residence. Graham writes also of the eldest son being looked upon as the head of the family and of brides of ages eight to ten years who live with their husband. Graham's predecessor, Isham, who was at York twenty years earlier, implies in his observations on Hudson Bay that on marriage the woman took up residence in her husband's tent (Rich 1949:101).

In similar fashion, the argument for matrilineality by Bishop and Krech is supported by their reference to Graham's (ibid.) declaration that men seldom send away the women with whom they had children. The latter were "maternal property," and parents would be without support in their old age. The James Bay records recall this practice; in one case, a Cree named Etap was raised by his "divorced" mother's new husband; others were treated similarly (Morantz 1983:82). However, a woman's right to her immature children, upon the termination of her marriage, is known among patrilineal societies, such as the East African Sonjo (Gray 1963:75), and is certainly a practice in our own society without widespread implications about matrilineality being drawn.

Two other eighteenth-century authors, Lahontan (Thwaites 1905, 2:457), writing in 1703 and Charlevoix (1761, 1:277) in 1761, indicate a bride service arrangement, which terminates after the birth of the first child and the family moves to the husband's paternal residence.

On another issue, Bishop (1974:343, 1975:153) chooses to ignore the eighteenth-century accounts when he attributes to early historic Cree and Ojibwa bands the practice of cross-cousin marriage, even though Graham (ibid.:175) said that the Hudson Bay people "never marry any of their own relations, not even cousins" (Williams 1969:175). If one accepts Graham's pronouncements on residence preferences, then why not also accept his views on marriage prohibitions?

Clearly, one can find in the records whatever one is looking for. But my concern at this point is not whether Cree or other subarctic Indians were matri- or patrilocal, but how we go about ensuring we are on the right track in reconstructing social organization.

There is another question, one to which everyone pays lip service, but which really has not been adequately tackled and probably must await more intensive case studies and linguistic analyses: the question of the degree to which the historic era shaped the structure of Northern Algonquian societies. The fact that anthropologists generalize about these societies (for example, Turner and Wertman 1977:83–95) is one indication of the strong similarities in these geographically far-flung societies. So many, if not all Northern Algonquian social and cultural institutions are very, very similar, leading one to consider seriously that rather than the fur trade being responsible for these similarities, perhaps these institutions have their origin in a common proto-Algonquian ancestral society. Much as in language, where a core or basic vocabulary changes very slowly, perhaps there is a core or basic cultural expression such as social organization or religious beliefs that is equally conservative. This position is referred to by Bishop (this volume) as a "persistence model" and by Slobodin (1980:53) as "retentionist" and is, as the latter says, an old unresolved issue. We would do well to heed Slobodin's (1980:57) warning that we must keep in mind the implications of such an overview, even though we may be a long way from understanding it. In other words, the fur trade alone should not be expected to explain subarctic rules of residence, inheritance, or other traits. Other processes were at work.

Another set of evidence that has been overlooked by ethnohistorians is the archaeological record, an issue raised also by Trigger (1982:151–52). Admittedly, there are serious shortfalls in eastern subarctic archaelogical data and the analysis of them, but these are exaggerated and do not justify its total disregard in the literature. If anthropologists truly intend to decipher aboriginal patterns of social organization, then it is the prehistoric record we must begin with, and not the always suspect accounts of adventurers or priests. The following outlines the kind of data that can be used to shed light on adaptations in the pre-contact James Bay regions.

Palynological studies (Chism 1978:2–6) indicate that in the northern section of the James Bay region, a closed boreal forest was characteristic from 6000 B.P. to about 2700 B.P., when an open forest, that is, areas of upland barrens interspersed with forest, succeeded and has continued to the present. Fauna, however, do not seem to have varied appreciably, and the same species found today, except for moose, were probably in James Bay about 6000 B.P. (Laliberté 1980:21). Similar studies for the region to the east, around Lake Caniapiscau, date the transition from closed to open boreal forest earlier, about 4400 years ago (Denton n.d.:21).

The principal archaeological excavations in this region have been conducted in four separate locations. A considerable collection of artifacts and data has been amassed from roughly one hundred prehistoric and protohistoric excavated sites and several hundred more that have been surveyed. Although a regional synthesis is probably premature, the kinds of questions that concern me here and that would be asked of the archaeological data, namely having to do with group size and diet, are readily answered. At the three principal excavation zones along La Grande (Fort George) River—Lake Washadimi (Chism 1978, Laliberté and Séguin 1983), Lake Kanaaupscow (Laliberté 1980), and LG-3 (Séguin and Mandeville 1980)—winter camps tended to be occupied by small groups of people ranging from three to ten individuals (Laliberté and Séguin 1983:419). Their diet was varied. Recent intensive osteological analysis (M. Julien, personal communication) confirms that a range of mammals, fowl, and fish comprised the aboriginal diet. The suggestion that these people were principally caribou-hunters is unfounded.

The remains of habitation sites are also of great interest. For example, at one site (Labliberté 1981:62), dated at A.D. 900, is a house structure, identifiable by post moulds and other depressions. It measures 4.25 x 3.0 metres and in its centre are the remains of a small hearth. Bone remains associated with this house are principally beaver, caribou, and duck (ibid.:53). Most of the other prehistoric sites reported by Laliberté and the other archaeologists display similar characteristics.

There are some notable exceptions. At LG-3, Séguin (1980) has unearthed what she interprets as a meeting place occupied during several weeks in the summer by an imposing group of people, estimated at some three hundred. This is on the basis of having found thirty-two concentrations of burnt bone corresponding, she suggests, to sites of habitation spread over an area of six thousand square metres. The homogeneity of the artifacts supports her view that this site was occupied at one time. No C14 dating has yet been undertaken, but the presence of a few pieces of Middle Woodland pottery, probably trade items, suggests a date earlier than A.D. 1000.

Two other sites showing a relatively large assemblage of people have been excavated and analyzed. At LG-3 a house structure, measuring 9.5 x 1.7 metres, suggests to one archaeologist (Mandeville 1980:42) a group numbering thirty individuals. On the basis of Iroquois pottery fragments and a piece of copper, its date is placed at the beginning of the seventeenth century.

Another contemporary longhouse, measuring 7.0 X 4.5 metres was discovered at Lake Kanaaupscow (Laliberté 1980:37–45). This camp would have housed fifteen to twenty individuals. The faunal remains and lithic materials indicate a base camp for hunting beaver and other animals (ibid.). These are the exceptions. Most northern James Bay sites are characterized by smaller, one-hearth camps.

Denton (1981b:3–4), working further inland at Lake Caniapiscau—the fourth excavation zone—expected to find, on the basis of ethnohistoric accounts and the presumed importance of caribou in this region, evidence for relatively large groups of thirty or more individuals, the lower range of Leacock's winter band of thirty-five to seventy-five persons. He was surprised to find instead that the most commonly represented camps were occupied by only ten to twenty persons in a single dwelling. The only longhouse, thirty-two metres long with six aligned hearths, was one dating to the seventeenth century and containing fragments of metal trade goods. One-third of this longhouse was used for ceremonial purposes. The remains of fish and water-fowl indicate a summer occupation.

The absence of attention paid by ethnohistorians to archaeological findings in their region of study indicates a decision to ignore this very important source. It is evident that subarctic archaeology will never yield the kind of well-rounded portrayals of prehistoric life one can assemble for more southern regions. However, the kinds of data needed by ethnohistorians to answer their questions about aboriginal social organization, namely data on the exploitation of resources and group size, are, as demonstrated above, accessible in the archaeological record. For James Bay we can at present reliably say that in aboriginal times, this region generally hosted small-scale winter-hunting groups whose resource base was diversified. It is hoped that as archaeological analyses progress, we will be able to determine whether larger scale congregations of people increasingly become associated with the fur trade; at the moment, this trend is signalled but not proven in the James Bay archaeological record.

Thus, archaeological data permits us to reject for James Bay the model of large, mobile bands formulated for adjacent regions in pre-contact and early post-contact times (Leacock 1954; Bishop 1974). Another model not applicable to this region is the one of "affluence" proposed by Bishop and Krech (1980:41) for early subarctic Athapaskans and Algonquians. Affluence (or poverty) involves, in part, a subjective evaluation, and it seems at first glance a hollow discussion. Yet, one indicator of relative scarcity of food resources is the fact that prehistoric James Bay people exploited the environment in comparatively small groups. The assumption held by students of social organization is that larger cohabitational groups may have been more desirable, but size was governed by availability of food. For instance, McFeat (1974:35–38) discusses the importance of the larger groups in bleeding-off interpersonal tensions, but sees the smaller-sized winter groups as arising out of "necessities imposed by the environment and task definition" (ibid.:35).

Another conclusion from the archeological data is that James Bay inlanders did not undergo dramatic changes when they became involved in the fur trade. A comparison of the archaeological record with eighteenth-century historic documents shows continuity in inlanders' social and economic organization. Throughout the eighteenth and nineteenth centuries, inlanders did not trade for European foodstuffs; they were primarily subsistence hunters. In contrast to homeguard populations, their greater distance from the seaside posts meant that they were little involved in the company's economic sphere, other than to trade furs. Unlike people traditionally dependent on the barren ground caribou, they did not have to shift ecological zones to participate in the fur trade. This continuity in resource use and social structure also suggests that Ray's (1975:33) proposition that transformation of the regional Indian populations occurred prior to the beginning of the direct trade phase is not applicable here. Thus, these findings, reaching back into prehistoric times, are similar to the assessment of "essential continuity" made by some scholars for some Northern Athapaskans (for a discussion, see Krech 1980:2–3).

CONCLUSIONS

This paper began with the question of whether the large, big-game hunting band model used elsewhere in the Subarctic could be extended to pre-contact and eighteenth-century eastern James Bay. To rely solely on seventeenth and eighteenth-century historic documents seemed less than satisfactory. For my dissatisfaction, I owe a debt of gratitude to John Yarrow, an Eastmain trader, who on 21 November 1752 gave a lengthy account of the structure of a beaver house he had seen when he accompanied a hunter about six miles from the Post; at last, he apologized for the length of his exposition with these words: "my Saying so mouch Conserning the bever house, being my Eight winter in houdsons bay and never Seed one taken before" (HBC B.59/a/21 fo.8). Thus began my scepticism on how much traders really understood of matters beyond the post.

Detailed descriptions of the archaeological and early historical data are the logical sources for answering questions about the early social conditions. The narratives of traders and others serve only as guides to directions in which to probe. The confused and sometimes contradictory accounts of traders cannot be relied upon to reconstruct social patterns. This is better left to the statistical or detailed analysis of the raw data.

Such an analysis for inlanders of eastern James Bay reveals a prehistoric and early post-contact social organization that is at variance with neighbouring peoples. The inlanders were "generalists" in subsistence activities and sufficiently flexible in their social structure. They were prepared, seemingly from prehistoric times onward, to meet all conditions, feast or famine.

With these social features already in existence in the 1700's, it is difficult to conclude that involvement in the direct fur trade produced significant changes for the inlanders in the form of structural realignments or in their mode of production. Throughout the period of study, they were mainly subsistence hunters. Food was always uppermost in their minds, and European foodstuffs were never a factor in their adaptations. Fur-hunting only complemented their subsistence activities. They were not the trapping specialists that Ray (this volume) and others describe for elsewhere in the Subarctic. There is therefore no reason to expect any substantial alteration in their social organization as a response to their participation in the fur trade. The production of thirty to forty beaver pelts and forty marten skins, for example, one man's hunt in 1742 (HBCA B.59/a/6 fo. 16d), could be carried out within a traditional subsistence orientation. Trapping marten, unpreferred and low-yielding as food, perhaps demanded some minor adjustment in laying up a stock of dried food or in allocation of duties. Beaver, of course, were eaten and would have been hunted anyway for food. A similar perspective is provided by Bruce Trigger (1976, 1:409) who, writing of the Hurons in the period before they suffered a number of devastating blows, comments that the changes brought about by the fur trade were ones of degree and enhanced rather than destroyed social relationships. Other ethnographers of Northern Algonquian groups—A.I. Hallowell (1955:119), Dunning (1959:76), and Turner and Wertman (1977:108), for example—view the fur trade from a perspective that is similar and perhaps best summed up by Hallowell's conclusion that the fur trade "supported and encouraged the perpetuation of their aboriginal ecological adaptation . . . hunting" (ibid.).

Elsewhere in the Subarctic, especially west of Hudson Bay, intertribal wars and epidemics are said to have been devastating events (Bishop and Krech 1980:35; Krech 1983) leading to changes in the orientation of subsistence strategies and social systems. Likewise, twenty years ago Service (1962:86) hypothesized that the fur trade precipitated a shift from patrilocal to composite bands.

For James Bay there were no such mortal events in Hudson's Bay Company times, not even the smallpox epidemic of 1782–83 which reached no farther than Albany on the west coast of James Bay (HBCA B.59/b/3 fo.12). There is one exception, as noted earlier: according to the *Jesuit Relations,* the James Bay Indians were previously victims of Iroquois raids. One such attack in 1665 at Lake Nemiscau (Thwaites 1896, 56:183) was said, to have resulted in the killing or capture of eighty of the local Indians. However, as one discovers that numbers of Algonquian groups each have not-too-dissimilar Iroquois stories, found even today in oral histories (Smith 1982), it is becoming increasingly difficult to accept such accounts at face value. Their widespread distribution requires that we investigate, if possible, such historic accounts to learn if Iroquois were as involved and implicated in mid-seventeenth-century events as oral histories and the one documentary note indicate them to have been.

Another unknown for this study is whether the smallpox epidemics of the mid-1600's reported for the area to the southeast (Thwaites 1896, 56:155) spread to the James Bay region. Even if they did not, there is an additional problem of whether the southeastern people, ravaged by epidemics and warfare, fled to the north, as Father Lalemant's relation of 1660 suggests.

Even assuming that all these disruptive events occurred, one can still only speculate about their repercussions. In the case of the James Bay inlanders, who were not specialized hunters grouped in winter bands, it is difficult to see what changes might have resulted. As reported earlier, pre-contact and early post-contact subsistence "affluence" did not obtain in this region because biological productivity is low and extraordinary climatic events and periodic population depletions are natural events; therefore, one must assume that starvation was known to these pre-fur-trade people and that long ago they had developed mechanisms to cope with such disruptive forces.

To the west of Hudson Bay, devastating events did occur and in greater magnitude (Krech 1983). Occurrences of inter-tribal warfare vastly increased and became more violent because of economic competition within the context of the fur trade and the use of guns (Driver 1961:354, 370). Epidemics, it is known, are more severe when introduced by alien populations (see Patterson and Hartwig 1978:4), but the effects of depopulation and displacement, not unlike that accompanying widespread starvation, have yet to be elaborated for all subarctic populations. While we have intensive studies showing adaptations to a changed resource base in the nineteenth century (see Bishop 1974; Rogers and Black 1976), we do not have such studies for prior social conditions. Did the various subarctic peoples who adopted and adapted to the fur trade have *in situ* flexible social organization of the sort described for them today (see Damas 1969)? If so, then the impact of the fur trade on such groups was only quantitatively not qualitatively different. This begs the question, admittedly, of determining their aboriginal social structure.

A further problem is that by the very nature of fragmentary historic data, we have been forced to make generalizations based on brief time periods such as twenty years of Graham or the Jesuits or of HBC district reports. Much as Bennett (1976:308), in his study of ecological processes, has differentiated between generalizations based on macro- and micro-social studies, so it seems useful to suggest that the variable "time" similarly affects generalizations in terms of their level and degree of applicability. Reported cases of ecological imbalance or of external pressures might show up in micro (time) studies as social upheavals or adaptations, but in macro (longer-term) studies could possibly be regarded as short-term adjustments. There is no doubt that future archaeological findings combined with a better understanding of the seventeenth- and eighteenth-century archival data will vastly improve the vantage point from which fur-trade accommodations are presently viewed. Such a perspective, beginning to be developed for James Bay and reported on here, is a prime example of this type of macro-temporal study.

Notes

Acknowledgements: The research for this paper was funded by the Ministère des Affaires culturelles of Québec through its James Bay Ethnohistory Programme. The final version was written under the auspices of a Social Sciences and Humanities Research Council postdoctoral fellowship. I wish to express my gratitude to both agencies and also the Hudson's Bay Company for granting me permission to consult and quote from their records on deposit on microfilm at the Public Archives of Canada. I also extend my appreciation to the other members of the symposium and in particular its organizer Shepard Krech, at the American Society for Ethnohistory meetings for their useful comments on an earlier draft of this paper. David Denton helped me gain a command and understanding of the considerable archaeological research in the area, for which I am most grateful. Any errors in interpretation are entirely my own.

1. $G/m^2/yr$ or grams per square metre per year refers to the amount of biological production by land plants, the basis for the production of land animals.
2. These time periods represent the middle years of the trading captain system and each one denotes a change in the intensity of competition between fur trading companies.
3. Made beaver (MB) refers to the standard of trade used by the Hudson's Bay Company. It represents the equivalent of one prime, dressed beaver pelt. The number of furs traded in the example of four canoes, seven men, and 250 MB was given as 150 whole beaver, 100 half-beaver, and 150 martens. Using the standard of trade of 1749 (HBC B.3/d/57 fo.12d), this works out to be 250 MB.
4. Their trade was grouped with that of three hunters from the north, the total of which was 74 MB.

References Cited

Angers, Lorenzo
    1971   Chicoutimi. Poste de Traite, 1676–1856. Ottawa: Leméac.
Audet, René
    1979   Histoire du caribou du Québec-Labrador et evolution des populations. *In* Dossier
            Caribou, F. Trudel and J. Huot, eds. Recherches amérindiennes au Québec
            9 (1–2):17–28.
Bennett, John W.
    1976   'The Ecological Transition: Cultural Anthropology and Human Adaptation. New
            York: Pergamon Press.
Berkes, Fikret, and Farkas, Carol
    1978   Eastern James Bay Cree Indians: Changing Patterns of Wild Food Use and Nutri-
            tion. Ecology of Food and Nutrition 7:155–72.
Biggar, H.P., ed.
    1922   The Works of Samuel de Champlain, Vol. 1. Toronto: Champlain Society.
Bishop, Charles A.
    1974   The Northern Ojibwa and the Fur Trade. Toronto: Holt, Rinehart and Winston.
    1975   Ojibwa, Cree and the Hudson's Bay Company in Northern Ontario: Culture and
            Conflict in the Eighteenth Century. *In* Western Canada. Past and Present. A.W.
            Rasporich, ed., pp. 150–62. Calgary: McClelland and Stewart.
    1978   Cultural and Biological Adaptations to Deprivation. The Northern Ojibwa Case. *In*
            Extinction and Survival in Human Populations. C.D. Laughlin and I.A. Brady, eds.,
            pp. 209–30. New York: Columbia University Press.
Bishop, Charles A., and Shepard Krech III
    1980   Matriorganization: The Basis of Aboriginal Subarctic Social Organization. Arctic
            Anthropology 17 (2):34–45.
Charlevoix, Pierre de
    1761   Journal of a Voyage to North America. 2 vols. London: Dodsley. (University
            Microfilms, 1966.)
Chism, James
    1978   Archaeology at Washadimi. Report presented to the Service de l'archéologie et de
            l'ethnologie, Ministère des Affaires culturelles, Québec. Typescript, 90pp.
Cree Way Project
    1975   Various oral histories collected at Rupert House, Quebec. Typescripts.
Damas, David, ed.
    1969   Contributions to Anthropology: Band Societies. Ottawa: National Museum of Man.
            Bulletin 228.
Davies, K.G. ed.
    1965   Letters from Hudson Bay, 1703–40. London: Hudson's Bay Record Society No. 25.
Denton, David
    1981a   Investigations archéologiques dans la région du futur reservoir Caniapiscau,
            Québec, 1979. Direction générale du patrimoine. Ministère des Affaires culturelles,
            Québec. Interventions archéologiques, No. 1.
    1981b   Variation in the Size of Prehistoric Co-Residential Groups in the Eastern Sub-Arctic:
            Evidence from the Central Interior of Quebec-Labrador. Paper presented at the
            Canadian Archaeological Association Meetings, Edmonton, April 27–30.
    n.d.   Prehistoric Settlement Systems and Adaptive Strategies in Central Quebec-
            Labrador. Typescript, 54 pp.
Driver, Harold E.
    1961   Indians of North America. Chicago: University of Chicago Press.
Dumais, Pierre
    1979   Les Amérindiens et le caribou des bois au sud du Saint-Laurent. *In* Dossier Caribou.
            F. Trudel and J. Huot, eds. Recherches amérindiennes au Québec 9 (1–2):151–59.

Dunbar, M.J.
  1968   Ecological Development in Polar Regions. Englewood Cliffs: Prentice-Hall.
Dunning, R.W.
  1959   Social and Economic Change among the Northern Ojibwa. Toronto: University of Toronto Press.
Falconer, William
  n.d.   Remarks on the Natives of Hudson Bay. *In* Records of William Falconer, 1768-1776. Vol. 1:19-62. MG19, D2. Public Archives of Canada.
Fitzhugh, William
  1972   Environmental Archeology and Cultural Systems in Hamilton Inlet, Labrador. Smithsonian Contributions to Anthropology, No. 16.
Francis, Daniel, and Toby Morantz
  1983   Partners in Furs. A History of the Fur Trade in Eastern James Bay, 1600-1870. Kingston and Montreal: McGill-Queens University Press.
Gray, Robert F.
  1963   The Sonjo of Tanganyika. London: Oxford University Press.
Hallowell, A. Irving
  1955   The Northern Ojibwa. *In* Culture and Experience, pp. 112-24. Philadelphia: University of Pennsylvania Press.
Hamell, George
  1982   The Magic of Glass Beads: Glass Beads as Crystals. Paper presented at the 81st meeting of the American Anthropological Association. Washington, D.C.
Hudson's Bay Company Archives (HBCA).
  HBCA A.11. London Inward Correspondence
  HBCA B.59/a/. Eastmain Post Journals
  HBCA B.98/a/. Kaniapiskau Post Journals
  HBCA B.133/a/. Mistassini Post Journals
  HBCA B.135/a/. Moose Fort Journals
  HBCA B.142/a/. Nemiscau Post Journals
  HBCA B.182/a/. Richmond Fort Journals
  HBCA B.186/a/. Rupert House Journals
  HBCA D.4. Simpson's Official Reports
Krech, Shepard III
  1980   Introduction: "Reconsiderations" and Ethnohistorical Research. Arctic Anthropology 17 (2):1-11.
  1983   The Influence of Disease and the Fur Trade on Arctic Drainage Lowlands Dene, 1800-1850. Journal of Anthropological Research 39:123-46.
Krech, Shepard III, ed.
  1980   Reconsiderations of Aboriginal Social Organization in the North American Subarctic. Arctic Anthropology 17 (2):1-63.
Laliberté, Marcel
  1978   La forêt boréale. *In* Images de la préhistoire du Québec, edited by C. Chapdelaine. Recherches amérindiennes au Québec 7 (1-2):87-98.
  1980   Rapport sur l'adaptation, le mode d'organisation et de subsistance des populations préhistoriques de la région de Kanaaupscow. Report presented to the Patrimoine autochtone, Ministère des Affaires culturelles, Québec. Typescript, 93pp.
  1981   Rapport d'analyse des sites GaGc-1, GaGd-4 et GaGd-13 du lac Kanaaupscow, Baie-James, Québec. Direction générale du patrimoine, Ministère des Affaires culturelles, Québec. Interventions archéologiques, No. 4.
Laliberté, Marcel, and Jocelyne Séguin
  1983   Trois Millenaires d'histoire au Québec subarctique: la région de Washadimi. Preliminary report presented to the patrimoine autochtone, Ministère des Affaires culturelles, Québec, Typescript, 500 pp.
Leacock, Eleanor
  1954   The Montagnais "Hunting Territory" and the Fur Trade. American Anthropological Association Memoir No. 78.

1955   Matrilocality in a Simple Hunting Economy. Southwestern Journal of Anthropology 11:31–47.
1969   The Montagnais-Naskapi Band. *In* Contributions to Anthropology: Band Societies. D. Damas, ed. Ottawa: National Museum of Man. Bulletin 228.
1981   Seventeenth-Century Montagnais Social Relations and Values. *In* Handbook of North American Indians. Vol. 6. Subarctic. William C. Sturtevant, gen. ed. June Helm, ed., pp. 190–95. Washington, D.C.: Smithsonian Institution.
Lehoux, Dénis, and Jacques Rosa
1973   Description des principales unités physiographiques de la région de la Baie James. Ottawa: Wildlife Branch, Department of the Environment. Typescript, 25pp.
McFeat, Tom
1974   Small Group Cultures. New York: Pergamon Press.
Mandeville, Jean
1980   Rapport des excavations du site archéologique, FjFp–4, Reservoir LG–3, Jamesie. Report presented to the Patrimoine autochtone, Ministère des Affaires culturelles, Québec. Typescript, 152 pp.
Martijn, Charles A., and Rogers, Edward
1969   Mistassini-Albanel: Contributions to the Prehistory of Quebec. Centre d'études nordiques. Travaux divers No. 25. Québec: Université Laval.
Morantz, Toby
1982   Northern Algonquian Concepts of Status and Leadership Reviewed: A Case Study of the Eighteenth Century Trading Captain System. Canadian Review of Sociology and Anthropology 19 (4):482–500.
1983   An Ethnohistoric Study of Eastern James Bay Cree Social Organization 1700–1850. Canadian Ethnology Service Paper No. 88. Ottawa: National Museum of Man.
1984   "Not Annual Visitors"—The Drawing in to Trade of Northern Algonquian Caribou Hunters. *In* Actes du quatorzième congrès des Algonquinistes. W. Cowan, ed. Ottawa: Carleton University. In press.
Normandin, Joseph L.
n.d.   Journal de Voyage que J.L. Normandin a fait dans le Domaine du Roi . . . en 1732. Margry Collection, vol. 9275. Handwritten transcript. MG7, 1A 3, Public Archives of Canada.
Oldmixon, John
1931   The Early History of Hudson's Bay. *In* Documents Relating to the Early History of Hudson Bay. J.B. Tyrrell, ed., pp. 371–410. Toronto: Champlain Society. (First published in 1708.)
Patterson, David K., and Hartwig, Gerald W.
1978   The Disease Factor: An Introductory Overview. *In* Disease in African History, G.W. Hartwig and D.K. Patterson, eds., pp. 3–24. Durham: Duke University Press.
Ray, Arthur J.
1978   History and Archaeology of the Northern Fur Trade. American Antiquity 43 (1):26–34.
Rich, E.E. ed.
1949   James Isham's Observations and Notes, 1743–1749. London: Hudson's Bay Record Society.
Rogers, Edward S.
1963   The Hunting Group-Hunting Complex among the Mistassini Indians. Ottawa: National Museum of Man, Bulletin 195.
1973   The Quest for Food and Furs. The Mistassini Cree, 1953–1954. Ottawa: National Museum of Man. Publications in Ethnology, No. 5.
Rogers, Edward S., and Black, Mary B.
1976   Subsistence Strategy in the Fish and Hare Period, Northern Ontario: The Weagamow Ojibwa, 1880–1920. Journal of Anthropological Research 32 (1):1–43.

Séguin, Jocelyne
  1980   Rapport des excavations du site archéologique F1Fo–1. Reservoir LG–3, Jamesie.
         Report presented to the Patrimoine autochtone, Ministère des Affaires culturelles,
         Québec. Typescript, 166pp.
Séguin, Jocelyne, and Mandeville, Jean
  1980   Rapport des excavations du site archéologique F1Ft–1. Reservoir LG–3, Jamesie.
         Report presented to the Patrimoine autochtone, Ministère des Affaires culturelles,
         Québec. Typescript, 81pp.
Slobodin, Richard
  1980   Some Recent Developments in Subarctic Culture History and Ethnohistory. Arctic
         Anthropology 17 (2):52–59.
Smith, Nicholas
  1982   Wabanaki-Mohawk Conflict: A Folk Tradition. Paper presented at the Fourteenth
         Algonquian Conference, Québec City.
Thompson, H.A.
  1968   Climate. *In* Science, History and Hudson Bay. C.S. Beals and D.A. Shenstone, eds.,
         vol. 1:263–86. Ottawa: Department of Mines and Resources.
Thwaites, Reuben Gold, ed.
  1896–1901   The Jesuit Relations and Allied Documents. 73 volumes. Cleveland.
  1905   Lahontan's New Voyages to North America. 2 vols. Chicago: McClung. (Reprinted
         and edited from the English edition of 1703.)
Trigger, Bruce
  1976   The Children of Aataentsic: A History of the Huron People to 1660. 2 vols.
         Montreal: McGill-Queen's University Press.
  1982   Response of Native Peoples to European Contact. *In* Early European Settlement
         and Exploration in Atlantic Canada. G.M. Story, ed., pp. 139–52. St. John's:
         Memorial University.
Trudel, François, and Huot, Jean, eds.
  1979   Dossier Caribou. Recherches amérindiennes au Québec 9 (1–2).
Turner, David, and Wertman, Paul
  1977   Shamattawa: The Structure of Social Relations in a Northern Algonkian Band.
         Ottawa: National Museum of Man. Mercury Series. Canadian Ethnology Service
         Paper, No. 36.
Tyrrell, J.B., ed.
  1931   Documents Relating to the Early History of Hudson Bay. Toronto: Champlain
         Society.
Waisberg, Leo C.
  1975   Boreal Forest Subsistence and the Windigo: Fluctuation of Animal Populations.
         Anthropologica 17:169–88.
Williams, Glyndwr, ed.
  1969   Andrew Graham's Observations on Hudson's Bay, 1767–1791. London: Hudson's
         Bay Record Society.
Wright, James V.
  1972   Ontario Prehistory. Ottawa: National Museum of Man. Archaeological Survey
         of Canada.

4

Sakie, Esquawenoe, and the Foundation of a Dual-Native Tradition at Moose Factory

Carol M. Judd

Until a decade ago little was known about the complexity of roles which Indians played in the subarctic fur trade. At that time, important work by Arthur Ray (1974), Charles Bishop (1974), and other scholars initiated the trend to redress the imbalances in information on various aspects of the trade. By describing the differing relationship of homeguard and upland Indians with one fur-trade post, this paper provides a few additional details in the larger picture being drawn by fur-trade historians. The post is Moose Factory. Although the cultural and social milieu there may have been unusual (conditions were different from those that prevailed at York Factory, which had a much larger hinterland), this post was chosen for this study because it was important, because the documentation for it was adequate, and because its limited hinterland brought trading Indians into the post annually or semi-annually, often enough for patterns of behaviour to be readily observable.

Most important for this study is that the records at Moose Factory for the time period from 1730 to 1750 (when the post was called Moose Fort) are virtually complete and unusually descriptive. Indians who traded at the post were named and in some cases described in detail; and editorial comments in the journal revealed the attitudes and beliefs of the officers in charge. This was particularly true during the three-year period (1741–44) when James Duffield was in charge at Moose Factory.[1]

Duffield ruled the fort with an iron hand. He trusted no one; he asserted his authority in all areas of the men's and officer's lives; a lonely and isolated leader, he confided only in his daily journal and in letters to his most intimate ally, Joseph Isbister, the factor at Fort Albany, a Hudson's Bay Company post about 100 miles north of Moose Factory.[2] This historical "accident" meant that personalities were discussed at length; it meant also that the activities of prominent Indians in the area were vividly portrayed and colourfully revealed.

In journals kept in later years, after Duffield's time, comments on the

principal Indian traders were more brief, but enough information has survived to cast light on the two main Indian groups who traded at Moose
Factory, by focusing on biographical accounts of their respective leaders. It is
important to note that all these journals reveal, for the mid-eighteenth century, the separate lifeways of the two main Indian groups and that these
formed a baseline for distinct and separate cultures that remained so well into
the present century (Judd 1981b:276–78).

By the time Moose Factory was permanently established in 1730, the
Hudson's Bay Company had been operating in the James Bay region for sixty
years. Indeed, the first post near the mouth of Moose River (distinguished
from later posts built on the same island as Moose Fort I) had been built in
1673 and operated for over twenty years before being seized by enemy French
forces. Years of neglect followed. Some Indians who had used Moose Factory
continued to trade at Albany, which could be reached only after crossing the
open and hazardous waters of James Bay. In fact, Moose Factory was
re-established only after natives threatened to take their business to opposition French traders, who were beginning to operate in the upper regions of the
Moose River, unless the post was opened once again (Judd 1981b:216–17).
More precisely, "upland" Indians were probably responsible for successfully
negotiating the reopening of Moose Factory, since the Indians who normally
spent the goose-hunting season and perhaps the summer in the general region
of Moose Factory retreated up the Moose River to more sheltered, inland
regions for winter.

Not surprisingly, when Moose Factory (Moose Fort II) was opened in
1730, an already well-defined pattern of native-European relations existed in
the James Bay region. Although the post was set up ultimately to answer the
demands of upland Indians who came down to the post on an annual or
semi-annual basis to trade furs, the arrival of British fur traders from Albany
with materials to build a fur-trade post immediately spawned a homeguard
band, which, in fact, had probably come with the traders from Albany.

This group of Indians was charged with the responsibility of providing the
Europeans with country provisions, especially geese and deer flesh. They were
paid with liquor, powder, and shot, although they traded other items as
well; because they were confined to hunting in the area of the post, they
expected to be given European provisions when their own became scarce.

During the first fall goose-hunting season, the Indians in the neighbourhood of the post brought in more than five hundred geese. On 13 October
1730, at the termination of the goose-hunt, the fur traders gave each hunter a
bottle of brandy. Since these Indians were not mentioned again in the post
journals for several months, it can be assumed that at the end of the goose-
hunting season they left the vicinity of the post to set up winter quarters in a
more protected area. They did not therefore resort to the meagre larder of the
fur-trade post during the lean winter months. The fur traders themselves used

a canoe (which they had received in trade for a gun) to set and haul nets for fishing. In that first fall season they harvested over seven hundred fish. During the winter they hunted partridges which abounded in the area, and by the beginning of the new year they had brought in over four hundred. Thus the traders did not rely fully on the homeguard for provisions but spent considerable time and energy procuring small game in the vicinity of the post (HBCA B.135/a/1 passim).[3]

During the first season of renewed operation at Moose Fort II, not enough trade goods had been brought in from Albany to enable the fur traders to obtain furs from the upland Indians. Upland Indians who came down to the post with furs to trade or who came to get "trust" or credit were sent on to Albany. Some of those who came indicated that they would rather go to the French traders, who were closer (on the Abitibi River), than cross the bay to Albany (HBCA B.135/a/1 passim).

The homeguard Indians, who probably passed regularly over the winter ice between Albany and Moose in any case, were used to carry messages between the two posts. In February a family of starving Indians came into the post. There are three equally likely explanations why these and others were "starving"—in fact, why starvation forms part of the permanent record of virtually all fur-trade posts (see, for example, Bishop 1974, Krech 1980): possibly, the traders were attempting to obscure the fact that some Indians were "guests" at the post for social reasons (perhaps as wives, for example) and provided an otherwise inexplicable drain on food; alternatively, Indians may have feigned hunger in order to avoid the difficulty of hunting; or the post may have been regarded as a refuge to which Indians increasingly resorted during times that were lean and when they were actually starving.[4]

Thus, by the end of the first season at Moose Fort II, the mechanism for socioeconomic exchange with homeguard Indians had been set. The seasonal migrations of homeguard Indians were geared to the needs of the post: they hunted geese in spring; hunted and fished along the Moose River or went off "hunting Eskimoes" on the eastern side of the bay in summer; returned toward the end of August to Moose Fort II for the fall goose-hunt; and in winter, headed off for quarters which were usually not more than a few days' travel from the bayside post. In this way, before a system of fur exchange was set up at Moose Fort II, the foundations of the homeguard system had been securely laid.

The homeguard band had a system of leaders, termed captains and lieutenants, which served the purposes of the traders by providing a core group with authority over other Indians. This system was almost immediately identifiable in the Moose records, but it is not clear whether it predated the fur trade; nor is it possible to state with certainty whether the Indians themselves or the factor chose the earliest-mentioned homeguard leaders.

Sakie was the first and most powerful homeguard captain whose career can be followed with any accuracy. He was first mentioned in the Moose journals in 1740, but he had probably been prominent at Moose and before that at Albany for many years. He had a large and loyal following of at least fifty and perhaps more than seventy-five of his own people and set up close social ties with the fur traders. The Hudson's Bay Company used him officially as liaison with the homeguard Indians in his capacity as captain of the goose-hunters. Sakie was accorded special treatment by the factors of the company; yet at times he appears to have been regarded more as a potential vehicle for manipulating the homeguard than as an equal. He was viewed with both ostensible respect and usually inward distrust as this excerpt from the Moose Post Journal shows:

> All our home Indians are here on the plantation awaiting for Sakie, the captain of the river, his brother being one of them, but as I am Informed he is gone for Albany and has put the chase upon us as he has done once before, But if he does but get there and not go nor send to the French, I am very Easy with him. (HBCA B.135/a/8 fo.25)

Thus Sakie was acknowledged to be powerful enough to keep a large group of Indians waiting for him to arrive. At the same time, the factor seemed powerless to control his actions and seemed most concerned whether Sakie had gone to trade with the French opposition traders. Nevertheless, the factor was extremely frustrated by this Indian's behaviour, declaring that "he plays a sure card, trades his goods at Albany, and then comes here under pretense of being captain of this river" (HBCA B.135/a/8 fo.25). Obviously, Sakie was no mere puppet of the fur traders.

Under the leadership of Sakie, the Indians who came to trade remained on the "plantation" (or cleared area) of the post for several days, drinking and smoking. For instance, early in June 1740 Sakie arrived in the vicinity of Moose Factory; on 9 June, following three days of continuous festivities, Sakie was still drunk and had traded for nothing but brandy. Three days later Sakie came into the post begging food. The factor, Richard Staunton, complained afterward that the Indians "would have been gone long ago if it had not been for him and he not coming in the spring according to his promise." Staunton lamented that Sakie had traded all his goods at Albany for two of the past three years, "and only comes here for a fine coat and what is else given him at this place." Despite appearing to take a hard line, the factor gave the Indian gifts of tobacco, oatmeal, and prunes. When they announced that they were all going deer-hunting, Staunton supplied "each man with what he wanted which was almost but everything, for Sakie himself had not one load of powder nor shot nor one pipe of tobacco nor one bit of provision" (HBCA B.135/a/8 fo.26).

Two weeks later Sakie returned to the post, "under pretense," the factor believed, "that his gun is broke but I am apt to think it is rather to get drunk." The factor announced that he would not give him one spoonful of brandy and that Sakie had brought nothing to trade. However, on 13 July, "Indians came here which from hence 32 days ago to go a deer hunting. They saying they have not killed one deer since they went which I do believe to be true for they all look very poor and have nothing to help themselves so I must relieve them at present" (HBCA B.135/a/8 fo.29). Thus, only when Staunton was confronted with additional evidence was he inclined to believe the hard-luck story of the Indian leader.

Two months later Sakie came in and told the factor that he was going away to hunt beaver because his eyes were too sore to shoot geese. The factor confided that it did not much matter where Sakie went, "for he minds nothing but drinking." The next morning, the journal related, "I got Sakie away but I was obliged to trust him to the value of 67 beaver besides giving him 1 gallon of brandy and one beaver skin in tobacco before I could get him away" (HBCA B.135/a/10 fo.5).

Clearly, the factor viewed Sakie as a mixed blessing at best and a drunken albatross at worst. Staunton did not deny that Sakie had uncommon influence among the homeguard, who were mainly goose-hunters and deer-hunters rather than trappers. The factor also perceived that the homeguard who performed this function sometimes encountered times of famine and had to be sustained from the provisions of the post. Despite his suspicions that some of the homeguard may have been attempting to dupe him, the factor felt an obligation toward his homeguard Indians.

That winter proved to be particularly bad, however. By mid-January Indians were flocking to the post for aid, and at least two starved before reaching it. Richard Staunton employed the men he was sustaining picking oakum until their strength returned enough to resume hunting. By the beginning of February, Staunton began shutting his gates to the hungry Indians, telling them that they had to hunt and fish, and if they refused, they must starve because he could not continue to feed them (HBCA B.135/a/10 fos.16–17).

The distress of the Indians in the vicinity of the post was not soon over, for the goose-hunt failed, owing to an unusually severe break-up. In early June, Staunton again faced a large crowd wanting food. Again, he showed them little sympathy: "In the evening 16 of our home Indians came to the factory for victuals and there was near 20 before so I shall serve them all alike, which is give them nothing, telling them it is enough for me to keep them in the winter from starving and not in the summer for them to be lazy" (HBCA B.135/a/10 fo.27).[5] Within two weeks they had all left to go hunting.

Three months later James Duffield replaced Richard Staunton, who left on the annual ship. One week after his arrival, Duffield condemned Staunton's actions toward the Indians. Duffield asserted that Staunton had "given in" to the Indians whom he allowed to overrun the place. Indeed, according to Duffield, "had Mr. Staunton continued a year longer the Englishmen would have victualled themselves and the natives made a new standard as best pleased them" (HBCA B.135/a/11 fo.3). For his part, Duffield threw the homeguard Indians out of the factory and would deal with them only at the trading window.

Although Staunton may have been generous when he could with the Indians, the record for the previous winter indicates that unprecedented scarcity had threatened the lives of Indians and traders alike. Indeed, Staunton had been forced to turn Indians away without assistance; those he was feeding he employed picking oakum, a tedious task which would certainly have driven a malingering Indian back to his traps.

Thus, there seemed to be an uneasy relationship between the Indians and the factors. A factor who was too trusting could be accused of being duped by wily Indians into supporting feasting rather than hunting. On the other hand, in times of real distress the Indians needed to be able to turn to the post for relief. The problem, then, came to be whether the factor in his judgment believed the Indians to be in distress or not. Since he had charge of the surplus food, he, of course, had the final authority. However, if he was not fair, the Indians, who were not slaves after all, might abandon the English post altogether and trade with the French in the upland areas.

Duffield's suspicions of the duplicity of the Indians who frequented the post did not stop at their apparently feigning hunger. He also thought they were engaging in smuggling with his own servants. He believed they were seeing the servants privately and exchanging goods for furs which the servants would then smuggle home with their personal belongings on the ship (for example, HBCA B.135/a/11 fo.13; B.135/a/14 fo.9).

Sakie seems to have been at the head of all intrigue that Duffield perceived to be taking place under his nose. Certainly, the factor believed Sakie to be the most clever homeguard as well as the most influential with whom he had to deal. No doubt because of this he wanted the captain of the river to believe that Duffield considered him to be an equal. In April 1742, Duffield "took Sakie up to my room, gave him a dram out of my glass. . . . I have represented that I run a very great risk of disobliging my great men (which is his own term for your honours) [the London Committee] in being so kind to him as I have been and therefore expect that he will act like a brother captain and not let me suffer on his account." This was said to cajole Sakie into repaying his debt to the post. Yet at the same time Duffield reproached the Indian for lying and acting unfairly, threatening to make a new captain of the river in his place. At the end of the meeting Duffield reported, "He has promised to be very good for the future, which time must explain, but expect a continuation of his usual artifices" (HBCA B.135/a/11 fo.56).[6]

Later in the spring Duffield gave Sakie a fine captain's coat, admonishing him "that he must not give it away, but appear like a captain in his own jurisdiction and use his utmost interest with all his Indians for my benefit." As added inducement the factor also gave Sakie a laced hat, one pair of stockings, a white shirt, two gallons of brandy, and one pound of Brazil tobacco. In addition he gave Sakie's wife a brass collar and stone ring (items which were not selling and which he hoped to "bring into fashion"). The factor then gave the Indian captain oatmeal "to make a feast" (HBCA B.135/a/11 fo.62).[7] Usually, trade with the homeguard did not include an elaborate trade ceremony. Individuals made their way to the trading window, bringing in a skin or two or a few geese for brandy or other goods. Twice a year after the goose seasons a feast was held at which captain's coats and other gifts were given away to the departing Indians.

The relationship between the factor and the captain of the homeguard continued to vacillate between congenial co-operation and sullen co-existence. On occasion, under Sakie's leadership, the homeguard band resorted to Albany when they did not like the treatment that was accorded them at Moose Fort. The factor continued to believe he was being duped by his home Indians who, he believed, often feigned starvation in order to take advantage of his humanitarian instincts. Because the homeguard had social as well as economic relations with the fur traders, the suspicion of smuggling also hung over them. In addition, fur traders and Indian women often formed clandestine family relationships which led to the growth of a large mixed-blood element in the homeguard group. This social and economic symbiosis led also to a dilution of cultural differences as the fur traders adopted the use of snowshoes, moccasins, and other Indian goods and customs, while the Indians adopted British dress and by 1744 they also began to adopt the more significant British burial practice.

In 1745, Sakie, the great captain of the homeguard Indians died "of a lingering consumption." The next day it was recorded in the post journal "26 November: We digged a grave and buried Sakie today and what home Indians was near the factory came to his burying" (HBCA B.135/a/16 fo.7). The following May, the factor designated a new captain of the river. He was the eldest son of Sakie's brother, who was also a lesser captain. Thus, although the factor apparently chose the new captain, he acknowledged in his decision the primacy of ties linking males in the most prominent local family (HBCA B.135/a/16 fo.17).[8]

When Captain Sakie's widow died in late May of 1747, she was accorded last rites according to a very elaborate English ceremony, thereby continuing the mark of respect that the traders at least superficially granted Sakie's family. On 27 May:

> In the afternoon we buried the queen alongside of the king, her husband, after the English fashion. We put her into a gun chest, and covered it with a flag, four English carried her upon their shoulders and four Indian women held up the pall. Old Chickatee (Sakie's own brother) and his wife walked next the corpse, and all the rest of the Indians in order after them, being about 30 Indians. I walked before the corpse to the burying place. When we came there and set the corpse down Chickatee made a short speech after their way. Then we put her into the grave and covered the corpse up. Chickatee interceded with me very much to rail it round like the Englishmen's burying place. I told him the Englishmen should do it when I had time. They all seemed to be vastly pleased when I said it should be done. (HBCA B.135/a/17 fo.17).[9]

Clearly, each side of the uneasy alliance found it necessary to curry the favour of the other. As leader of the homeguard, Sakie had felt compelled to comply with the demands of the fur traders, who were not averse to threatening to name a new captain. In that sense at least the ultimate power seemed to reside with the factors. The fur traders, for their part, harboured private feelings of distrust about the homeguard, but usually found it necessary to at least pretend to respect them.

Joseph Isbister, factor at Albany, observed privately to George Howy, factor at Moose Fort, after the death of Sakie, "I cannot say that I am sorry for the death of Sakie, but if it had been Snuff the Blanket too I should have liked it better" (HBCA B.135/a/16 fo.12). While Sakie was the most prominent homeguard during his lifetime, Snuff the Blanket (or Esquawenoe), a leader of the upland Indians, was even more famous. Although Isbister can be forgiven for mentioning the two together, they and the two groups they represented should not have been confused. Their relationship to the post and indeed their interrelationship was clearly defined and separate. There existed ties of friendship and kinship between the homeguard and upland Indians, but differences between the groups were also important; as well, there were differences in the way the Hudson's Bay Company traders dealt with the two groups, and these fostered the development of a dual-native tradition in the Moose Factory area.

The upland groups travelled and lived great distances up the waterways that fed Moose River. They may have travelled as far afield as Fort Timiskaming, established by the French in 1720 as a depot and headquarters post that sent traders out in several directions to trade with Indians on their own lands (Mitchell 1977). More likely, however, they normally confined themselves north of the height of land and sometimes traded at Lake Abitibi. Indeed, French traders may have established seasonal posts far down the Abitibi River, for in 1730 some upland Indians indicated they would trade with the French who were closer than Fort Albany (HBCA B.135/a/1 fo.7), and in 1743 James Duffield reported that the French pedlars were on the main branch of the river about sixty miles upstream from Moose (HBCA B.135/a/13 fo.1). Although some upland Indians regularly travelled down the Moose River to trade with the English, many traded also with the French or had access to French goods when members of their families traded with the French, for it was not uncommon for a prominent trader at Moose Fort to have a father, son, or brother who was prominent among French traders.

Like Sakie, Esquawenoe frequented the Moose-Albany area for many years. He was a great captain, along with other upland leaders such as Shimata, Achmet, and Pethay, but of all the uplanders Esquawenoe came to the post most regularly and attracted the attention of the fur traders most frequently. Thus Esquawenoe's long association with Moose Fort can be followed with some precision. He can therefore be used as a kind of representative of the relationship between uplanders and the Hudson's Bay Company bayside post and between uplanders and homeguard.

Esquawenoe was first mentioned by name in the Moose journals in the winter of 1740, just before the first mention of Sakie. Like Sakie, he had also probably already visited the post many times. In February 1740 the factor reported that he gave Esquawenoe a gallon of brandy and a pound of Brazil tobacco to feast up in the country with his young followers. The journal added, perhaps by way of justification, "he promises great matters this spring" (HBCA B.135/a/8 fo.15). To receive such lavish gifts, Esquawenoe was, it appears, already highly favoured at Moose Factory. On the other hand, sometimes lavish gifts were given in an attempt to win the loyalty of the uplanders. That the upland Indians might trade with the French was the greatest fear the Hudson's Bay Company had of these trading partners, who were also their principal source of furs.

This fear perhaps lay behind the formal trading ceremony which accompanied trade with the upland visitors. The record indicates that when the uplanders arrived at the post, some came with flags flying in their canoes. Others beached their canoes across the river and set up a large, smoky fire as a signal that they wished to be met by the factor of the post. Usually trade was accompanied by formal speeches with the upland leaders being taken into the factor's private chambers and afterwards into the warehouse. The followers were obliged to trade at the window and were not allowed to enter the storage area for trade goods. Upland captains received coats and other gifts during another ceremony at the completion of trade.[10]

Before trade began, the uplanders traditionally spent from several hours to one day with the homeguard Indians, drinking and making merry. The factor viewed this social custom as an example of crafty homeguard Indians victimizing innocent uplanders, for the homeguard apparently relieved the uplanders of some of their furs during this festive occasion. In a sense this action should have meant nothing to the fur traders because they presumably collected the value of the furs in any case. Nevertheless, if the uplanders were unhappy with their treatment at Moose, they would go to the French.

Unfortunately, the only representation of the custom came from the English traders, who may not have understood it. Although the Hudson's Bay Company interfered with the tradition, eventually obliterating it, it is possible that the uplanders, who were intelligent and resourceful, orginally accepted the homeguard as middlemen and thus deserving of the so-called "pillaged" furs (for example, HBCA B.135/a/11 fo.61).[11]

The interference of the English company in Indian traditions can be interpreted as attempting to manipulate or control their trading partners. But control of the uplanders was difficult to obtain, and it had to be at a price. The factors at Moose were forced to give lavish gifts to their upland Indians; they were forced to allow the uplanders to accumulate large debts; they had to be satisfied often with collecting the Indians' less valuable furs, realizing that the French were getting the smaller, more valuable furs; they also had to accept that their partners were shrewd traders who were skilled at turning a reasonable profit.

In 1742 the factor at Moose Fort described Esquawenoe's trading skills: "This man is the grand politician of all being a free agent travelling about, sometimes to the French, at others to Albany and this fort, never drinks but has always his senses about him, makes the best of his market at all places" (HBCA B.135/a/11 fo.69).

In line with the post's efforts to prevent the uplanders from transferring their loyalties to the French, the factor at Moose Fort traded and gave them brandy that was mixed with no more than one-quarter water; if he believed they had just come from the French, he often gave them their brandy in an undiluted state. The homeguard were treated differently. They were paid in brandy that was usually watered-down by one-third when they brought in their geese and deer flesh (Ray and Freeman 1978:137).

This paper has mentioned the close social ties between the upland Indians and the homeguard. Both groups were also tied socially with the Indians who traded most often with the French: the homeguard captain, Sakie, had a brother who was a prominent French captain, while Esquawenoe's son was also a major captain among the French.[12] Because of the intimate connections between the three groups of Indians, the British fur traders were sometimes inclined to suspect that they were all involved in duplicity or treachery against the post. For example, during the spring trading season in 1745 the factor's suspicions were aroused:

> 10 May 1745: The upland Indians traded a great many goods today as our two captains, Sakie and Esquawenoe, and our home Indians being all here, I gave them their coats and made a feast to them of brandy, oatmeal, bread, prunes, pipes and tobacco to make the uplanders merry. I fired all our great guns and small arms to let them know what they have to trust to if any of them should come to beset us. Captain Esquawenoe and some of our home Indians have a scheme in their heads, I believe, to surprise us, so came to the gates and called out to us, they see a great many canoes a-coming. They wanted to come in but we would not let them in and kept a good watch all night long.
> 11 May: The upland Indians made an end of trading this morning and went all away directly. I asked our captain and homeguard were the canoes was they saw last night. They told me there was none, only some of the Indians was got drunk and made others believe they see a great many canoes upon the river. After the upland Indians went away I would not let any of the homeguard come into the factory all day to let them know I was angry for what they did last night. (HBCA B.135/a/15 fo.13).

Normally, the factor suspected the homeguard of nothing more serious than feigning hunger to get free food, but in this instance, because they were associating with the uplanders, the homeguard shared in the more serious accusation. In this case the fur traders believed the uplanders to be capable of plotting to destroy the post. This fear was doubtlessly rooted in the fact that the uplanders had easy access to the French, who remained enemies of the English fur-trading concern, and was heightened during the wars between the two mother countries.

Another reason, perhaps, for the upland Indians being more vulnerable to suspicion was that the fur traders apparently had no control over who were the upland leaders. For example, in 1744 Achmet, an old upland captain, died. Shortly afterward his three sons came to the fort to announce that Achmet's oldest son had been appointed to succeed him. The son was wearing his father's captain's coat and carrying his flag. "After he had traded," the factor related, "took him up to my room with captain Esquawenoe to smoke a pipe then re-delivered his flag exhorting him to trade in his father's steps and bring us all his interest" (HBCA B.135/a/14 fo.38). In at least this case the factor also secretly approved of the choice, for after two more of the sons came in, the factor commented that they "richly deserve encouragement, being quiet, sober and peaceable people" (HBCA B.135/a/14 fo.41). The factor may also have been impressed with the nine hundred beaver skins that they had brought to trade.

After Sakie died, the relationship between the upland Indians and the homeguard may not have been as close as it formerly had. Esquawenoe was probably present when Sakie's successor was chosen, and he was probably also present in 1747 when the factor, George Howy, provided the ingredients for a great feast in honour of over one hundred Indians (including four captains) who were trading at the post. However, his name was not mentioned on either occasion (HBCA B.135/a/17 fo.15).

Indeed, Esquawenoe was not again mentioned by name in the Moose post journals until 1750, when he was described as "an old captain" en route to his winter quarters. The factor gave him gifts in return for his promise to spread the word among upland Indians to come down to the bayside post in the spring to trade. True to his word, the Indian brought in eleven canoes of traders, but for their numbers, the factor complained that they traded little (HBCA B.135/a/21 fos.3,20).

During this time the British fur traders seem to have become increasingly concerned about the possibility of French attacks. In the fall of 1747 Moose Fort learned that the British had taken Cape Breton (Louisbourg) and that Britain was again at war with France. The factor, John Potts, sent word inland that there would be few French goods available during the coming year, but the English ships were well stocked; therefore the uplanders who usually traded with the French would be well advised to come to the English posts. He also sent a tantalizing selection of gifts up the river as an added inducement. The factor's initiative paid off, for in the spring many "French" Indians came in. Extraordinary defensive precautions were taken while the strangers were trading at the post, however, as this example shows: "22 April 1748: The Indians trading and drinking: six of our people upon guard, two at the gates, three upon the sheds, and one upon the house with their muskets, cartridge boxes, bayonets, pistols etc. I am resolved to keep the same guard all the time of trade, night and day" (HBCA B.135/a/18 fo.26).

The factor's efforts were rewarded, but at the cost of a heavy drain on gifts which largely nullified the benefits of additional trade. His motive, however, was to acquaint the "French" Indians with the good terms that were available at English posts and thus to reap a long-term benefit from their continued allegiance. This, apparently, did not occur.

Nevertheless, the fear of possible enemy attack lingered. In 1751 the fort took alarm from an Indian report that the French were coming. Upon hearing the news, the factor hurried to the spot at which the sighting was reported but found nothing but canoes of home Indians paddling off and kettles still hung over smouldering fires (HBCA B.135/a/21 fo.26). Although the fort took elaborate defensive precautions, the attack never occurred. Nevertheless, the fort remained skittish for several seasons, and the outbreak of new hostilities in 1756 only increased the tension.

In the meantime, Esquawenoe continued to make regular visits to the post. He was mentioned only briefly and often brought in few goods (HBCA B.135/a/21 fo.20; B.135/a/26 fo.23). Only in January 1757 did the journal make a more lengthy comment about the aging captain:

> Old Captain Snuff the Blanket with his wives and two sons came in for relief in a very bad condition, there being neither partridge, fish, nor venison to be got, and this is known to be the first time of him coming in the winter. Am afraid it is very bad with the Indians who are gone up the country as well as with those who are near us. He brought a few beaver in, part of his debt. (HBCA B.135/a/29 fos.14–15).

Esquawenoe was apparently wintering closer to the fort than he had when he was younger, and after this experience he announced that he was going further up the river and would not return until the ice had gone out. When he returned at the end of May, he was almost entirely without goods. He brought the news of the death by starvation of three goose-hunters. This news, on the heels of the death of the captain of the goose-hunters, one of the leading deer-hunters, and several other homeguard Indians and their families, was the last blow of a devastating winter which the factor described as "the hardest winter and most fatal among the Indians as has been known for these many years" (HBCA B.135/a/29 fos. 15, 22, 29). Fortunately, an abundant goose season brought needed relief to the hard pressed Indians.

For two more years Esquawenoe was mentioned only sporadically. He came to the post, took "debt," and in the winter had to come in for "relief" (HBCA B.135/a/31 fos. 4,13). Then, in June 1759, the old man suddenly became the most important item in the journal.

> 3 June 1759: . . . in the evening I was informed that old Captain Snuff (who has been mediating the destruction of the trade of this place these four years past) has acquainted all the uplanders that had then been down that he intended to destroy the English and to take the factory, and that he had prevailed with all our home Indians to assist him, but that they told him they thought at present they were too weak, upon which he told the uplanders not to bring down any more goods to the factory, but to inform the French that if they would meet him at a particular place, he and all the Moose River Indians would assist them to take the fort. . . . I called the factory, acquainted them with the information I had received, and in order to quash so villainous an attempt it was unanimously agreed to take him into custody and to effect it in as peaceable manner as possible.

The old man was seized and put in irons. Once he was in custody, the journal relates that his wives and indeed most of the Indians on the planation agreed that the rumour had been correct (HBCA B.135/a/31 fo.28).

Four days later the old captain hanged himself in his cell. The anticipated attack never took place. For thirty years Esquawenoe and his followers had given no cause for suspicion to their British trading partners. He was an intelligent and wily man, earning a reputation as a "sly cunning fox" (HBCA B.135/a/11 fo.69), who traded with both French and English, depending on where he could get the best bargain. As he had got older, however, he had taken on some of the tasks of homeguard Indians where necessary. Once he had led the goose-hunters; at least once he had brought fish into the post.

As he grew older, however, he seems to have brought in fewer furs than he had during his prime years as a hunter. The fact that he also began to come in for relief during lean winter months suggests that he wintered close enough to the English to receive succour when necessary. This would imply that rather than being in league with the French he was drifting ever more into the orbit of the bayside post. Despite his close association with the Hudson's Bay Company, he had remained aloof and independent in many ways, visiting the post only infrequently and seldom relying on its stock of provisions except to see him through a bad winter.

In the end Esquawenoe paid a high price for his seeming independence, for he was never able to escape the distrust of the English fur traders. The uplanders, because of their more distant association with the post, were vulnerable to the suspicion that they were plotting treachery against it. As the leader of the uplanders, Esquawenoe was vulnerable to being accused of leading the treachery. Indeed, several times in the course of a generation of honest dealings, the great upland captain and his kin were suspected of being involved in plots against the post. The fact that none of the feared events ever occurred did not seem evidence enough to spare the old man the terrible indictment against him and the ultimate indignity to which he was subjected.

Esquawenoe's freedom and ceremonial respect were more illusory than real. The homeguard Indians had long since given up their independence to attach themselves not only to the needs but also the security of the trading post. The uplanders had retained a more independent lifestyle but at the price of both security and ultimate trust. Sakie and his wife had, after all, been buried with great ceremonial honours. In contrast, Esquawenoe's wives asked that the great upland leader be buried without the Indians seeing him (HBCA B.135/a/31 fos.29–30).

The differences between the two leaders and their groups were real; yet they should not eclipse the similarities between those native groups who chose to live close to the post and act mainly as provisioners and those who spent most of the year in interior woodland areas.

In the lives of Sakie and Esquawenoe can be seen the beginnings of a dual-native tradition at Moose Factory that continued well into the present century. As the years passed, the homeguard worked more and more in jobs around the post, while uplanders, if they worked for the Hudson's Bay Company at all, tended to do so in transport to supplement their trapping income. When they camped on Moose Factory Island, the two groups seem to have stayed on different parts of the plantation.

In this paper, it has been shown that a division between the two groups developed both in the way they treated Moose Factory and its residents and in the way the traders treated them and their leaders, from the earliest days of the re-establishment of the post. Many questions remain. Was Moose Factory unusual? Was its hinterland situation typical? For that matter, were Sakie and Esquawenoe—two leaders who stand out strikingly in the Moose Factory journals—really as representative as they seem to be? More research on these important subjects is needed before more definite answers can be offered. Nevertheless, in some fur trade regions at least, homeguard and interior groups, though closely connected by friendship and kinship networks, developed separate and distinct lifeways.

Notes

1. The Moose Post Journals from 1741–44 (HBCA B.135/a/12–14) provide the basis of the Duffield material. Post journals in general provide the most important records for studying social aspects of native life in the region of fur trade posts.
2. Duffield's heavy-handed justice made him very unpopular with his men. He probably also was paranoid, suspecting that everyone was his enemy and out to destroy him (see Pannekoek 1979). In my view Pannekoek underplays Duffield's paranoia and largely accepts the deluded factor's observations as accurate. These, of course, portray the men at the post as much more scheming and vengeful than they probably were.
3. Indeed, the fur traders never relied solely on the efforts of the homeguard Indians for country provisions, and as the years passed they went further and further afield in search of game. In especially lean years the men might scatter from the post to tents where they hoped to be able to live off the land. They also traditionally trapped furs whenever their regular duties permitted (see, for example, HBCA B.135/a/10 fo.9).
4. Also see Arthur Ray's paper in this volume. His work elsewhere (Ray 1974) is also the best source for the relationship between homeguard, middlemen, and interior Indians in the prairie west.
5. On 9 May 1741, Staunton had told them "2 Indians came in from ye Southward for Victuals saying they can't kill any Geese, but I sent them away as they came without giving them anything. Telling them if they will not Hunt they must starve for I had not anything to give them, for I have had but one goose killed from the South this spring." One week later they salted their first geese of the season, and on May 22 there was reported to be "not one Goose in the Marsh, and the Indians almost starved" (HBCA B.135/a/10 fos. 25–26).

6. Duffield's statement suggests that he believed he had the power to name a new captain of the river (that is, the homeguard).
7. These were usually generous gifts, certainly reserved only for the most influential leaders. Note that Sakie may have been inclined to give away his captain's clothes, as was traditional among more western groups. See especially Ray (1974).
8. There may have been more than one captain of the homeguard because on 4 May 1747, with over one hundred Indians on the plantation, the factor gave a coat to each of four captains. Some of them may also have been uplanders (HBCA B.135/a/17 fo.15).
9. This burying ground has not definitely been located, although there is a strong possibility it was somewhat west of the factory, where in 1967 a road grader turned up traces of Indian grave goods. These were described in Edward Rogers et al. (1972); see also Luegar (1981:143) and Judd (1981a:73–4).
10. Almost every spring some mention was made in the post journals of the trading ceremony with uplanders. There was an especially full account in 1742 (HBCA B.135/a/11 fos.69–73).
11. See Ray (1974) for a full explanation of the concept of middlemen. Ray's middlemen worked in a vast hinterland, however, and did not normally enact "rites of passage" at the post itself.
12. Sakie's brother who traded with the French was Muntango; another brother, Chickatee, was a homeguard captain. Esquawenoe's son was not mentioned by name (HBCA B.135/a/15 fo.14).

References Cited

Bishop, Charles A.
  1974 The Northern Ojibwa and the Fur Trade. Toronto: Holt, Rinehart and Winston of Canada.
Hudson's Bay Company Archives (HBCA)
  HBCA B.135/a/1–31. Moose Post Journals, 1730–1759.
Judd, Carol M.
  1981a The Changing Faces of Moose Factory. In Moose Factory Heritage Survey, 1980–81, Final Report. Arthur J. Ray. ed., pp. 45–135. Ontario Ministry of Culture and Recreation.
  1981b An Uncommon Heritage: A Brief Social History of Moose Factory, Ontario. In Moose Factory Heritage Survey, 1980–81, Final Report. Arthur J. Ray, ed., pp. 210–95. Ontario Ministry of Culture and Recreation.
Krech, Shepard III
  1980 Introduction: "Reconsiderations" and Ethnohistorical Research. Arctic Anthropology 17 (2):1–12.
Luegar, Richard
  1981 An Archaeological Survey of Moose Factory, Ontario. In Moose Factory Heritage Survey, 1980–81, Final Report. Arthur J. Ray, ed., pp. 136–88. Ontario Ministry of Culture and Recreation.
Mitchell, Elaine Allan
  1977 Fort Timiskaming and the Fur Trade. Toronto: University of Toronto Press.
Pannekoek, Fritz
  1979 "Corruption" at Moose. The Beaver, Spring: 4–11.
Ray, Arthur J.
  1974 Indians in the Fur Trade: Their Roles as Hunters, Trappers, and Middlemen in the Lands Southwest of Hudson Bay, 1660–1870. Toronto: University of Toronto Press.

Ray, Arthur J., and Donald Freeman, eds.
    1978   "Give Us Good Measure," An Economic Analysis of Relations between the Indians
           and the Hudson's Bay Company before 1763. Toronto: University of Toronto Press.
Rogers, Edward, Donald Webster, and James Anderson
    1972   A Cree Burial, Moose Factory, Ontario. Arctic Anthropology 9 (1):27–34.

The Trade of the Slavey and Dogrib at Fort Simpson in the Early Nineteenth Century

Shepard Krech III

In July 1822, one year following the coalition of the Hudson's Bay and North West Companies, W. Ferdinand Wentzel began to construct a post at the confluence ("the forks") of the Mackenzie and Liard Rivers. Wentzel, a clerk in the Hudson's Bay Company (HBC), was acting on orders given by Chief Factor Edward Smith to A.R. McLeod, chief trader and manager of the Mackenzie River District; Smith was undoubtedly following the advice of George Simpson, governor of the HBC's Northern Department (Rich 1938:242). Wentzel soon erected some buldings and began to carry out the rest of his task, which was to take charge of The Forks; to attract to it natives who formerly traded at an earlier post that for a time was located on this spot, but who in recent years visited two other posts (Forts Alexander and Liard) in the region; and to make the post secure in provisions. For the summer trade, Wentzel had powder, ball, shot, knives, a "very deficient" three pound supply of tobacco, and "We had likewise 2 Kegs of H. Wines an article of very little consequence in this quarter—where the natives have never been indilged in that pernicious liquor to any excess" (HBCA B.200/a/1 fo.1).

The Forks—the name soon changed permanently to Fort Simpson— immediately became the trading centre of many Northern Athapaskan Slavey and Dogrib Indians and in the next decade attracted as well an increasing number of Cordillera-dwelling Mountain Indians (called Dahotinne and Umbahotinne) and, for a while, a few Kaska (called Nahanny) (see Krech Ms). Fort Simpson also became the main depot for the Mackenzie River District, the vast region north and northwest of Great Slave Lake and the northwesternmost district in the Hudson's Bay Company Northern Department.

The principal aims of this paper are to describe the trade of the Slavey, Dogrib, and other Northern Athapaskans at The Forks or Fort Simpson in the first several decades of the nineteenth century and to analyse the various impacts of the trade upon them. Unfortunately, it is difficult to describe the exchange in any detail before 1821, because so few documents pertaining to the first two decades of the nineteenth century (and before) in the Mackenzie River region have survived. In contrast, following the amalgamation in 1821 of the Hudson's Bay and North West Companies, the involvement of the Hudson's Bay Company in this region intensified, and the emphasis it placed on journals, reports, account books, and correspondence spread to this region. For this reason, the temporal focus in this essay is on the 1820's, the first decade of HBC monopoly control in this area.

This research is aimed in part at filling major ethnological and geographical lacunae in historical studies of the fur trade. Most accounts of the trade which include a discussion of this northern region, published in the nineteenth and twentieth centuries, are either brief sections of more comprehensive studies of the fur trade or, in a few cases, seemingly random collections of data; often, they focus overwhelmingly on the rivalry among trading companies, on the officers and servants of the Hudson's Bay Company, or on exploration (for example, Ballantyne 1848, Bryce 1900, Butler 1872, Innis 1970, Rich 1967, Willson 1900). In recent years, anthropologists, historians, and geographers have published several significant studies of Indian participation in the fur trade (for example, Bishop 1974, Heidenreich 1971, Ray 1974, Ray and Freeman 1978, Trigger 1976); none, however, focus on Northern Athapaskans in the northwestern Canadian Subarctic.

In recent decades, several researchers have shown an interest in nineteenth-century native adaptations in the Great Slave Lake and Mackenzie River regions, but as a rule their research has not been based on extensive research in the Hudson's Bay Company Archives, the major repository of primary documents. Since 1975, some notable exceptions, firmly grounded in historical research, have appeared: full-length analyses of native adaptations and the results of contact (Janes 1975; Yerbury 1980); briefer analyses of the trade and its various impacts (Sloan 1979; Krech 1983); an ethnohistory of the Yellowknife (Gillespie 1975) and of Yellowknife-Dogrib conflict (Helm and Gillespie 1981); and several specific debates about demographic processes (Krech 1978, Helm 1980), and about the effects of Cree-Athapaskan warfare specifically or contact in general (Janes 1976, 1977; Helm 1977; Yerbury 1977, 1978). In these studies and in others focused in part on the historical era, the lines have become drawn between those who think that the era of the fur trade, in spite of its new mercantilistic impulses and attendant diseases, had little impact on native people and that basic aboriginal cultural patterns persisted among natives who remained essentially independent of the trade throughout the nineteenth century (see, for example, Asch 1976; Janes 1975, 1976; Smith 1976; Helm 1980); and those who disagree, stating instead that the nineteenth-century fur trade had a noticeable impact on the demographic and social arrangements of people in their territories (for example, Krech 1978, 1983; Sloan 1979; Yerbury 1980). There is even a disagreement over the terminology to use for historical eras: some favour a long, stable "contact-traditional" era, while others prefer a briefer, more neutrally labeled "early fur trade" era (see Krech 1983, 1984 for a discussion).

The data presented in this essay should be placed in the context of these debates and issues. Did the fur trade have an impact on the Slavey and Dogrib in the early nineteenth century? To what degree were they involved (or changed) economically? To what degree were they dependent on or independent of the trade? While this paper emphasizes economic adaptations, it is also interested in whether the trade affected the relations between ethnic groups or whether it was accompanied by new diseases. After all, the economic exchange was not carried out in a vacuum, and to make most sense of this exchange it must be placed fully in a context that included these other factors.

The research reported here is based almost exclusively on the rich and for this region largely untapped documents in the Hudson's Bay Company Archives (HBCA). Immediately following is a brief, admittedly selective reconstruction of Slavey and Dogrib adaptations in the first two decades of the nineteenth century, a time on the very threshold of continuous, intensive, direct trade in this region. This is as close as one can get to a baseline aboriginal reconstruction on the basis of historical materials. Next, this paper will scrutinize in detail various aspects of the exchange itself, and then it will explore the broader context of interethnic relations and of diseases brought by traders. Finally, the matter of fur-trade dependence, alluded to above, will be returned to.

SLAVEY AND DOGRIB ADAPTATIONS, 1800–1820

In the early nineteenth century, the Slaveys and Dogribs who traded at The Forks (Ft. Simpson) exploited a territory of roughly 80,000 square kilometres and came to the post from distances of more than 250 kilometres (Fig. 1). For the most part, this territory is part of the Arctic Drainage Lowlands ecozone (McClellan 1970), a subarctic region typically characterized by a continental climate; boreal forest dominated by white spruce, poplar, willow, and some birch, with a ground cover of lichens, mosses, and, in season, cranberries, blueberries, and other edible berries; numerous lakes and rivers, in which such important food species as whitefish, inconnu, lake trout, and loche are found, and which serve as important habitats for a variety of breeding birds or resting spots for migrating waterfowl; a variety of large faunal species, including moose, elk, barren ground and woodland caribou, bison (mostly southwest but also northwest of Great Slave Lake), black and grizzly bear; and smaller animal species, including beaver, fox, marten, mink, otter, muskrat, lynx, hare, porcupine, wolf, and wolverine. The distribution of resources in this vast

FIGURE 1

territory was not uniform; it appears that the richest portions were southwest of the Mackenzie River, where there was the greatest variety of faunal species; east of the Mackenzie River, resources (with the exception of barren ground caribou) became relatively scarce as the boreal forest changed first to transitional taiga, then to a tundra zone. Fishing lakes were located both east and west of the Mackenzie River.

The Dogrib lived northeast of the Mackenzie river, from Horn Mountain and Lac La Martre north to Great Bear Lake. In 1823, they were "divided into Six families" and "occupied the Whole of the East of the Mackenzie River as far as Martin Lake—and then continue North to Great Bear Lake"; and they were said to "[amount] to about two Hundred Men and Boys capable of pursuing the Chase," who had "5 leaders who possess little or no authority"

(HBCA B.200/e/1 fo.3). The "six families" were probably regional bands. The Slavey lived south and west of and along the Mackenzie River. They also were distributed and organized in bands; in the early 1820's, a major distinction was made between "Rocky Mountain" or "Forks" Indians and "Beaver Indians." Both were Slavey. The latter, who numbered approximately seventy hunters, lived along the Liard and upper Mackenzie Rivers and traded at Forts Liard and Simpson. The "Rocky Mountain" or "Forks" Slavey numbered "about 40 to 50 Hunters," had two leaders, and were said to "form an intermediate race between the Dog Ribs and Beaver Indians—and are properly speaking a Mixture of both—altho at present considered a distinct people." Their territory or "Hunting Grounds" were described as "bounded on the South by the Nahanny River a Large Stream which Falls into the Rivière aux Liard—and on the West by the Rocky Mountains until they reach the Mountain River that discharges itself into the Main Stream somewhat to the Southward of the Great Willow Lake River" (HBCA B.200/e/1 fos.3–4, Wentzel Ms.c).

The Slavey and Dogrib were fishers and hunters. While Slaveys were reported in 1807 to "subsist upon every species of animals, birds and fish, making no exception," it is clear that whitefish, trout, inconnu, and other species of fish were of great importance, especially in winter. Good fisheries were located east of the Mackenzie River at Willow, Hornell, and Fish Lakes, which were "fishing abodes for many families of Natives"; southwest at Trout Lake, where before 1807 the traders "got a great quantity of peltries . . . it being a fishing place for a few families"; and northwest at Cli Lake(?) (Wentzel 1960:82–83,89). These and other lakes were said to "abound in fish—which afford the Natives an easy subsistence—a mode of life they seem from habit to be fond of indulging in" (HBCA B.200/e/1 fo.1). The Dogrib and Slavey fished with nets made by twisting the inner bark of willow and measuring in some cases 10 x 40 yards, with 4½ inch mesh. They also used wood, bone, bird claw or beaver rib hooks, and caribou antler spears. Fish were eaten raw, roasted, or boiled with hot stones in wattap kettles (Wentzel 1960:83, Ms.c:2; Keith 1960:115; McKenzie Ms.:21; Franklin 1828:63).

For subsistence, the most important large animals were moose and caribou. In summer and winter, men chased these animals, with the help of dogs, into babiche snares set in hedges or barriers; and in spring, they ran them down in crusted snow. A man also hunted caribou by placing the skin of the head and neck of a caribou over his own and, imitating the animal, gaining the centre of a herd. Nine-foot spears with bone blades, willow bows, and arrows tipped with flint (and—increasingly—guns) were used to kill these animals (Wentzel Ms.c:3, 1960:82–89 passim; Franklin 1823:244, Keith 1960).

Beaver also were important for subsistence, more so west of the Mackenzie River where they were more abundant than in some regions east of the river—near Great Bear Lake, for instance—where there were fewer. Beaver were subject to depletion, and as early as 1800 Indians reported that "their Lands are now so Barren that there is No more Beavers to be found—what few there was they have already destroyed" (Thompson Ms.). In fall, beaver were trapped in wooden traps placed on top of their lodges; in winter, they were sometimes killed after the lodges were broken into with trenches (chisels); increasingly, they were shot spring and fall (Wentzel 1960). Liard River Slaveys—for whom beaver were very important for clothing and food— marked individual, unowned beaver lodges as their own, although sanctions for trespass were unclear (Keith 1960).

Hares were important for both subsistence and clothing. Chief Factor Edward Smith remarked that "the Natives have a peculiar fondness of hunting the Wood Rabbit—which afford them besides nourishment under reinment for the Winter" (HBCA B.200/e/1 fo.1d); and that the Slavey remained "where there is plenty of dry wood and Hares" and tended not to move until "the want of either fuel or Rabbits drives him to another spot" (HBCA B.200/e/3 fo.1).

Caribou, moose, and beaver, as well as hares, were important for clothing. Slaveys who lived along the Liard and Mackenzie Rivers used beaver skins for clothing (Wentzel 1960, Thompson Ms.). Dogribs and some Slaveys who lived in areas where beaver were less frequently found (or where they had been more rapidly depleted because of the trade) or where caribou were plentiful used caribou or hares for clothing. There were differences between winter and summer clothing and between men's and women's clothing: caribou or moose skin clothing, with the hair off, was worn in summer, and caribou skin with the hair on or a beaver robe and capote and moose skin leggings were used in winter. In some groups, men were more likely to use beaver skins, while women used hare-skin thongs woven like a mat for an undergarment, robe, and trousers-like leggings. Some of this clothing was fringed and ornamented with quill-work (Keith 1960; McKenzie Ms.:20; Wentzel 1960:86).

Slaveys and Dogribs who visited The Forks to trade came from seasonal fishing, hunting, and trapping camps where, in winter, they lived in two-family, square or oblong spruce log and moss houses with a single central fire and where they pursued traditional subsistence and other maintenance activities (Keith 1960; Wentzel 1960). It is difficult to say how large or transitory the camps were, although gatherings at fishing lakes appear to have consisted of more than several families and to have lasted for some time: "weeks and even months" were spent in one spot (Keith 1960:116), fishing, snaring hares, or living off caribou or moose meat cached in fall or obtained from snares in winter (Wentzel 1960:89; Thompson Ms.). In these camps, men were hunters, fishers, and responsible for setting up or striking camp; with women, they were responsible for collecting wood; and women cooked, made clothing, and tended the children. Women were "indulged" and said to have some influence over men, compared with Chipewyan and Yellowknife women (Keith 1960; Wentzel 1960; Franklin 1823:290).

The traders were struck by what they regarded as "perfect equality" between families (Keith 1960:90). The families and lodges which associated with each other did so surely in part on the basis of kinship. Polygyny, early marriage, and initial matrilocality, and the care provided by youngest sons for aged parents (Keith 1960:114-15 passim) also were important in ordering group composition. Leaders, who were likely to be good hunters and have many moose snares, had little authority; some were said to have been obeyed "only in hopes of being recompensed" (Keith 1960:69; Wentzel 1960; HBCA B.200/e/1). Meat was shared widely in obligatory channels; not to ask for meat was to risk being "considered as no friends" (Keith 1960:90), and the hunter received the smallest share (Keith 1960; Wentzel 1960).

Advent of the Trade

Had these Slaveys and Dogribs been significantly affected by the European fur trade by the time that Wentzel (re)established The Forks in 1822? Prior to the 1780's, the effects of the trade in this region were surely limited to indirect participation in the trade at Fort Churchill via Yellowknife and Chipewyan middlemen (and direct participation of a few); and to fatalities and territorial changes resulting from the incursions of armed Crees who came north at least as far as Great Slave Lake (see Mackenzie 1970:174, 238). Neither the degree of participation in the Churchill trade nor the extent of mortality or territorial change are known at this time.[2]

In the 1780's, the trade extended more significantly into this region. In 1786, the North West Company established Slave Lake Post on Great Slave Lake for the Yellowknife and Chipewyan. For one year a rival establishment competed with this post (Mackenzie 1970:168). The first year, the trade was not very successful; it seems that the post clerk "remained quietly waiting for the furs," which Indians obtained mainly in trade from more distant groups (Wentzel 1960:94; see also Mackenzie 1970:429). In contrast, there was "great success" the following year, when many Indians visited from up to 200 miles away, "often starved" in the process, but left behind at their camps some men to help procure food for women and children who also remained (Wentzel 1960:95). In 1789, the year of Alexander Mackenzie's exploratory voyage down his "River Disappointment" (the Mackenzie River), trade was conducted for the first time on the north side of Great Slave Lake with the Yellowknife and Slavey and at Lac la Martre, where Slaveys or Dogribs, or both, traded five packs of martens and other furs (Mackenzie 1970:229,438).

Two years later, trade was conducted again on the north shore of Great

Slave Lake, but the Slavey trade was reportedly "not of great consequence . . . being entirely in Martens." Thus, some thought was given to shifting the post south to the mouth of the Slave River, where Slaveys "may either come themselves or allow the Red-Knives to be their carriers" (Mackenzie 1970:444). In the early 1790's, more trade may have been carried on (with "success and ease") at Lac la Martre (Wentzel 1960:95).

The posts on Great Slave Lake were still considered too far off for all but the closest Mackenzie River Slaveys and Dogribs, so in 1796 Duncan Livingstone built a post 130 kilometers down the Mackenzie River from Great Slave Lake, perhaps below Horn River. Livingstone's success for the next three years was "great" (Wentzel 1960:95): sixty-nine packs of furs were produced in 1799 alone (Mackenzie 1970:476).

Livingstone's post was closed in 1799 (perhaps because Livingstone was killed that summer). The next year, trade in this region shifted north to Rocky Mountain House, opposite the mouth of the North Nahanni River, and to Great Bear Lake, where the North West Company encountered opposition— perhaps of the XY Company. At Rocky Mountain House, John Thompson traded powder, ball, shot, guns, alcohol, kettles, tobacco, beads, and other goods for the furs and provisions of Slaveys and Dogribs. He was frustrated at the low volume of trade, a result, he thought, of Indians who "pass their whole lives doing nothing else but Fishing" (Thompson Ms.). The first post at The Forks was established by the North West Company in 1803, and for the next three years, the trade ranged from thirty-six to fifty packs of furs. In 1804, there was competition from the XY Company. After 1806, the trade continued but with mixed results and a gradual decline, ending in mismanagement, threats of native hostilities, and, in 1815, closing of the posts and abandonment of the region. From 1817–20, the trade was shifted to Fort Alexander, near the mouth of Willow Lake River, and in 1821 The Forks was reopened (Wentzel Ms.c).

The effects of this early trade, which was direct and in Slavey territory from the early 1790's on, included additions to and some substitutions in Slavey material culture; mortality from diseases; and hostilities owing to middleman trading. In 1804–1806 at The Forks, Slavey arrived from seasonal camps located up to eight and ten nights off, sometimes leaving "no men at the lodges," in order to trade provisions and beaver and other furs for kettles, guns and ammunition, and dry goods. They received gratuities such as awls, flints, gunworms, small knives, tobacco, and rum. Dry goods as well as guns and iron works were desired, and the Slavey were finicky customers; on one occasion, some were "much displeased at the shortness of the capots—for they observe that they are not children but men and these capots are so short that the musquetoes in summer eats all their Backsides" (Wentzel Ms a:27,55). Guns and ammunition were important, and by 1810, Liard River Slaveys were said to be "pretty expert" in shooting moose. Copper and brass kettles also were greatly desired, although many could not afford them (Keith 1960:69, 115).

If many could not afford trade goods, it was because they preferred to trade provisions, which Wentzel and perhaps others did not encourage beyond a certain point; some Dogribs or Slaveys complained that Wentzel "speaks too strongly for Hair, that Meat has not hair & This seems to disatisfy them & gaves them cause for discontent, it appearing to them an impossibility to pay their Debts wt. furs only" (Wentzel Ms b:9303). Some Indians amassed large debts; the debts of some were "so great that they believe that they will not ever pay them," and there were complaints that "the Country here around is now too poor to furnish scarcely the means of subsistance" (Wentzel Ms a:48, Ms b:9308). While Wentzel did not encourage the provision trade among the majority of Slaveys and Dogribs, he did recognize the need for native provisioners; accordingly, he often hired natives as fort hunters, and supplied them with guns and ammunition or with "collets" or snares, with which they shot and snared moose and caribou; or they collected hares and grouse or brought fish from camps on fishing lakes. Wentzel also sent some of his men to camp with the Indians, a policy not without difficulty. In 1805, there was an incident involving a North West Company man and a Slavey woman, and as a "consequence of letting men have their will with Indians," a Slavey named Pouce Coupe, who "has always been a good Hunter for the Fort & a good Indian for the White People . . . is now almost the reverse—through the means of a *Canadien Beast"* (Wentzel Ms a:42).

Tensions in this early fur trade period also resulted from Chipewyan exploitation of resources in Slavey territory; in 1806, some Slaveys were "in general exasperated at the disappointment they have met with from the Montagniers who had already . . . occupied the Country they were sent to in order to Hunt the Beaver" (Wentzel Ms b:9307). And there were tensions from the aggressive middleman trade that Yellowknifes had with Slaveys and Dogribs (Keith 1960:112).

In these early years of the nineteenth century, a few diseases affected the Slavey and Dogrib. In 1804, Indians who traded at The Forks were "sick all summer"; in the winter of 1805–1806, Indians near Great Bear Lake were in a "Sickly state," and others from Horn Mountain reported that "diseases rage *wh* astonishing fury" and that several died. By 1807, "the death of many natives" had adversely affected the trade at The Forks (Wentzel Ms a:44, Ms b:9301, 1960:95).

While some Slaveys and Dogribs were without doubt not affected by the trade during these decades, others just as surely were. Some suffered from diseases, others the aggression of the Yellowknife or the trespass of Chipewyans. Some may not have had trade goods in their possession, but others surely did; a minimum of 93 and as many as 125 of the 204 adult males who traded at Fort Simpson in the 1820's had outstanding balances at Forts Alexander and Liard in 1821. By this time many Slaveys were armed with guns, had axes and ice chisels, and were said to look for "a country capable of supplying [their] wants and of affording [them] the means of purchasing those articles, which from long habit, have become indispensible to [their] existence such as Iron works, Kettles, Guns & ammunition which [they] barter from the Whites with Peltries" (Wentzel Ms. c:2). On the other hand, the traders did complain that some Indians considered the use of earth trenches to obtain beaver in winter as "too laborious a labour"; that some were "so very indolent that only that part of their wants, which they can not do without will they exert themselves to kill a few Skins to procure"; or that an Indian "idles away his time in winter, and contends himself when the fine weather sets in to trap a Martin, and pick up a Beaver here and there with his Wooden Traps Fall and Spring" (HBCA B. 200/e/3 fo.1).

In summary, the Slavey and Dogrib were fishers and hunters who depended a great deal upon fish for subsistence and upon animals (including beaver) for clothing as well as food; who lived in a quasi-sedentary fashion with some food stocks, in multi-family camps, especially in winter; of whom some by 1810 or so eagerly sought kettles, iron works, dry goods, and guns but others seemed content with few goods; who were affected by Indian middlemen who wished to obtain furs or who made territorial incursions to obtain animals directly; and who experienced the disruptive and fatal effects of new diseases. Even in the earliest period of contact, it is difficult to sort putatively aboriginal from historical adaptations.

In the next decade the Slavey and Dogrib became even more involved in the exchange and increasingly exposed to the potentially adverse effects of interethnic contact and alien diseases; this next decade is examined in some detail, beginning with the economics of the exchange.

THE TRADE, 1821-30

On 10 February 1825, a Slavey trading leader named Sekellebethaw or Mountain arrived at Fort Simpson with seven "followers," after a ten-night trip from their camp(s) west of the Mackenzie River. It was Sekellebethaw's first visit in five months, since the preceding September. The trading group brought seventy-eight martens, fifty-eight beaver, thirty-three lynxes, five black bears, and some moose skins and provisions. Chief Factor Edward Smith remarked: "Not one of the party but Paid His debts in full and something over—in consequence they got 3 Quarts Indian Rum and 1 foot Tobacco as a gratuity—with which they passed the evening in the best Good humour" (HBCA B.200/a/5 fo.31d). They exchanged their furs and skins for goods roughly equivalent in value (Made Beaver). The goods included powder, ball, shot, powder horns, and a gun, all related to the traditional subsistence quest (and to the provision exchange), and which together formed over 50 per cent of the total value in Made Beaver (MB) exchanged; tobacco, 17 per cent of the total exchange; iron works, such as axes, knives, and hand daggers; dry goods like cloth, leggings, a bonnet, and gartering; and other items, such as a comb, tin dish, skin scraper, and tobacco box. Following the exchange, the group left; Sekellebethaw would not appear again at Fort Simpson until June 1825.

In all aspects—the distance travelled to Fort Simpson, the timing and brevity of the visit, the presentation of tobacco and—up to 1826—rum, the types and values of furs and goods exchanged, and the length of time before the next trip—this visit by Sekellebethaw was typical of the trading visits of the Slavey and Dogrib during the 1820's, a conclusion based primarily on an analysis of over sixteen hundred exchanges by two hundred trappers in the period from 1822 to 1827 (HBCA B.200/d/3a, 10a).[3]

The Pattern of Trade

The seasonal pattern of trade at Fort Simpson was governed in part by conditions of travel that in turn were most influenced by the break-up of ice in mid-May and freeze-up in November; in part by the arrival of the "outfit" of winter trading goods in the late summer or early fall and of extra goods from Great Slave Lake just following break-up; and in part by the degree to which travel over the distance between the post and hunting and fishing locales interfered with these traditional subsistence activities. The trade built in late winter toward a pronounced peak in late May and June; fell to a moderate level in the summer and early fall months; was practically non-existent in November, when travel conditions were hazardous; and peaked again in December.

Both individuals and groups of up to twenty men arrived to trade. The groups, or trading bands, were sometimes preceded by the arrival of a youth with a "tally stick." When the main band arrived, a gift of rum (until 1826), tobacco, and sometimes other goods was presented to the trading leader; then, furs and provisions were exchanged for trade goods.

The use of tally sticks announced the arrival of a group and allowed for a preliminary gift. It also indicated that the Slavey and Dogrib understood the approximate value, in Made Beaver (MB), of their furs. For example, on 5 January 1827, Bedzebethaw, a Dogrib trading leader, sent two "couriers" ahead of him and his main group of seven "followers" with a small stick notched with 180 "X" marks for the number of MB in furs they were bringing. The two asked for tobacco, were given three feet and some vermilion, and left the next day. One day later, Bedzebethaw and his band arrived with ninety martens, sixty-four beaver, ten lynxes, four otters, two large bears, two small bears, five hundred and thirty muskrats, and one wolverine; these furs were worth 181 MB. He also brought sixty-four tongues and ninety pounds of fresh meat, both probably of caribou (HBCA B.200/a/8 fo.27).

One year before, this same leader (of eleven men this year) sent two young men from Willow Lake, east of the Mackenzie River. One asked for a pipe of tobacco, for "he'd been two moons without smoaking." A tally stick was used by one of the young men, who

> rising up and going to His traveling knapsack—laid a small Stick on the Table—saying this is what I was told to say—and this is What I was told to deliver—and squatted down on the hearth and began to light His Pipe—On the Stick their was 25 Marks X upon denoting that they had as many furs in Made Beaver—they were deserving of some attention and sent back the messengers with 4 feet Tobo and a little Vermilion—in the Evening the party made their appearance with every man His bundel on his back—and delivered 103 Beaver, 6 Cats, 66 Martins, 1238 Musquash, 1 Black Bear, 1 Wolverine, and all their Provisions Was, 4 Deer Tongues, 6 Beaver Tails, 6 lbs Grease, 16 lbs fresh Meat, and 6 lbs fish roes—the interpreter being absent deferred their final settlement for the day (HBCA B.200/a/6 fo.57).

Gift-Giving: Alcohol, Tobacco and Chief's Clothing

When Indians arrived at Fort Simpson, they sometimes received alcohol, tobacco, and other goods as presents or rewards for good behaviour, that is, for successful trapping. The presentation of alcohol was never very great in this region, and it was halted in the mid 1820's. The trend toward prohibition was evident as early as 1822, and two years afterward, the Council of the Northern Department resolved that the "use of Spirituous Liquors be gradually discontinued and that they [the Indians] be liberally supplied with the requisite necessaries particularly the article of ammunition whether they have the means of paying for it or not." After 1826, liquor no longer was brought into the department, either for Indians or for servants and officers of the company (Fleming 1940:24–170 passim).

At Fort Simpson, these changes had little effect, in large part because, as stated before, the Indians were not "indilged in that pernicious liquor to any excess" (HBCA B.200/a/1 fo.1). Prior to 1827, Indians received alcohol as a present, especially when their trapping return, provisioning, or services met with approval. For example, in the summer of 1822, five Indians received alcohol and tobacco "in the shape of a Present for their good behavior during this summer, with a kind of speech adopted to impress them with industrious notions—how far they will observe its tenor time only can show" (HBCA B.200/a/1 fo.10). The quantities of alcohol presented in the early 1820's were not excessive compared to other regions of the Subarctic, but then there was no reason, such as competition, why they should be. In 1822, eight Indians were "pleased" with five pints mixed rum given them; the following year, nine Dogribs arrived, and "5 Quarts weak Grog and 3 feet Tobacco Was given them as a present.—Which they drank quietly in the House"; in June 1826, thirty-nine men from three trading bands received twelve quarts of mixed rum and a fathom of tobacco and spent a "most jovial night"; in March 1823, a band of ten Slaveys, absent for one year, arrived with over two hundred martens, forty-five beaver and other furs

> in consequence of which they got 2½ qts Mixed Rum in a present for which they seemed well satisfied, in course of their Drinking they proposed a Dance which was agreed by all the Party, they danced for some time, keeping constantly going round in a ring and keeping time, to their whimsical song"; and in early June 1826, Slaveys and Dogribs who arrived to trade together with Slaveys hired as Fort hunters "forming in all a party of upwards of 50 Hunters—got 11 Quarts Indian Rum and 1 Fa Tobacco with some Vermilion to paint themselves . . . and they passed the night in the best humor smoking and dancing (HBCA B.200/a/1 fos.14, 35–36; B.200/a/3 fo.26; B.200/a/6 fo.19; B.200/a/7 fo.9).

The only exception to this placid behaviour was a demanding Slavey trading "Chief" named Grand Cheveux, who arrived at Fort Simpson in October 1822, and "his Highness wished to show us some Montagnies haughtiness by *ordering* me to send him not less than a Fathom of Tobacco—which I did—and he, I believe, was thoroughly smug for having ventured so far for I did not spare him being more severe than I should otherwise have been, had he not been the Chief & well known to me" (HBCA B.200/a/1 fos.11–12). The following June, Grand Cheveux arrived with Robe de Castor, another Slavey leader, and the trader "granted the usual Clothing to one of the Chiefs, & a Jacket, Shirt & Duck Trousers to the other with 3 feet of Tobaccoo & 23 half pints of Indian Rum—observing at the same time that it would be the last Dress they should receive—unless they proved themselves more deserving than this year." Later that same month, Grand Cheveux was hanging about the Fort, "becoming troublesome" in his demands for alcohol, which were "rather increasing than decreasing." His demands were not met, however, and Grand Cheveux left until December 1823, when he and others arrived, and there was "now a full assembly of them yet all was quiet as they are never allowed Grog enough to make them intoxicated" (HBCA B.200/a/1 fos.49–50; B.200/a/3 fos. 17–18).

After 1826, alcohol was not presented at Fort Simpson. In January 1827, a band of Dogribs arrived from Horn Mountain with over seven hundred martens, seven hundred muskrats, sixty-four beaver, and other furs, "the whole in the Highest order and Prime." The leader received one-half pound of tobacco and a "deserving junior" one-third pound. Others were given as presents a capote, some iron works, or a lesser amount of tobacco. One man had a slight debt erased. In May, others came and "spoke of their usual allowance of Grog at this season—Tobacco was given them with which they appeared as pleased." Each received a present of one-half pound tobacco, a shirt and breechclout. They smoked and "according to their usual Custome danced in the evening" (HBCA B.200/a/ 8 fos.30–30d, 45d).

Thus, it should be emphasized that rum was given as a present for good behaviour and that the HBC traders tried to use gift-giving (of rum, tobacco, and other goods, and of "chief's" clothing) as an incentive to trap furs. As a further example of this policy, in April 1824, eighteen Slaveys arrived from west of the Mackenzie with one hundred twenty-four martens, eighty beaver, and other furs. Edward Smith remarked, "this Party has been frequently to the Fort in course of the Winter and give us assistance in Provisions, and worked tolerably well in point of the Furs Hunt. In consideration of which we gave them 6 Quarts of Indian Rum, a little Vermillion and ½ ftm Tobo. with a Looking Glass—with this present they were highly satisfied and had their frolick in peace and quietness" (HBCA B.200/a/4 fo.4d). Two months later, the trading leader Grand Chefre arrived with six men and over one hundred beaver: "This good exertion of theirs with the consideration of the old man's influence obtained for him 4½ Quarts mixt Rum a bit of Tobo, a bit of Cloth and Ribbd and a little vermillion to rig out a Cap, of which the old *Foguie* was extremely proude, and spent the evening with his followers and about 18 visiters in great harmony" (HBCA B.200/a/4 fo.7d).

The presentation of clothing to trading leaders or "chiefs" was dependent upon their success in trapping and in inducing others to trap. At the outset of the decade, Chief Factor Edward Smith noted in one of his reports that "we give no Gratuities worth noting [compared with other districts], nor is there an Indian now at the Post, considered worthy of receiving the clothing of a Chief, they are all divided into small parties, and every family goes according to their own ideas without a leader" (HBCA B.220/e/3 fo.1d). In time this would change, as numbers of both Dogribs and Slaveys arrived in trading groups, although many Slaveys continued to come to Fort Simpson in very small groups or individually. Leaders were clothed following successful trade. For instance, in June 1824, a Dogrib leader named Ethethawebethaw arrived with forty beaver, ninety-six martens, and other furs. Edward Smith "Gave a Kind of Cloathing to the Chief (for he has brought to the Fort this Winter ninety-five skins in Furs,) consisting of a check shirt, a cotton hand.kf., a pr of Bath. Coating Trousers, a short Coat, and ½ a Circle Feather, with 6 Quarts of Mixt

Rum, with which him and his Party [-?-] themselves peaceably" (HBCA B.200/a/4 fo.7d).

It was possible for a leader to be "declothed" if his trapping success declined. This happened to Grand Cheveux, a Slavey trading leader. In November 1825, he sent his son and two others to Fort Simpson from his camp near the area known as the rapids on the Liard River, "saying as He done but little he was ashamed to come Himself—this Indian from Misfortunes in His familie by deaths—has done little or anything for this many years past—owing at same time a heavy Balance of long standing—sent Him payment for the few Skins brought by His Son—and word that His debt amounting to sixty Made Beaver (which he never was able to have paid) was given up—and expected he would exert Himself—as the all he had to depend upon was what he would bring—which he would in future Trade and get no more debts—a footing to which we would Wish to bring the Whole of the Indians of this Post" (see below) (HBCA B.200/a/6 fo.50). The following June (1826), Grand Cheveux regained his status: "The Grand Cheveux who was for many years considered a Chief amongst his tribe, had from bad behavior lost his usual clothing for two winters back, but having in course of last winter again retrieved his character, he was presented with his usual present, which consisted of a Chiefs Scarlet Coat, 1 Pair Blue Cloth Trousers, 1 Laced Hat, 1 Cotton Shirt, 1 Cotton Handkf, ½ Circle feather and 1 Fm Tob" (HBCA B.200/a/7 fo.9).

One final note here concerns Indians who came to Fort Simpson for the first time, who often received a present. In April 1825, for example, three "Nahanny" whose visit was their first received a gratuity of four measures of powder, fifteen balls, some shot, one half foot of tobacco, one awl, two knives, two flints, a scraper, and a fire steel (HBCA B.200/a/6 fo.7).

The Exchange: Furs and Goods

On their visits, Slaveys and Dogribs brought beaver, martens, lynxes, bear and moose skins, muskrats, provisions, and the occasional fox, mink, otter, wolf, and wolverine. These furs and provisions were obtained and traded in different months of the year. For example, beaver were shot or trapped in wooden traps in the spring and early fall and traded in May and June and again in November and December. Occasionally, Indians arrived in midwinter, requesting chisels in order to break open beaver lodges (HBCA B.200/a/5 fo.20d; B.200/a/11 fo.10d), but this was not common practice. Rather, wooden traps or guns and shot were used in spring and fall. Steel traps were rare in the 1820's. The fur season ended "in Trapping and Shooting Beaver at the opening of the small Rivers in May—in the Winter they make little or any use of the Chizel to Work Beaver—their reasons are in long

Complaints of the Cold in Winter—and the fear of Want of Provisions makes them [retire?] to places where their is plenty of Rabbits" (HBCA B.200/a/5 fo.19). Competing also with the beaver hunt was summer and fall fishing: in July 1822, one band "required assistance of some meat to conduct them below, where they intend to Hunt—I [Wentzel] granted them the supply they required [117 pounds were given], and that with a better grace, because I wish to prevent them from flying to the fishing Lakes—in order to secure a Fall Hunt of the Beaver—otherwise they would not make any" (HBCA B.200/a/1 fo.56). High water in late summer could "annihilate them trapping Beaver," as it did one September (HBCA B.200/a/3 fo.7).

In contrast to the pattern for beaver, lynxes and martens were snared and trapped throughout the winter and traded from November through June. There is some indication that early and later winter were the most important times; for instance, some Indians arrived in December 1825, and there were "no expectations of them doing much in the fur way until the fine weather sets in—then they will begin to trap martins" (HBCA B.200/a/5 fo.19).

Provisions were obtained during the late summer and early fall hunt (when skins were prime for clothing) and traded at Fort Simpson from August through October. In the early 1820's, some pressures were exerted on Indians not to trade before August because too much low quality meat was in the storeroom. In June 1823, for example, "All the Natives equipped here this Spring have orders not to come in with Provisions until the Latter end of August—This measure has been adopted with a view to save expenses, as we have a Superabundance of Poor Provisions on Hand—throughout the whole Department" (HBCA B.200/a/1 fo.47).

The exchange in provisions was substantial, and it was dependent in part on several "Fort hunters," who were Slaveys or Dogribs, or both, outfitted with ammunition and other supplies and hired to kill moose, caribou, hares, and other animals. In 1826 alone, provisions received at Fort Simpson included approximately 18,000 pounds of fresh meat, 14,000 pounds of dry meat, 900 caribou tongues, 1,800 hares, and 3,000 fish (HBCA B.200/d/11 fo.18).

The numbers of furs exchanged varied from year to year. The numbers exchanged in seven years from 1824 to 1831 are presented in Table 1. These data reveal several trends. Most noticeable are the decline in the trade of beaver, especially in 1831, probably as a result of overhunting; the rise in the lynx trade through the late 1820's, followed by a decline in 1831 because of the cyclical decline in lynx population (coupled with the hare population, which crashed in 1830); the decline in marten in 1831, perhaps owing to an inexplicable population shift; and the mid-late 1820's rise in the muskrat trade, the result probably of the organization of the Dogrib trade. The trade in moose-skins was affected by snow conditions; in April 1830, for example, many moose

TABLE 1: FUR RETURNS AT FORT SIMPSON

	1824	1826	1827	1828	1829	1830	1831
Beaver	1330	1394	2472	1982	1837	1369	715
Coatings and Cuttings (lbs.)	55	—	90	91	55	121	73
Castoreum (lbs.)	55	49	95	66	91	52	19
Bear	65	68	88	111	81	187	111
Fox	7	14	4	15	11	17	18
Lynx	484	1044	1669	2865	2771	1657	251
Marten	2065	5103	1985	1510	1052	870	488
Muskrat	2453	3631	5034	3685	4068	2233	1881
Mink	4	28	2	26	0	29	4
Otter	9	15	6	8	24	18	12
Wolf	0	1	3	5	8	1	8
Wolverine	10	15	11	15	17	36	32
Swanskins	14	—	8	34	—	24	15
Moose Skins	23	—	—	—	—	—	36
Caribou Skins	0	—	—	—	—	—	60

Source: HBCA B.200/d/4, 10b, 13b, 17, 23, 32
Note: Beaver, bear, fox, and otter are totals; (distinctions large or small and common or fine are combined).

were killed in very deep snow, and "like the others [the Indians] continued the distruction of the Animals to no purpose—the whole remaining on the feild except the Skins" (HBCA B.200/a/11 fo.43).

Furs and provisions were exchanged for a limited range of goods: tobacco; guns and ammunition; kettles, knives and other iron works; dry goods such as capotes and blankets; bracelets, awls, combs, and other miscellaneous items. Table 2 lists "outfits" of trading goods, most of which are for the Indian trade distributed at Fort Simpson in the fall, and the inventories at the end of trading season in spring. (Some goods—vests, playing cards, men's shoes, tea, flour, sugar, etc.—destined exclusively for HBC officers and servants have been omitted.)

In the late 1820's, inventories were in general very low and some goods were completely traded out (see below). Guns traded readily: for example, twenty-six of twenty-nine sold in 1824–25, none were on inventory in 1827, and the same was probably the case in 1828 and 1829, when the traders could not ship in enough of any type of goods to satisfy the demand. Powder, ball, shot, powder horns, and other items associated with guns also exchanged in considerable quantities. Iron works, such as axes, knives, hand daggers, files, and one type of chisel also seem to have been popular. For instance, in 1827–28 and 1828–29, there were exchanges of approximately 170 and 130 axes, 450 and 320 knives, and 230 and 200 files; of seemingly large quantities of tobacco and a number of tobacco boxes; of 100 capotes and over 100 shirts each year; and of roughly 100 awls each year.

TABLE 2: OUTFITS AND INVENTORIES AT FORT SIMPSON, 1823-29

	Outf 1823	Inv 1824	Outf 1824	Inv 1825	Inv 1827	Outf 1827	Inv 1828	Outf 1828	Inv 1829
Guns	30	9	20	3	0	25	—	38	—
Shot (bags)	3	1	2	0	0	5	0	5	—
Ball (bags)	6	1	4	1	1	7	0	5	0
Gun powder (kegs)	5	1	4	2	1	7	0	7	1
Gun flints (ct.)	6	4	8	2	1	1	0	14	0
Gunworms	36	0	144	96	144	288	216	144	36
Powder Horns	4	2	21	4	5	24	—	18	—
Axes	74	—	77	13	26	178	25	142	35
Hand daggers	45	36	9	8	1	8	—	36	—
Knives	144	40	144	54	31	497	72	288	30
Crooked knives	—	—	—	—	30	—	15	—	18
Files	120	34	87	7	32	204	0	198	0
Chisels	80	33	166	83	8	—	28	55	0
Skin scrapers	—	—	—	—	3	—	9	—	0
Awls	288	96	288	144	84	—	0	144	0
Beaver traps	—	—	—	—	—	—	—	4	—
Twine (skeins)	22	18	22	5	66	22	55	61	95
Net thread (lbs.)	15	2	0	0	58	2	38	8	40
Br. & cop. ktls. (lbs.)	104	45	90	37	15	99	58	176	—
Fire steels	72	12	—	—	240	—	48	36	60
Twist tob. (rls./lbs.)[a]	4	55	3	—	192	7	28	7	80
Tobacco boxes	20	2	21	2	7	64	0	44	0
Demerara rum (kegs)	3	1	2	—	0	0	0	0	0
Blankets	57	10	66	3	4	126	—	144	—
Strouds (pieces)	7	20	5	2	1	10	—	15	0
Gartering (rolls)	14	7	8	7	0	7	0	5 gr	0

Item									
Cloth (yds.)	—	—	4	—	2	77	—	75	—
Cotton (yds.)	—	—	—	—	—	86	—	78	—
Capots	70	38	54	33	9	92	—	109	0
Chief's coats	4	1	4	5	2	—	—	0	—
Jackets	7	9	—	—	—	—	—	—	—
Shirts	29	19	21	18	1	119	—	158	—
Sleeves (prs.)	20	17	7	—	4	—	0	—	—
Trousers	16	15	7	9	10	36	0	46	3
Handkerchiefs	82	48	10	17	—	82	—	144	—
Hats	6	6	—	—	17	14	5	9	5
Belts	59	20	10	1	3	48	—	21	—
Coat buttons	36	0	—	—	24	72	—	48	2
Needles (ct.)	2	5	1	4	6	0	3	6	5
Thread (lbs.)	1	15	2	—	8	9	6	8	0
Women's scissors	5	1	7	0	11	12	0	0	0
Combs	48	18	29	30	38	24	0	60	0
Pl. & fing. rings	144	—	144	324	648	—	324	—	—
Copper wrist bands	18	4	—	—	—	—	—	—	—
Looking glasses	—	—	3	13	13	6	—	16	—
Beads (lbs.)	30	0	10	1	61	22	41	19	27
Vermilion (lbs.)	3	2	2	2	1	3	0	3	0

Source: Adapted from HBCA B.200/d/4,17. All figures rounded off to the nearest whole number.

a. outfits are rolls, inventories are pounds

These somewhat limited impressions of the exchange, gained from an examination of outfits and inventories, are augmented considerably by an examination of the Indian accounts (HBCA B.200/d/3a, 10a), which provide a far more personal glimpse of the exchange. Examples of two of the more than two hundred Indian accounts used in the analysis here are provided in Figure 2, part of the account of Shedaisbethaw (HBCA B.200/d/10 fo.10) and in Table 3, "Transactions of Tithica, 1822–27." The types of data that can

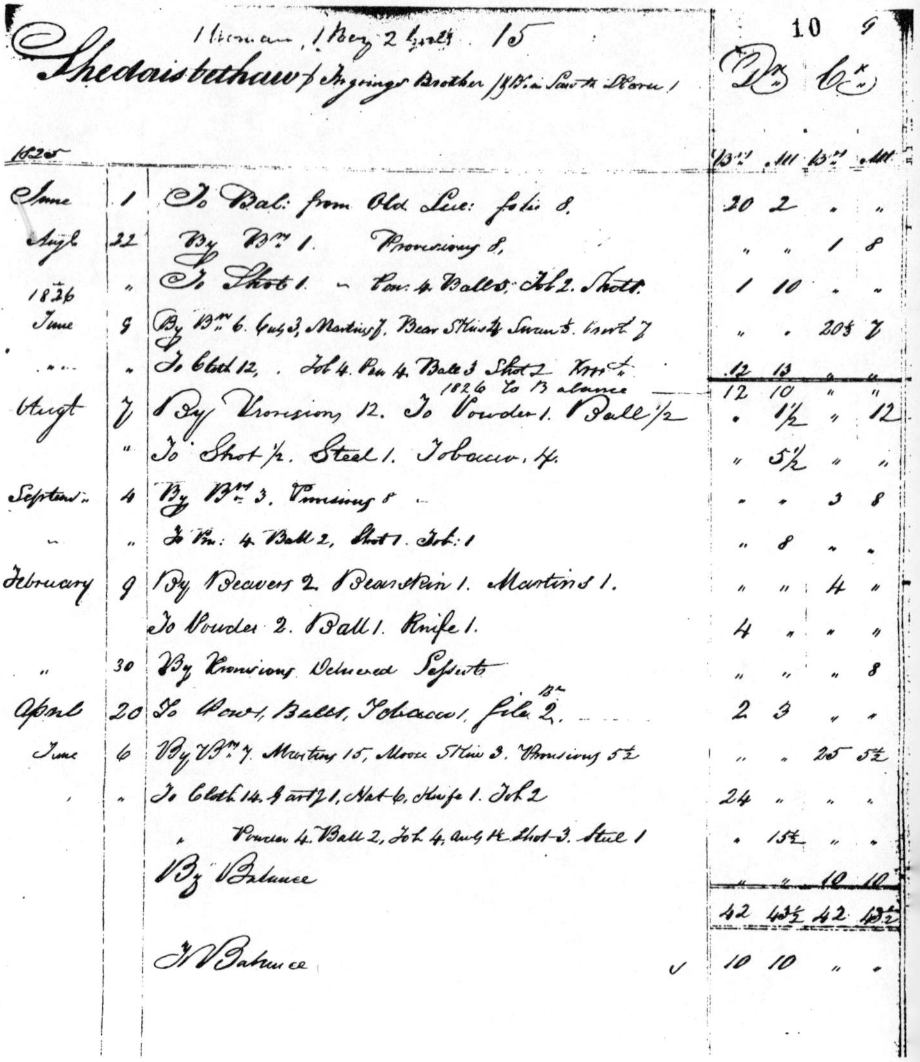

FIGURE 2

TABLE 3: TRANSACTIONS OF TITHICA, 1822–27

Date	Debit Br	Mt	Credit Br	Mt	Beaver	Lynx	Marten	Muskrat	Bearskin	Otter	Mooseskin	Provisions	Tobacco	Powder	Ball	Shot	Knife	File	Kettle	Axe	Gun	Firesteel	Dagger	Ice Trench	Brayette	Bonnet	Cloth	Capot	Gartering	Blanket	Comb	Buttons
18 Oct 1822	10	2	4	14	4							14	4	6	4		3			2						2						
18 Oct 1822	15	16	12	7	6							7																	1	9		
27 May 1823		4				1								1	3																	
14 Jun 1823				9			5			balance Ft. Liard																						
19 Oct 1823				8	2	1																							1			
25 May 1824	30	14	18	1	7	1	5		4		3	9	3	4	3	2					20	1	2				5	3				
2 Jul 1824							3			1																						
20 Aug 1824	8	8	5	10								8	2	4	2												2					
18 Oct 1824	9	11		27	8	14			2		3	10	3	5	3					3							2					
20 May 1825	28	3	3		2				5					4															10			
4 Sep 1825	3		11	10	8	1	2	1			8	10	1	1	1		1	1	8	2				2						8		
22 Nov 1825	11	4	2	2			2					2		2	2		1															
22 Dec 1825			8	10	6		2					10	2	3	2																	
13 Feb 1826	7			14								14	2	4	3																	
26 Feb 1826	12	9	10											2	2									2			10				1	1
13 Apr 1826	5		3												3																	
19 Jun 1826	10	2	13	2	7			1			3	4	2	4	1												2					
7 Aug 1826	4				2								2	1		2		2														
28 Aug 1826	5						3																									
28 May 1827	4	2			3	5					2	2	1	2	1																	
28 May 1827	12				balance								1	1	1	1																

be extracted from these accounts are obvious and include: the values (in MB) of specific furs, provisions, and goods exchanged; the total credit in furs ("Br" or "beaver" credit) and provisions ("Mt" or "Meat" credit); the total debit, likewise figured as debit in goods exchanged for "beaver" or for "meat" credit; and balances outstanding in 1822 and 1827. Provisions could be exchanged for a limited set of goods—mainly tobacco, powder, ball, shot, and knives; in contrast, furs could be exchanged "down" for these goods or for any other goods in the Indian trade inventory. These accounts show both the relative value of various furs (and provisions) brought by Slaveys and Dogribs to exchange and their selection of goods, within the constraints both of what was available on inventory and of the limited set of goods for which provisions could be exchanged.

Beaver, marten, lynx, and provisions were the most important items exchanged by Dogrib and Slavey trappers and hunters, in terms of the value they received (their credit in MB). Table 4 shows the mean values in Made

TABLE 4: MEAN VALUES (IN MB) OF FURS AND PROVISIONS

Beaver	31.1	Mooseskins	3.9
Provisions	30.0	Bear	2.5
Marten	22.3	Otter	0.6
Lynx	12.8	Castoreum	0.6
"Furs"	9.1	Wolverine	0.2
Muskrat	4.8	Wolf	0.1
		Fox	0.1

Source: Computed from HBCA B.200/d/3a,10a

Beaver of the furs and provisions exchanged by 204 trappers in the period from 1822 to 1827. The average trade of a trapper or hunter during this period is shown, and it is clear that the most important items brought to exchange were beaver, provisions, and martens. The provision trade, exceeded in value only by that of beaver, was important for the Dogrib and Slavey as well as for the Fort Simpson traders.

The use of notched tally sticks, discussed above, indicates that the Slavey and Dogrib understood the approximate value, in Made Beaver, of their furs. While the Hudson's Bay Company had its own pricing system to evaluate the yearly fur returns (Table 5) and thus the annual profit, this system was not strictly comparable to the exchange rate for furs in specific districts. In the mid 1820's, George Simpson wrote Edward Smith, "We are desirous that every encouragement should be afforded the Indians to increase their exertions, and to that end you are at liberty to reduce the Tariff if you consider it advisable.— Both the Gov. & Committee and the Council are desirous that they should be liberally dealt with and that fair prices should be given for their Furs" (HBCA D.4/90 fos.119–119d).

TABLE 5: PRICE (IN STERLING) FOR EVALUATION OF RETURNS,
OUTFITS 1822 AND 1827

	1822	1827
Beaver Large Fine	26/ 2	30/ 6
Large Common	18/11	30/ 6
Small Fine	—	13/ 6
Small Common	—	13/ 6
Cutting & Coating (lb.)	14/ 6	12/ 3
Castoreum (lb.)	—	16/ 3
Bear Black	24/ 4	19/ 8
Brown	16/—	15/ 2
Fox Cross	5/ 5	12/ 2
Red	6/ 9	4/ 6
Silver	106/ 6	63/ 4
White	—	2/ 8
Lynx	5/ 8	9/ 6
Fisher	6/ 4	—
Marten	5/ 4	7/ 9
Mink	—	2/11
Muskrat	6d	10d
Otter	18/ 1	16/ 4
Wolf	3/ 6	10/—
Wolverine	5/ 9	5/—

It is of interest that in 1833, just after the end of the decade under scrutiny here, Chief Factor John Stuart wished to do just the opposite: tighten the tariff for furs. He wrote to the managers of Mackenzie River District posts: "According to the Present mode of valuing Furs Property is sold in the most distant parts of Mackenzies River for far less value than at Norway House or the Winipic District where the cost of Transport is comparatively triffling. Not that the Standard Tariff Price is less here than at those places for in most things it is the same but that the Furs are priced at a higher value beyond their real worth." Stuart suggested a different evaluation for furs: two small beaver equal to one large beaver; a bear or otter equal to one MB, unless large and prime; no fewer than ten large or fifteen small muskrats per MB; a "full size and prime" lynx equal to one MB but a "small and common" one only one-half; alterations in provisions were suggested but left to the "discretion" of managers. Martens were to remain at three per MB (HBCA B.116/a/11 fos. 12–13d).

There were reactions to these suggested changes—from Slavey arriving at Fort Liard who "complain of the reduction in the price of the Musquash of which they happen to have more than a usual quantity" (HBCA B.116/a/11 fo. 23d) to Governor George Simpson, who wrote to Edward Smith that "It is with much concern we learn that Mr Stuart has altered the Tariff of McKenzie's River, as regards the Indian Trade, which we consider to have been

injudicious and improper, as the prices usually charged during your adminis-
tration were sufficiently high; you will therefore be pleased to revert to former
prices" (HBCA D.4/20 fo.16d).

There are few statements in post journals or reports, beyond the fairly
general ones just mentioned, that allow one to discover the precise relationship between the tariff for furs and the degree to which small (cub) or
unseasonal (summer) furs, or those damaged in preparation, detracted from
the value of pelts. In fact, the actual exchange rate for specific furs must be
inferred from journal entries listing the numbers of furs brought on specific
trading trips and from account books data showing the value in MB of the
transactions on those particular trips. This has been done for selected transactions, and the results—the number of pelts per Made Beaver—are found in
Table 6.

In these transactions, the number of beaver pelts per Made Beaver ranges
from 0.7 to 2.3, of lynx pelts from 1.1 to 2.0, of marten skins from 1.2 to 7.5,
and of muskrats from 9.1 to 14.3. The averages (medians) are 1.1 beaver, 1.3
lynx, 3.6 martens, and 10.6 muskrats. These compare favourably with infer-
ences which may be drawn from Stuart's comments (above) that one beaver,
one lynx, three martens, or ten muskrats were worth one MB. The deviations
from the averages in the cases of beaver, lynx, and muskrat are slight compared to marten; perhaps the extremes in marten pelts (1.2 and 7.5) are errors;
or perhaps the pelts in these two cases were very large and well-prepared or
very small, poorly prepared and unseasonal, respectively. The different

TABLE 6: NUMBER OF PELTS PER MB IN TWENTY
SELECTED TRANSACTIONS, 1822–27

	Beaver	Lynx	Marten	Muskrats
7 Nov 1822	1.0			
7 Feb 1823	1.0		3.1	
7 Mar 1823	1.4		4.8	
23 May 1823	0.9	2.0	1.2	
4 Jun 1823	1.1	1.0	3.5	14.3
12 Jun 1823	1.0		3.4	
10 Jul 1823	2.3		3.6	
3 Jun 1824	1.3		4.8	
28 Nov 1824	1.0		3.6	
11 Dec 1824	1.1		7.5	
10 Feb 1825	1.8	1.3	3.1	
13 Apr 1825	1.3		5.5	
28 May 1825	1.2	1.1	4.1	
7 Jun 1825	1.6	1.3	3.1	
21 Nov 1825	1.1		5.0	
8 Dec 1825	1.0		3.2	
7 Apr 1826	1.3	1.4	3.6	12.6
20 Apr 1826	0.7		4.4	9.1
31 Jan 1827	1.3	1.4	3.7	10.6
7 Jan 1827		1.3	3.9	10.0

numbers in all cases suggest that the Fort Simpson traders were evaluating each fur according to its size and quality and discovering the most flaws in marten pelts. Smith told the managers of all posts in the Mackenzie River District (and presumably took his own advice) to no longer accept summer furs, because of their inferior quality, and to make sure that furs were properly cleaned and stretched "and when any neglect is found . . . the Skin or Skins brought in by them in bade condition to be reduced in Value" (HBCA B.200/b/4 fos. 18–19). That individual pelts differed in value meant that some haggling may have taken place, although how much or how intensive was not recorded.

Guns, ammunition (powder, ball, and shot), tobacco, and dry goods (blankets, capotes, and cloth) were the goods most highly esteemed by Dogribs and Slaveys, in terms of debit in MB or value expended. Table 7 shows the mean value in MB of goods selected by the Slavey and Dogrib;

TABLE 7: MEAN VALUES IN MB OF TRADE GOODS
EXCHANGED BY 204 TRAPPERS, 1822-27

Powder	19.0	Powder horn	0.7
Tobacco	13.4	Tobacco box	0.7
Gun	12.2	Ice trench	0.7
Ball	10.6	Firesteel	0.5
Blanket	10.1	Stroud	0.3
Capot	8.0	Comb	0.3
Cloth	7.6	Hat	0.3
Kettle	5.8	Molton	0.2
Shot	5.7	Breechclout	0.2
Sundries	4.6	Beads	0.2
Axe	2.5	Flint	0.2
Knife	2.5	Shirt	0.2
Leggings	1.9	Sleeve	0.2
File	1.7	Bracelet	0.1
Dagger	1.5	Button	0.1
Gartering	1.3	Tin Dish	0.1
Belt	1.1	Scraper	0.04
Brayette	0.8	Vermilion	0.04
Bonnet	0.7	Awl	0.02
		Razor	0.01

Source: Computed from HBCA B.200/d/3a,10a.

within limits imposed by the outfit they chose to spend 39 per cent of their credit for guns and ammunition, 31 per cent for dry goods, 14 per cent for iron works and 12 per cent for tobacco.

Guns and ammunition were highly valued (and expensive items; see Table 8) and were obviously related both to the subsistence quest and to the trade in provisions (which as already noted, were exchanged mainly for powder, ball, and shot). Guns were one of the first items requested in the trade; for example, in March 1828, a band of Mountain Indians arrived and "being Strangers and unarmed they all call for Guns." There were none left in the outfit that year, so "to satisfy their demands" on this and another occasion, the post manager traded to them a gun he purchased from one of his men. The year before, two Slaveys had acted as intermediaries in the Mountain Indian trade, but "found themselves disapointed having Traded their Guns with the Dahotinnes— Wanted others have had none to give them" (HBCA B.200/a/8 fo.42; B.200/a/9 fo.25d).

Many guns apparently did not last very long. Some were not durable and others were misused. For instance, in May 1828, one man "burst his Gun

TABLE 8: VALUES IN MB PAID FOR PARTICULAR TRADE ITEMS

1 MB
yew-handled knife
brass inlaid knife
crooked knife
roach knife
clasp knife
small file
small axe
hatchet
steel tobacco box
horn comb
tin dish
1½ feet tobacco
firesteel

2 MB
fine knife
brass inlaid knife
cartouche knife
earth chisel
small dagger
9" file
small axe
hatchet
steel tobacco box
small copper kettle
3 feet tobacco
cap
small belt
bonnet
brayette
small capot
breechclout
razor

3 MB
half axe
small copper kettle
tin dish
earth chisel/ice trench
hand dagger
small blanket
plain 3 pts. blanket
cotton shirt
flannel shirt
checked shirt
leggings
powder horn
small capot
tobacco box
bonnet

4 MB
rose belt
narrow scarlet belt
powder horn
tin pan

5 MB
small capot
cotton shirt
jacket
flannel shirt
blanket
powder horn

6 MB
second hand gun
belt
jacket
vest
wool hat
blanket
capot
shirt

8 MB
second hand gun
copper kettle
capot 3 Ells
plain 2½ pts. blanket

9 MB
copper kettle
capot

10 MB
second hand gun
covered copper kettle
blanket 4 Ells
plain 3 pts. blanket
duffle blanket
steel trap
capot

12 MB
second hand gun
covered copper kettle
cloth capot
striped blanket
chief's coat

14 MB
second hand gun
covered copper kettle

16 MB
blue capot

18 MB
duffle blanket

20 MB
gun

25 MB
gun

yesterday by puting a Ball on Shot to fire at a Moose deer—that came Near Him When He Was Watching Beaver—thus he lost both His Gun and the Deer"; another arrived in February 1830 "rather displeased because he did not get a gun careless in the extream of their Guns, that few among them (the Indians) have a Gun the second year thats Good for anything" (HBCA B.200/a/9 fo.32d; B.200/a/11 fo. 27d). In other cases, workmanship was clearly at fault: in 1824, one Indian "complained of the badness of His Gun He got another—during summer He burst His Gun and remained Criple for some time—Here other individuals among the Indians have the same complaint burst their Guns—Three of them With Wilsons name & One Barnett." In 1830, these guns were still being traded; one Indian arrived, with the cock broken off his gun: "this is one of Wilsons guns many is the criple his Guns have made among the Indians, and on many occasion have they gone hungry to bed either from their bursting or breaking" (HBCA B.200/a/5 fos.13d–14; B.200/a/11 fo.29). On defective or undesirable guns, it was remarked that "its a loss to the Company to import a bade article—as often it is sold at an undervalue from regular Standard" (HBCA B.200/b/5 fo.14d).

Despite these flaws, guns and ammunition remained highly desired, which is attested to by the high proportion of their credit that Slaveys and Dogribs spent on these goods. If neither guns nor ammunition remained, however, Slaveys and Dogribs would trade for other items—as in the case of one man who, in late September 1827 "came in to see if the Boat was arrived to get a Gun for His Skins in Store—tired Waiting he asked payment for them in Other Goods—which he get and departed for Lac du Saule [Willow Lake] in a bade humore having with an Old Gun which he carrys in lieu of a better missed on a Moose deer at the end of this Island—the none arrival of the Boat causes us many losses and disapointments" (HBCA B.200/a/9 fo.9d).

The trade in kettles, knives, axes, and other "iron works" was not very great, since only 14 per cent of credit was spent on these goods; moreover, the trade in this category was mixed: kettles were esteemed, but items like earth trenches were not. Kettles, axes, and other iron works were among the first items traded by groups new to the trade. In 1828, for instance, some Mountain Indians arrived, but "Was short of Guns and Kettles to meet [their] demands . . . which is to be the more regreted—they being strangers"; two years later, more arrived, wanting specifically guns and ammunition, kettles, knives, and other iron works, and "we had the means of meeting their demands—and the Trade was soon over Skin for value—their Wants compleated as far as their means of purchase would admitt" (HBCA B.200/a/9 fo.25; B.200/a/11 fo.38d). Some of the Slavey and Dogrib were adamant in their demand for a trade in kettles; in March 1830, one man came with lynxes to trade for a kettle; there were none, so "he left payment for one whpn there will be one to give him—and that will not be before the Arrival of next Outfit" (HBCA B.200/a/11 fo.35).

Broad, earth chisels or trenches were traded or lent occasionally in order to break into beaver lodges in winter, but as Edward Smith commented (in 1825), "the [Earth] Chizel is not in general use among the Natives of this River to work the Beaver in Winter. Nor can all our arguments get the better of their lazy habits—to induce them to make use of the Chizel the Price . . . was reduced from 6 to 3 Made Beaver still they purchase no more of them than they did before—this accounts for the number of Common Beaver sent out from this River yearly" (HBCA B.200/a/6 fo.48). In the mid-1820's, the Fort Simpson blacksmith was making small axes out of earth chisels, "which has been long a dead Stock on hand"; there was a "ready market" for these small axes (which in fact, were exchanged only eight days after they were made) (HBCA B.200/a/5 fo.17d).

Axes and knives, though not high-priced (Table 7), were traded in large quantities at Fort Simpson (Table 2). At times, there were problems with axes: in the early 1820's, there were "complaints from Indians of the Badness of their Axs—and our own being in the same state"; at one point "Indians complain[ed] daily" of the axes. Again in the late 1820's, axes were "the Worst I have yet seen from the Factory. the evil appears to be in the Temper" (HBCA B.200/a/1 fo.29; B.200/a/3 fos.21,31; B.200/a/11 fos.19–20). In these years, a blacksmith was kept busy repairing axes and guns and making axes from broad chisels, crooked knives from old files, and awls, fire steels, and, in the late 1820's, beaver traps for the trade (HBCA B.200/a/8–11 passim).

Throughout the 1820's, the trade in dry goods was steady and significant, in that Indians allocated 31 per cent of their credit to blankets, capotes, leggings, etc. In 1823, Edward Smith remarked of the Slavey: "they appear as fond of Goods as their neighbors the Chipewyans when they can afford to get any, they are very [fond?] of Good Capot or Blanket" (HBCA B.200/a/3 fo.18). The trade by Slaveys of beaver pelt capotes depended in part on the supply of dry goods, and in some years, as happened in 1827–28, all dry goods had been traded by late winter. In April, some Slaveys arrived and "we made a shift to settle them in the Articles the most necessary—they were all clothed in Beaver and having no Capots—was necessited to allow them to return with their Beaver Coats—however they promised to bring them in June" (HBCA B.200/a/9 fo.29). Some capotes were regarded as inferior in quality, and Indians took them only "from necessity and with reluctance at a reduced price"; others, of a large size, with buttons and a hood, they "cheerfully" took at a higher cost to them. Other dry goods were also useful: handkerchiefs were "a Good Article for the Trade"; striped gartering was traded, although other kinds were not; trousers "find a ready market"; and the quantity of strouds "never ought to be reduced" (HBCA B.200/e/8 fos.6d–7d).

In the late 1820's, the demand for dry goods was so high that blankets, capotes, and cloth were among the first items completely traded out; in

February 1828, "Dry Goods is nearly out and scarcely anything remains except ammunition and Tobacco"; in March 1829, "scarcely any thing remains in the sheap of dried Goods"; and in November 1829, two Slavey "wanted each a blanket more than we could allow & were disappointed at a refusal" (HBCA B.200/a/9 fo.23; B.200/a/10 fos.26d–27; B.200/a/11 fo.15). And in January 1830, "The Indians complains much of the qualitie of the Strouds, and with some right, being this year more than 2/3rds Blue N.C. & B.C. plain common Blue and plain Common White, all inovations in Trading Articles for Indians is dangerous. Strouds is all the same Price to them, and ought to be continued the same qualitie" (HBCA B.200/a/11 fo.22d). These Indians knew what they liked and what they did not, and took steps to ensure a favourable trade in terms of the quality and type of goods and price.

The trade in dry goods may have been relatively great in the 1820's because traditional beaver-skin clothing (capotes) were being exchanged; also, there may have been particular pressure placed on the exchange of dry goods in the late 1820's and early 1830's because of the population crash of hares, an animal important for clothing; demographic and genealogical data do show that the trade in dry goods (as well as the total trade) was significantly greater if a trapper had a wife and children than if he had neither.

As mentioned above, a major difficulty in the late 1820's was shipping enough goods to Fort Simpson to satisfy the Indians' demand for them. During a few years, the HBC traders at Fort Simpson were in debt to the Indians. This happened quite quickly: in 1824, 150 Slavey and Dogrib were a total of over 2,300 MB in debt; by the spring of 1829, the situation was reversed and the Hudson's Bay Company was approximately 600 MB in debt to the Slavey and Dogrib. "This . . . growing evil" continued in 1830, when over 200 Indians at Fort Simpson were still owed roughly 625 MB by the Company (HBCA B.200/d/6,27; D.5/3 fo.419).

Some traders thought that the Company's inability to supply goods would be "a clog on their [the Indians'] exertions" (HBCA D.5/3 fo.420). A direct relationship between supply of goods and return of furs was seen: "the more the Indians are restricted in their wants with the means of prompt payment at Command the less they will do" (HBCA B.200/b/5 fo.22). Certainly, the Indians were greatly disappointed in the lack of goods (although they did not become openly agitated, as Indians in other places did). In March 1828, some Slaveys arrived and "when they were told that they had no more Goods to expect from us the Whole being gone—were quite reasonable—and observed ammunition and Tobacco Was all they Wanted for the Summer—and any of their relations that would kill more Furs than the debts they were due—could have no objections to trust us until the Arrival of the Boats in August—when they would be sure of payment" (HBCA B.200/a/9 fo.26). Two years later, Chief Factor Edward Smith forecast gloomily: "The stress for Goods will be more severely felt than last Spring, our promises to the Indians have not been fulfilled, and the Gentlemen write that in spite of their best endeavors the Natives from a continual dissapointment in not getting their Wants with Furs in hand will return again to their usual habits of indolence and indifference for the Whites" (HBCA B.200/a/11 fo.30). At the end of the decade, Smith considered the limited outfits to be the most serious disadvantage of the trade in the District: "Having done what we could to gain the confidence of the Natives, with unremitted attentions to their wants—we had established that Character among them becoming the Representatives of a respectable Company—to meet our views their exertions continued to augment, while Outfits imported was inadequate to the demands. in their little wants many have been disappointed, and leaves the establishments ill pleased" (HBCA B.200/e/9 fo.4d).

The shortage of goods was owing to several factors, one of which was the expansion of the trade at Fort Simpson itself and in the district as a whole. In 1830, George Simpson wrote approvingly to Smith of the "great attention you have paid to the business" of encouraging Indians to trade more and agreed to Smith's request to expand the outfit. But in 1829, Fort Halkett was established west of Fort Liard, and this new post strained further the outfit of trading goods. The shortage of goods was also the result of the reduction of men and inventories in the general context of Simpson's "Oeconomy." Yet there was a conflict between reducing the number of men on one hand and being able to transport into the district sufficient goods for the trade on the other. (It was even more difficult to feed and otherwise maintain in the district in winter a large contingent of men needed for the transport.) Thus, the outfit for the winter of 1829–30 was "too limited to meet the demands of the season—a Fifth Post to equip and Eight extra Men—Leaves us more deficient for the Other posts than last year—which was not enough to pay any of the Trade of the season" (HBCA B.200/a/11 fo.6).

One consequence of inadequate supplies was the discontinuing of the debt system: "from this want of property the debt system (altho proposed some time before) was discontinued from necessity and the loss is more nominal than otherwise—being only a Few back debts that never would have been paid—we purpose now to continue and give no more debts." Excepted were fort hunters, who "will require some things in advance—which will be paid of every Spring—and be the same as giving no debts" (HBCA B.200/b/4 fo.18, B.200/b/5 fo.11d).

By the early 1830's, this problem of limited outfits had ended, but it would recur, caused once more by pressures on a limited outfit from expansions of the trade westward.

INTERETHNIC RELATIONS

One of the priorities of the Fort Simpson traders was to organize the travel and trade of native people in order to minimize the threat of disputes or hostilities. Indians were discouraged from roaming widely and from trading at posts to which they did not "belong." In 1822, for example, Wentzel gave "no Debts" to two Indians who came from near Fort Liard because he "desired them to return to their own Establishment" (HBCA B.200/a/1 fo.6). Efforts to control the trade were more successful within the Mackenzie River District than between it and the neighbouring Athabasca District. The clerks were stymied by the closing of a post on Hay River; by the wandering propensisties of Chipewyans and the trading desires of Yellowknives; by the more favourable (for Indians) tariff at Fort Resolution, which remained in the Athabasca District; and by a less-than-co-operative attitude between managers of the two districts. The latter affected the trade at Fort Simpson; in 1823, a report came from Willow Lake "that in consequence of 3 men having been sent to Martin Lake from Slave Lake with a view to trade with the Slaves—Many Indians who have received advances here will go there, by which it would appear, that all [fettish ?] & discontinued Indians resorting hither will make that place, a refuge to cheat the Company of the advances they have already got at this Establishment" (HBCA B.200/a/1 fo.24).

In the 1820's, different ethnic groups converged for the trade at Fort Simpson and encountered one another near their seasonal camps. For the most part, interethnic relations were fairly placid; however, relations between the Slavey and Chipewyan were sometimes tense and between the Dogrib and Yellowknife were marked by outright hostilities. Each of these is examined briefly.

Slavey-Chipewyan Relations

In the 1820's, Chipewyans traded with Slaveys and trespassed on Slavey territory; both trade and trespass were upsetting, the former insofar as the Fort Simpson traders were concerned and the latter for the Slavey themselves. In the early 1820's, goods were traded at Fort Simpson "at an advanced price on the Fort Chipewyan Indian tariff—this again varies according to utility and luxury": blankets were marked up 25 per cent, iron works 40–50 per cent, guns 67 per cent, but knives not at all (HBCA B.200/e/1 fo.2, B.200/e/2 fo.2). It is clear that the different price of trade goods in the Athabasca and Mackenzie River Districts caused problems. In 1823, Slavey and Dogrib were said to be "much spoiled, from their frequent visits from the Chipewyans and Yellow Knives, as well as from their intercourse at the different Posts with strangers that know nothing of this Trade with them, the rate at which the goods is sold to them shown there has been some mismanagement in this many articles being sold the same Price as to the Chipewyans, which this great expense of bringing the Goods here can but very ill admit" (HBCA B.200/a/3 fo.11).

Two years later, Edward Smith clearly recognized that the Chipewyan acquired their "Necessarys much cheaper at Slave Lake than our Indians in this River—they can afford to barter their property with the Slaves and have handsome Profits—While the McKenzie River Indian stil pays it cheaper than from the Compy. Stores—at Slave Lake or Peace River a Chepewyan gets a Gun for 12 Skins comes among our Indians sels it for 17 Skins—by this barter the Chipewyan gains 5 Skins and the Slaves has it Three Skins Cheaper than from their own Traders—Will take the earlyest opportunity to acquaint Our Athabasca friends of this evil—which if not timely stoped may be followed up with some disagreeable consequences between us and our Indians" (HBCA B.200/a/6 fo.4).

There was a reason other than to trade with Slaveys that led Chipewyans to Slavey territory: to break open beaver lodges, an action to which the more timid Slavey did not strongly object. In March 1823, some Chipewyans "fell in with" the Slavey Grand Cheveux and "trenched most of the Beaver Lodges that many of the Indians from here had found previous to the meeting" (HBCA B.200/a/1 fo.32). Although the Fort Simpson traders objected and Edward Smith told some Chipewyan to "Keep Clear from the Indians of this River—and to return no more to their hunting Grounds" (HBCA B.200/a/6 fos. 42–43), these difficulties did not end and in 1827 some Slavey were

with a party of the Slave Lake Chepewyans toward the latter part of the Summer—and while together they found a spot where their was 10 or a doz of Beaver House—and which the Chepewyans told the Slaves not to Work on any account—thus they dictate to the Slaves on their Owen Lands—their Leder now askes advice what to do wheither to Work the Beaver or leave them to the Chepwyans who are to return—sent them word to work them—I have long since represented to the Athabaska Gentlemen the necessity of endeavoring to keep their Indians near home—or they will continue to harase the Slaves (McKenzie River Indians) until the same Catastrophe is acted over again was with the Copper Indians (HBCA B.200/a/9 fo.17).

By the end of the decade, the effects of Chipewyan hunting were clear: "The idea of husbanding the Country laying between the Hay, Liard River and the McKenzie as far as this district extends in the direction of Hay River has long since drawn our attention. The native indians would never have ruined it—since 1826 it has been overrune. . . . The only plan to preserve the few

Beaver still remaining in this track is to endeavor to keep the Chepewyan indians to their own lands" (HBC B.200/b/6 fos. 30d–31).

Dogrib-Yellowknife Hostilities

The "catastrophe" mentioned above refers to the hostilities that erupted in 1823–24 between the Dogrib and Yellowknife. In June 1823 a report reached Fort Simpson that "all the Martin Lake Slaves were coming this way—flying in a manner from the Red Knives who had murdered 4 of their women this year—from which they apprehended warfare" (HBCA B.200/a/1 fo.51). In the fall, the Dogrib retaliated and killed at least five Yellowknifes between Great Bear Lake and Lac la Martre: "The Dog Ribs of Martin Lake had posted themselves there in the latter part of summer to watch the Copper Indians on their way to Great Slave Lake—they Met as the Story goes when the Ice began to form on the borders of the Lake—The Copper Indians expecting, no harm fell a sacrifice to the treachery of their enemies—The Dog Ribs doe not intend to stop here their intentions (as report says) more to keep the Whole a profound secret from the Traders until the Whole of the Copper Indians had been distroyed" (HBCA B.200/a/3 fos.35–36).

Reports of an even larger conspiracy came to the Fort Simpson traders, although Wentzel admitted, "I do not comprehend the business very clearly—for as observed before—these Indians appear to conceal"; regardless, the traders "understand also that the Hare Indians of Bear Lake have joined the Slaves as allies in this War, and it is whispered that the whole of the Martin Lake Dog Ribs intend to proceed in Summer towards the Barren Lands to destroy all Chepewyans and Red Knives they shall chance to fall in with—besides they express a wish to get the Mackenzies River Slaves to become one of their allies too" (HBCA B.200/a/4 fos.1–1d).

It is clear that the Marten Lake Dogrib regarded themselves as long-suffering, the Yellowknife as aggressors, and their own hostilities as fully justified. Kanoobaw, a Marten Lake Dogrib, reported in 1824:

We suffered our Wives, our Daughters and our Mothers to be taken from us, with their Children. Our Furs also, this we considered of little importance, they were only Skins of Animals, but even our Nets upon which our existence depended, were likewise taken from us, and frequently our Axes, Guns or whatever was most useful or necessary to our maintenance, and left us destitute of means to procure us a subsistance, that it has not seldom happened that many of our friends and relations have died in consequence of starvation! (HBCA B.200/a/4 fo.2d)

Repercussions of the Yellowknife-Dogrib war were noticeable by May

1824, when four Horn Mountain Indians arrived at Fort Simpson and "crossed to the other side. fear of the Dog Ribs and Red Knives has driven them this way for the summer" (HBCA B.200/a/4 fo.6d). In October, there was a rumour that the Hare intended to join the Yellowknife and attack posts in the Mackenzie District. In November, two Indians arrived from a Marten Lake Dogrib group who were near old Fort Alexander, ten nights to the north. Edward Smith commented: "They come from a party of the Martin Lake Indians drove from their fear of the Yellow Knife Indians to the Borders of this River—being no more on their own Lands consequently follows to them Starvation—they have eat some of their Skins and fear Much Cold Weather Now fast aproaching—they have Guns and Amunition Animals are not scarce—poor Wretches they are no Hunters" (HBCA B.200/a/5 fo.17).

Causes and Consequences of Interethnic Tensions

The involvement of the Slavey and Dogrib with the neighbouring Chipewyan and Yellowknife respectively was produced in large part by the fur trade. Prior to 1820, Yellowknife middlemen controlled the trade of the Dogrib and others at Great Slave Lake. In 1812, Yellowknifes were said to "very generally make free booty of any white property collected" by Dogribs and Slaveys "for the purpose of traffic, in order to produce a few necessaries" (Keith 1960:112; see Wentzel Ms. c:2), and Dogrib abandoned some country north of Great Slave Lake because of their fear of Yellowknife hostilities (Franklin 1823:291). While mistrust, enmity, warfare, and wife-capture between the Dogrib and Yellowknife may have antedated the arrival of the European fur trade, the Yellowknife clearly were motivated by middleman profits to exploit the more timid Dogrib. The consequences of these hostilities, in addition to fatalities, involved permanent as well as temporary territorial changes and starvation, owing to flight to areas where resources were poorly known. In one instance, Dogribs went west of the Mackenzie River into mountains "where they found nothing but Mountain Goat . . . their Dogs they had all distroyed and in one instance some had recourse to the bodies of their deceased Children who had previously died from Want—What a picture of disstress and we can do nothing to alevate their sufferings . . . they will now live as Rabbits is plenty" (HBCA B.200/a/5 fos. 19–19d). Chipewyan involvement with the Slavey in the 1820's also was produced by the fur trade—by Chipewyan desire for beaver on Slavey lands and for middleman profits. By the mid-1820's, the problem was serious, and "our Indians the Slavey and Dogrib are hemmed in on all sides by those of the Athabasca District that of Slave Lake in particular" (HBCA B.200/a/6 fo.4). The advantage to the Chipewyan was clear; as Edward Smith commented in the mid-1820's, "This Trade is lucrative to the Chepewyans getting the Goods at 50 p. cent cheaper than the McKenzies River Indians can afford to under value us in their Clandestine dealings with the Indians of this River" (HBCA B.200/a/6 fos.25-26).

Chipeywan trespass and middleman trade was produced in part by the depletion of beaver stock in the Athabasca District and by company efforts to "nurse" or "recruit" the country, that is, to allow beaver populations to increase following depletions. In the late 1820's, there were complaints from Fort Chipewyan "of the poverty of the hunting grounds usually frequented by the Home Guards of that Establishment"; this was caused, George Simpson thought, by each post manager who, compared with his predecessor, "has been more anxious to establish for himself the reputation of a Pack Master or first rate Indian Trader" (HBCA D.4/18 fo.9). Simpson recommended that the Chipewyan be encouraged to go the barren grounds "for a few years, and instead of directing their attention to Beaver Hunting to enjoy themselves among the Rein Deer" (HBCA D.4/18 fo.9d).

At the close of the 1820's, the trade in the Mackenzie River District was further interfered with (from the standpoint of the company) by Beaulieu, a half-breed who spent time with the Dogrib and Yellowknife when he was young, and who was an interpreter for the North West Company in 1820 and an interpreter and hunter for Franklin on Great Bear Lake in 1825 (Franklin 1823:142; 1828:51).

In March 1827, nine Indians arrived at Fort Simpson after an eleven-day trip from Bedzebethaw's camp on Willow Lake, east of the Mackenzie River, reporting that Beaulieu and other Chipewyans who had been working for the Franklin expedition wintered there and "carried off part of their Hunts to swell again the Athabaska Returns" (HBCA B.200/a/8 fo.37d). The next year, Beaulieu intended "being a resedenter" again among the Marten Lake Dogrib (HBCA B.200/a/10 fo.7d). In 1829, in an attempt to remedy or at least control this situation, Beaulieu was "employed to remain" at Lac la Martre, and in a verbal agreement "was provided a recompense of in goods of 8 to £10 yearly at Mens Tariff" (HBCA B.200/e/9 fo.2). The next year, Beaulieu and others with him continued working for the Mackenzie River District, some at Lac la Martre and some at Willow Lake. Smith remarked, "Beaulieu will Continue his services in this Quarter—to keep them as much as he can on this side of Marten Lake where there is Furr bearing animals" (HBCA B.200/a/11 fo.42d).

In 1831, Beaulieu interceded in what seems to have been the last Dogrib-Yellowknife altercation: a report came from him "saying the YellowKnives had again lifted their arms against the Marten Lake Slaves—thus far Beaulieux has succeeded in keeping them from Retaliating—without the Copper Indians (Yellow Knives) make advances for a peace with the Slaves more blood will be spilt" (HBCA B.200/a/13 fo.12). However, blood was not

spilled, and insofar as the Dogrib and Yellowknife were concerned the following decades were peaceful.

DISEASE AT FORT SIMPSON, 1820-30

The emphasis on open lines of communication and on the efficient, rapid
transportation of goods into the Mackenzie River District, together with the
tendency of natives to congregate at trading posts, waiting for the arrival of
the outfit of goods, virtually ensured the dissemination of colds, measles,
influenza, whooping cough, and other contagious diseases (see Ray 1976;
Krech 1983).

The progress of a "severe and infectious cold" in 1830-31 was typical. On 4
August 1830, the Mackenzie River brigade left Portage la Loche, the height of
land south of Lake Athabasca, with the winter outfit. The following day, "a
severe and infectious Cold . . . got Among us," and two men were too sick to
work; this cold may have arrived at Portage la Loche with the outfit from
York Factory, although Edward Smith commented that the water was high
and "muddy and Warm as Milk—which may be the Cause of our sickness."
On 10 August, Fort Chipewyan was reached, but more men were sick: "its
painful to see so many suffering and unable to assist them." Ominously, "the
Indians [were] much worse than the Men." When Fort Resolution came in
sight on 18 August, many men—Smith included—complained of pains in the
throat, head, and breast. Two days were spent at this post, where all but
three—two Hudson's Bay Company servants and one Indian—recovered.
The Indian was "still very unwell" enroute to Fort Simpson on 23 August. The
next three days, the brigade saw, met, and camped with Indians along the
Mackenzie River, until Fort Simpson was finally reached on 27 August.

In September, many Indians arrived at Fort Simpson; some were sick and
at one point, Smith commented: "of such Company ["invalids"] we have too
Many." Several were sick in October, and by 1 November "for this some time
past a severe Cold has attacked every individual of the establishment—and
does not much abate of its violence." The winter of 1830-31 was difficult:
many were sick (and at least one died—in November—from sickness), and
many starved, owing in part to the great, cyclical decline in the hare population and in part to the inability of sick men to hunt. By March 1831, Smith
wrote: "the stress of the Winter has been throughout—none of the indians has
escaped privation" (HBCA B.200/a/12 fos.3-30d).

Diseases which at other times affected Slaveys and Dogribs trading along
the Mackenzie surely arrived in similar fashion. Understandably, fewer afflic-
tions arrived before 1820 than after, as a result of the more erratic conduct of
the trade in these early years. However, those that did arrive were surely no

less disruptive than later diseases; they may have peaked in intensity in the winter of 1805–1806, when they were said to "rage *wh* astonishing fury" near Horn Mountain (see above).

In the period from 1819 to 1823, Indians (Chipewyans) trading on Great Slave Lake and to the south in Athabasca District were affected by measles, dysentery, and a severe cough that may have been influenza. Many Indians who traded at posts in Peace River and at Forts Chipewyan and Resolution died. In 1820, George Simpson spoke of "great mortality" among the Beaver (Rich 1938:61) and John Franklin estimated that "one-third of the Indians" in the region died (1823:137). Sickness—influenza apparently—prevailed at Fort Resolution in the winter of 1822–23 (HBCA B.181/a/4). Indians trading at Fort Simpson seem to have escaped the deadly onslaught of the years from 1819 to 1822, although there are no post journals until the summer of 1822 to confirm or deny this. During the winter of 1822–23 some sickness and a few deaths were reported; Grand Cheveux, a trading leader, said in the spring of 1823 that "many of them were sick" and that his father had died in winter (HBCA B.200/a/1/ fo.49). This winter, at least, conditions were far worse at Fort Resolution.

The Fort Resolution epidemic may have travelled north in the summer of 1823, for by fall, "Some unusual sickness has taken hold of some of [the] Dogs" at Fort Simpson, and in December, "An elderly man arrived from a party of Indians below the Fort with a Story of Woe—saying his Son in law, His Brother, His Wife, His Daughter, and Himself Were all sick." By mid-December, "More complaints of sickness . . . it appears to be generall" (HBCA B.200/a/3 fos.12–19 passim), but by late February 1824, this illness seems to have run its course.

In 1827, highly communicable whooping cough struck Fort Simpson. On 3 November, "The Children of the Fort this some time is attacked with a severe Cough which we fear is the Hooping Cough." One week later, the "Children Worse and Worse" with what by then had been identified definitely as whooping cough (HBCA B.200/a/9 fos.13–14). The epidemic spread among Indians trading at Forts Simpson and Liard and affected children and adults who had never before contracted the disease. At Fort Liard in mid-December, "the Hooping Cough was raging with all its violence among the people of the Fort and the Hunters the latter was unable to hunt—all they could doe was to Snare Hares." Indians living between Forts Simpson and Liard were also affected and among them "all was sickness and discontent" (HBCA B.200/a/9 fo.17d).

This contagion arrived in a usual way: "it was brought from Norway House by the Athabaska to Fort Chipewyan—and our last Boat from thence brought it here"; the first part of the winter outfit arrived at Fort Simpson on 27 August and the last part on 17 October. Whooping cough came with the August boat, since it had reached Fort Liard by mid-September. So many

Indians had waited at Fort Simpson for guns which were coming with the October boat, and the mid-November comment, "its impossible now they can escape," while true, was too late (HBCA B.200/a/9 fo.14d). By March 1828 the disease was over, not, however, before some children died and hunting activities of the sick were adversely affected.

A question of some interest is whether the epidemics of the 1820's (and before) had any demographic impact on Slaveys and Dogribs who traded at Fort Simpson (Krech 1978, 1983; Helm 1980). This question is not easily answered, at least in part because census figures for this decade are incomplete and subject to more than one interpretation. Before 1820, there are no reliable population estimates, although in 1807, Wentzel—including it appears Liard River Slaveys with those who traded at The Forks—estimated a population of "about" two hundred men and three hundred women and children, figures he admitted were guesses (Wentzel 1960:85–86).

Four estimates were made of the Fort Simpson trading population in the 1820's (Table 9). While the intent here is not to analyse these data, some provisional comments may be appropriate. First, the 1827 total is a 13 per cent decline from 1825 and the 1829 total is a 16 per cent rise from 1827. Secondly, it is difficult to interpret these changes. Very briefly, the changes may be the result of various factors, including: (1) an overestimate in 1825, where a ratio of 4:1 was used to project the total population from the number of adult males, whereas a 3:1 or a 3.5:1 ratio may have been more appropriate; (2) a population loss between 1825 and 1827 caused by disease or starvation, or both; (3)

TABLE 9: 1820'S CENSUS DATA ON THE FORT SIMPSON
TRADING POPULATION

	1823[a]	1825[b]	1827[c]	1829[d]
Rocky Mountain or Forks Indians	40–50[e]	240[f]		
Horn Mountain or Dogrib Indians	200[e]	760[f]		
Dogrib and Mountain Indians			703[g]	
McKenzies River Indians				620
Martin Lake Indians				115
Nahanny			60	72
Dahotinne			105	
Umbahotinne				202
Totals		1,000	868	1,009

Sources and notes (see text):
  a HBCA B.200/e/1
  b HBCA B.200/e/3
  c HBCA B.200/e/7, B.200/a/8 fo.45
  d HBCA B.200/e/9
  e hunters only
  f These figures based on the ratio of 1 hunter: 4 total population
  g 563 of these 703 were listed with hunters who had debts and 140 with those without debts

the organization of the Cordillera trade by 1829; (4) a greater knowledge by 1827 and 1829 of the trading and non-trading populations (HBCA B.200/a/8 fo.45; cf. HBCA B.200/e/3 fo.1).

Any but very tentative conclusions are difficult to make. Obviously, diseases struck Slaveys and Dogribs trading at Fort Simpson in the 1820's. Some diseases found "virgin-soil," in the sense that they affected adults and children, male and female alike. They were transmitted readily during the summer transport of trading goods and disseminated via the fall aggregations (and subsequent dispersals) of Indians at the post. Because adult males were sick—or died—the subsistence quest was probably adversely affected, a situation exacerbated by the traditional custom of destroying one's property following the death of a relative. How many died from epidemics is difficult to say, although it appears that the Fort Simpson natives fared far better than Indians in the Peace River region and elsewhere in the Athabasca District, or those farther north at Fort Good Hope in the 1820's (Krech 1978, 1983).

ON DEPENDENCE

In the 1820's, the Slavey and Dogrib collected and exchanged furs and skins for ultimate consumption in European markets. If we wish to put their activities in the broadest context (and in the language of those whose analyses are of this context), then these Indians were at the farthest remove in an economic system termed an external arena (Wallerstein 1974, 1980). This arena was linked to the major world-economy through the fur trade, one of the "rich trades"; the subarctic geographical region would not be considered a so-called peripheral section of the world economy until production there was in goods that were "essential for daily use"—such as bullion, leather, and sugar, the production of which elsewhere in the New World transformed social structures (Wallerstein 1974:302,337; 1980:273n).

While the Slavey and Dogrib can thus be placed in one economic system linked to another (the world economy) through the fur trade, it is of greater interest here to specify the degree to which they were *dependent* on this fur trade. At the outset of this paper mention was made of the intuition of anthropologists that native culture and society in this region persisted in the nineteenth century and that the trade was relatively insignificant; that, in other words, natives were not particularly dependent on the trade.

To discuss this issue, there must first be some agreed-upon definition of "dependence." If dependence means simply, reliance on another (entity) for aid or support, then there are many who would argue that Indians in this general region were dependent on the trade—from H.M. Robinson (1879:335), who wrote that "the company feeds, clothes, and wholly maintains nine-tenths of the entire population"; to E.E. Rich (1960:35; 1967), who on separate occasions proclaimed that "however independent [the Indian's] nature might be, he was not economically independent" and that "within a decade of Indians becoming acquainted with European goods, tribe after tribe became utterly dependent on regular European supplies." More recent studies of subarctic Indians focus on economic dimensions of dependence, although they do not necessarily agree with Rich's proclamations. For example, Ray (1974:155–56), in part following Daniel Harmon's observations, portrays the Ojibwa as the most dependent of several tribes, because they relied upon guns, ammunition, iron works, and other goods without which they could not obtain a living; and Bishop (1974:189–94) states that by 1850, Northern Ojibwa were dependent on the post for nets, guns, fish hooks, snare twine, and other "supplies necessary for survival." In contrast, Morantz (1980:39) seems to favour a definition of dependence that is more appropriate to political science: "This term [dependence] implies that the Indians were under the domination of the Europeans, that they lacked the ability to direct and control their lives." It becomes clear, however, that Morantz is primarily interested in economic indices of dependence, because she argues, for the James Bay Cree at least, that "Rich's claim [of economic dependence or economic subservience] is grossly exaggerated" (1980:40).

In this early fur-trade era, dependence seems best defined in terms of economic indices: Indians were most dependent on the trade when they relied totally upon guns, ammunition, fishing equipment, and other goods (food and clothing included) necessary for their survival and obtained only through the exchange of furs, provisions, and services at the trading post. (Admittedly, the hypothesis that in the absence of such goods, Indians would not survive, would be difficult if not impossible to test.)

Defined this way, it does not appear that the Slavey and Dogrib were very dependent on the trade at Fort Simpson in the 1820's. For one thing, no food was traded. Certainly, there was no trade in such store goods as flour and sugar, which remained luxuries to the officers and servants of the Hudson's Bay Company in this region in these years. Several times, Indians wished to exchange their furs for provisions, but they were refused, because the Fort Simpson traders were never assured of a sufficient quantity for themselves (HBCA B.200/a/4 fo.12). The only exceptions (which seem to have been few) occurred when traders wished to prevent Indians from going to fishing lakes or when Indians were truly starving. For example, one band arrived in June 1826 and received as a gratuity rum, tobacco, and vermilion, and with the vermilion "they beged a small Piece of Grease being so destitute of Provisions"; they were given some dry meat. On another occasion, in the early 1820's, more Indians who were starving *were* supported: "Many of the Natives likewise was supported with subsistence and several Maintained at the establishment—amounting to no less than 40 Persons at a time." But, again, this seems to have been more the exception than the rule (HBCA B.200/a/6 fo.19; B.200/e/1fo.2d).

Was the trade in other goods sufficient to speak of "dependence" in this decade? An answer here might be found in the trade of some who were "major consumers"—those Slaveys and Dogribs whose trade was among the greatest in the five-year period from 1822 to 1827. Table 10 presents the trade of five "major consumers": Enouellebethaw (A), François Noir (B), Grand Cheveux (C), Bosseux (D), and Touyabethaw (E). Each of the five had an outstanding debt in 1822 (at Fort Alexander or Fort Liard). Each had a total debt in 1822–27 ranging from 291–405 MB (and possibly greater: the accounts of two are incomplete—six months missing in both cases), 75 per cent of which was for guns, powder, ball, shot, kettles, capotes, blankets, and tobacco. It is difficult to estimate how many trade goods these Indians had in their possession in 1822; certainly, they had some, since all had outstanding debts (and a quite large one in the case of François Noir). In contrast, one can be very precise about how many goods these five Indians bought for themselves and their families (a total of six wives, twelve boys, and ten girls)—and others perhaps?—from 1822 to 1827: ten guns and enough powder and ammunition to fire them; roughly 240 feet of tobacco (and seven tobacco boxes); ten kettles, twenty-one knives, nine daggers, thirteen files, seventeen axes, three ice chisels and one beaver trap; nineteen blankets, ten capotes, nine leggings, six belts, and some cloth (63 MB worth); and minor quantities of other items.

This does not seem to be an overwhelming quantity of goods, and one would be hard pressed to argue that these goods (guns and ammunition, kettles, blankets, and capotes)—though useful—had become fundamental to the survival of people, one of whose major occupations during this decade was fishing. Furthermore, activities designed only to procure trade goods do not seem to have been the major focus of Slavey and Dogrib life in the 1820's. The Slavey and Dogrib, it is true, were dealing as individuals with the HBC traders, but there is no way of telling what happened to the trade goods each acquired; possibly, the goods were shared, as the meat from the animals whose pelts and skins were traded surely was. In other words, although individuals were engaged in activities which resulted in an accumulation of more personal property, there is no sign of marked change in the domestic mode of production.

Returning to the "major consumers": in two cases (François Noir and Enouellebethaw) additional goods may have been purchased and recorded in the "Fort Hunters" debt book, which has not been preserved in the archives. These two Indians were in a category of fort hunters, a sort of homeguard of fifteen to twenty men (and their families) who shot and snared large and small animals and birds for the company traders. They came to the post frequently

TABLE 10: VALUES IN MB OF GOODS PURCHASED BY
FIVE "MAJOR CONSUMERS," 1822–27

	A	B	C	D	E	Totals
Powder	26	32	66	75	58	257
Gun	65	50	40	25	40	220
Blanket	46	37	32	49	44	208
Tobacco	37	10	33	38	44	162
Ball	9	17	29	38	36	125
Shot	6	13	33	40	16	108
Kettle	22	0	24	18	42	106
Capot	20	34	22	1	24	101
Cloth	15	3	17	10	18	63
Axe	7	3	13	7	10	40
Sundries	0	27	1	0	5	33
Belt	4	8	4	3	12	31
Knife	7	4	7	6	5	29
Gartering	6	5	3	5	8	27
Leggings	6	6	6	3	6	27
File	4	0	8	8	4	24
Dagger	4	8	0	9	2	23
Brayette	0	10	2	6	0	18
Tobacco Box	2	3	3	2	7	17
Strouds	4	5	0	0	6	15
Hat	0	8	0	4	0	12
Bonnet	0	2	4	6	0	12
Molton	0	1	0	0	10	11
Steel Trap	0	0	0	10	0	10
Ice Trench	0	0	3	3	4	10
Fire Steel	0	0	0	3	4	7
Shirt	0	3	0	3	1	7
Powder Horn	0	0	3	3	0	6
Jacket	0	0	0	6	0	6
Flint	0	0	2	3	0	5
Comb	1	3	0	0	0	4
Tin Dish	0	0	0	4	0	4
Sleeves	0	0	0	0	3	3
Breechclout	0	0	0	0	3	2
Total debt, 1822–27	291	292	355	390	405	1733
Outstanding debt, June 1822	130	212	79	44	21	
Total Debt	421	504	434	434	426	

Source: HBCA B.200/d/3a,10a

(far more often than indicated in the account books), where they were given
ammunition and sinew or twine for hare snares ("no. 1 twine twisted double
. . . they say its as good as their own snares"), and then they proceeded, as in
February 1826, "to be the support of this place" (HBCA B.200/a/6 fo.71). But
this homeguard did not live permanently at Fort Simpson, and the composi-

tion of the fort hunters group seems to have changed as some men quit and others were hired in their places. In the formal ways of the company, a fort hunter was supposed to request discharge; in one instance, a hare hunter named Bosseux's Son asked to see his father, but "being refused he appeared in bade homor—the remender of the evening—at this place we have always much trouble to keep the Hunters to their duty—as they are treated with every lenity even to indulgence—I can atribute their dislike to act in the capacity to no other cause—than that of not having it in their power to indulge in lazzeness." Two days later, Chief Factor Edward Smith relented, and "to keep Him here against His will he would be of no use to us—made a virture of necessity and granted Him leave of absence" (HBCA B.200/a/8 fo.25d). When a hunter quit he gave as a reason, if he gave one at all, the desire to visit his sick father or to work for his father-in-law: "One of [the hunters] got married lately and since has done Nothing—its generally the Case among these Indians we lost the services of one of our Hunters the last year from the same cause" (HBCA B.200/a/5 fo.42). In this decade, then, the fort hunter category—including men who hunted, guided, interpreted, or voyaged for the company—was not large. Although it was composed of those men who were most wedded to the post and the exchange and while "its generally the case with them every Spring to remain at the establishment until downright famine drive them away" (HBCA B.200/a/6 fo.15), even these men lived for much of the year in the bush, away from the post, and continued a fairly traditional (though perhaps the most "individualized" and "acculturated" of all) style of life. They were as likely to hunt for themselves or to trap furs as they were to hunt for the post.

Dependence on or independence of the fur trade must, I think, be measured in additional ways in order to give a more complete picture of the context and effects of the trade. If—as argued so far—goods exchanged at the post were added to, or in some cases supplanted, the traditional inventory of material culture and if fur-trapping was incorporated into the traditional seasonal round, then to what extent was survival in that traditional round dependent upon a successful accommodation of fur-trapping and trading? Successful accommodation especially entailed not letting the trade interfere with traditional subsistence activities. And here, it is possible to argue that, in the 1820's, the trade interfered in the following ways: diseases, to which Indians were susceptible, accompanied it; interethnic hostilities, between the Dogrib and Yellowknife especially, were spawned by it; and enthusiasm for the trade and for trade goods led to lengthy, more frequent, and perhaps inopportune visits to the trading post.

As the first two of these points have been discussed at length in previous sections of this paper, I shall comment only on the third here. The visits of Slaveys and Dogribs (and other Indians) to Fort Simpson increased in the

1820's: the numbers of visits in the six years beginning in 1822 are 153, 286, 216, 284, 411, and 296 (in a year in which the account book ends in June). These Indians came in large part because they wanted trade goods (there are a number of other possible reasons to come, including visiting other Indians on the way or at the post). They were interested traders, exchanging some of their goods, if possible, at a profit with Mountain Indians or some of their furs, at a more favourable price, with Chipewyans who received the main profit. Although they did not, as a rule, feel cheated in an exchange which brought the Hudson's Bay Company substantial profit—to the contrary, in one case at least, "one of them on getting 2 knives (Yew Handled) for 6 Martins began to dance and Sing as if He had procured something of greater Value" (HBCA B.200/a/3 fo.31)—they complained if guns, axes, strouds, or other goods at Fort Simpson were of poor quality or in low quantity or if the exchange tariff was tampered with (as John Stuart did in 1833). It is true that some Slaveys and Dogribs were not enthusiastic about travel to the post: in January 1827, one youth was sent to Fort Simpson by "His father who has not seen the Fort since June 1825—such is their independence of us"; five months later, a census revealed a larger population than expected, because "formerly we was not aware that many who had no debts kept them selves at home lazzeness to travel to the Fort to get their wants makes them give their Furs to those that come" (HBCA B.200/a/8 fos.30,45). But it is also the case that most Indians came and many of these from great distances. Often enough, in mid-winter, Indians came from afar: in 1824, Marten Lake Dogribs came from ten and fourteen nights off and Slaveys from ten nights away; the following year, from twelve and twenty-two nights; in 1827, twice from ten nights; and in 1828, from seventeen nights. These treks of from twenty to thirty days round-trip may have had some effect on traditional adaptations; they may have removed adult males at awkward times, awkward that is from the standpoint of the procurement of subsistence resources. (On the other hand, men may not have made these lengthy trading trips unless they left behind adequate supplies of meat and fish.)

It is in this broader context that involvement in the fur trade and dependence on the post and on European goods must also be understood. The effects of the trade surely varied from one individual to the next, from one band to another, and one ethnic group to the next. As Morantz (1980:39) has stated for the eastern James Bay area, "the effects were neither monolithnic nor total." For the Mackenzie River in the 1820's and at Fort Simpson particularly, one can but agree, underlining, however, that effects there were during this early fur-trade era, demographic, economic, and territorial adjustments among them, and that Slavey and Dogrib adaptations can be understood only by embedding them firmly within the historical context of this fur trade.

Notes

Acknowledgements: I wish to thank Charles Bishop and Toby Morantz for their critical reading of this essay; Shirlee Anne Smith, Keeper, Hudson's Bay Company Archives, for assistance; Rene Gadacz for research assistance; Carl Mehler for his map; the Hudson's Bay Company for permission to use and quote from its Archives; and the American Philosophical Society and George Mason University for financial support.

1. In the late nineteenth century, the number of Dogrib bands seems to have been reduced to four, but the Dogrib still lived in the same region—from the southern shore of Great Bear Lake south to Great Slave Lake and east to the source of the Coppermine River. Four Slavey bands, living in the same general territory as "Rocky Mountain" and "Beaver" Indians in the 1820's, were distinguished at the same time (Petitot 1891:363).
2. There is a pressing need for a comprehensive examination of the Churchill records in order to determine, if possible, the degree of participation of Chipewyans, Beaver Indians, and other Northern Athapaskans in the trade prior to the 1780's.
3. The coding, programming, and analysis by SPSS of account books data was accomplished with the assistance of Madeleine Kennedy, Academic Computing Services, George Mason University.

References Cited

Asch, Michael I.
    1976 Some Effects of the Late Nineteenth Century Modernization of the Fur Trade on the Economy of the Slavey Indians. Western Canadian Journal of Anthropology 6(4):7–15.

Ballantyne, Robert M.
    1972 Hudson's Bay or Every-Day Life in the Wilds of North America. Rutland, VT: Charles E. Tuttle. (Originally published 1848.)

Bishop Charles A.
    1974 The Northern Ojibwa and the Fur Trade: An Historical and Ecological Study. Toronto: Holt, Rinehart and Winston of Canada.

Bryce, George
    1900 The Remarkable History of the Hudson's Bay Company. London: Sampson, Low, Marston and Company.

Butler, William Francis
    1968 The Great Lone Land: A Narrative of Travel and Adventure in the North-West of America. Rutland, VT: Charles E. Tuttle. (Originally published 1872.)

Fleming, R. Harvey, ed.
    1940 Minutes of Council Northern Department of Rupert Land, 1821–31. London: Champlain Society.

Franklin, John
    1823 Narrative of the Journey to the Shores of The Polar Sea, in the Years 1819, 20, 21, and 22. London: John Murray.
    1828 Narrative of a Second Expedition to the Shores of The Polar Sea, in the Years 1825, 1826, and 1827. London: John Murray.

Gillespie, Beryl C.
1975   An Ethnohistory of the Yellowknives: A Northern Athapaskan Tribe. Contributions
to Canadian Ethnology, 1975. D.B. Carlyle, ed., pp. 191–245. National Museum of
Man Mercury Series. Canadian Ethnology Service Paper 31. Ottawa.
Heindenreich, C.E.
1971   Huronia: A History and Geography of the Huron Indians, 1600–1650. Toronto:
McClelland and Stewart.
Helm, June
1978   On Responsible Scholarship on Culture Contact in the Mackenzie Basin. Current
Anthropology 19:160–162.
1980   Female Infanticide, European Diseases, and Population Levels among the
Mackenzie Dene. American Ethnologist 7:259–85.
Helm, June, and Beryl C. Gillespie
1981   Dogrib Oral Tradition as History: War and Peace in the 1820's. Journal of
Anthropological Research 37:8–27.
Hudson's Bay Company Archives (HBCA)
HBCA B.116/a/11. Fort Liard Journal, 1833–34.
HBCA B.181/a/4. Fort Resolution Journal, 1822–23.
HBCA B.181/d/2. Fort Resolution Accounts, 1825–26.
HBCA B.200/a/1–13. Fort Simpson Journals, 1822–1832.
HBCA B.200/b/1–6. Fort Simpson Correspondence, 1822–1831.
HBCA B.200/d/3a–32. Fort Simpson Accounts, 1822–1832.
HBCA B.200/e/1–9. Fort Simpson Reports, 1822–1830.
HBCA D.4/18,20,90. George Simpson Outward Correspondence, 1827, 1830–31,
1843.
HBCA D.5/3. George Simpson Inward Correspondence, 1823–1830.
Innis, Harold A.
1970   The Fur Trade in Canada. Rev. ed. Toronto: University of Toronto Press.
Janes, Robert R.
1975   Dispersion and Nucleation among Nineteenth Century Mackenzie Basin Athapaskans: Archaeological, Ethnohistorical, and Ethnographic Interpretations. Ph.D.
dissertation. Department of Archaeology. University of Calgary.
1976   Culture Contact in the 19th-Century Mackenzie Basin, Canada. Current Anthropology 17:344–45.
1977   More on Culture Contact in the Mackenzie Basin. Current Anthropology 18:544–56.
Keith, George
1960   Letters to Mr. Roderic McKenzie, 1807–1817. In Les Bourgeois de la Compagnie du
Nord-Ouest. Vol. 1. L.R. Masson, ed., pp. 65–132. New York: Antiquarian Press.
(Originally published 1889–90.)
Krech, Shepard III
1978   Disease, Starvation and Northern Athapaskan Social Organization. American
Ethnologist 5:710–732.
1980   Northern Athapaskan Ethnology in the 1970s. Annual Review of Anthropology
9:83–100.
1983   The Influence of Disease and the Fur Trade on Arctic Drainage Lowlands Dene,
1800–1850. Journal of Anthropological Research 39:123–146.
1984   Ethnohistory and Ethnography in the Subarctic. American Anthropologist.
In press.
Ms.   On Nahani.
Mackenzie, Alexander
1970   The Letters and Journals of Sir Alexander Mackenzie. W. Kaye Lamb, ed. Cam-
bridge: Hakluyt Society.
McClellan, Catharine
1970   Introduction to Special Issue: Athabascan Studies. Western Canadian Journal of
Anthropology 2(1):vi–xix.

McKenzie, Alexander
   Ms.   Journal of Great Bear Lake, 1805–1806. Victoria: Provincial Archives of British
           Columbia.
Morantz, Toby
   1980   The Fur Trade and the Cree of James Bay. *In* Old Trails and New Directions: Papers
           of the Third North American Fur Trade Conference. Carol M. Judd and Arthur J.
           Ray, eds., pp. 39–58. Toronto: The University of Toronto Press.
Petitot, Emile
   1891   Autour du Grand Lac des Esclaves. Paris: Nouvelle Librarie Parisienne
Ray, Arthur J.
   1974   Indians in the Fur Trade: Their Roles as Hunters, Trappers, and Middlemen in the
           Lands Southwest of Hudson Bay, 1660–1870. Toronto: University of Toronto Press.
   1976   Diffusion of Diseases in the Western Interior of Canada, 1830–1850. Geographical
           Review 66:139–57.
Ray, Arthur J., and Donald Freeman
   1978   'Give Us Good Measure': An Economic Analysis of Relations between the Indians
           and the Hudson's Bay Company before 1763. Toronto: The University of Toronto
           Press.
Rich, E.E., ed.
   1938   Journal of Occurrences in the Athabasca Department by George Simpson, 1820 and
           1821, and Report. London: Hudson's Bay Record Society.
Rich, E.E.
   1960   Trade Habits and Economic Motivation among the Indians of North America.
           Canadian Journal of Economics and Political Science 26:35–53.
   1967   The Fur Trade and the Northwest to 1857. Toronto: McClelland and Stewart.
Robinson, H.M
   1879   The Great Fur Land or Sketches of Life in the Hudson's Bay Territory. New York:
           G.P. Putnam's Sons.
Ross, Bernard R.
   Ms.   Letter from Mr. Ross to George Gibbs, with detailed information relative to Chipe-
           wyan tribes, with abstract of McKenzie River District, June 1, 1858. Ms. 144a, BAE.
           Smithsonian Institution.
Sloan, W.
   1979   The Native Response to the Extension of the European Trade into the Athabasca
           and Mackenzie Basins, 1770–1814. Canadian Historical Review 60:281–95.
Smith, David M.
   1976   Cultural and Ecological Change: The Chipewyan of Fort Resolution. Arctic
           Anthropology 13(1):35–42.
Thompson, John
   Ms.   Journal of John Thompson, Esq., McKenzie River, Winter 1800–1801. Montreal:
           McGill University Libraries.
Trigger, Bruce G.
   1976   The Children of Aataentsic: A History of the Huron People to 1660. 2 vols. Mont-
           real: McGill-Queens University Press.
Wallerstein, Immanuel
   1974   The Modern World-System I. New York: Academic Press.
   1980   The Modern World-System II. New York: Academic Press.
Wentzel, Willard Ferdinand
   Ms.a   Journal of W. Ferdinand Wentzell, Winter 1804–05, At The Grand River.
           MG19/C1, vol. 8. Ottawa: Public Archives of Canada.
   Ms.b   Fragment of Journal by Wentzel at Grand River Near McKenzie's River 1805 &
           1806. MG19/E1, pp. 9298–9308. Ottawa: Public Archives of Canada.
   Ms.c.   Account of Mackenzie River, 1821, MG19/A20. Ottawa: Public Archives of
           Canada.
   1960   Letters to the Hon. Roderic McKenzie 1807–1824. *In* Les Bourgeois de la Compag-

nie du Nord-Quest. Vol. 1, L.R. Masson, ed. pp. 75-153. New York: Antiquarian Press. (Originally published 1889-90.)

Willson, Beckles
1900   The Great Company: History of the Honourable Company of Merchants-Adventurers Trading into Hudson's Bay, 1667-1871. 2 vols. London: Smith, Elder.

Yerbury, J. Collin
1977   On Culture Contact in the Mackenzie Basin. Current Anthropology 18:350-52.
1978   Further Notes on the Ethohistory of the Mackenzie Basin. Current Anthropology 19:458-9.
1980   The Social Organization of the Subarctic Athapaskan Indians: An Ethnohistorical Reconstruction. Ph.D. dissertation. Department of Sociology and Anthropology. Simon Fraser University.

6

The Microeconomics of Southern Chipewyan Fur Trade History

Robert Jarvenpa and Hetty Jo Brumbach

INTRODUCTION

The general goal of this study is to understand the rapidly changing material adaptations of the Chipewyan Indians in the late fur-trade economy of north-central Canada. Methodologically, it addresses the role of fur-trade documents in assessing the interplay of economic behaviour and ecological energetics at the local level. Certain kinds of documents, particularly business account books, provide unique insight into the production and exchange behaviour of individual Indian hunters. In essence, the study is an exercise in combining archival material with other forms of evidence in explaining how people coped with the material conditions of local ecosystems and the political economy of the Euro-Canadian fur market.

A focus on individual variability is compatible with recent developments in ecological anthropology. There is a growing interest in individual strategy, theories of choice, and actor-based decision models (Netting 1974:43–45; Orlove 1980:245–58). Attention to the process by which individual actors make choices among alternative resources places an emphasis upon intra-cultural variability rather than treating groups of people as behaviourally homogeneous. One analytical advantage to such an approach is the close focus on mechanisms linking environment and behaviour. However, we concur with Bennett's (1976:273) and Barlett's (1980:549) position that a holistic approach to *adaptation* must consider both short-term "adaptive strategies" and longer-term "adaptive processes." One may view individuals as constrained by the groups and social systems which envelop them, but it is equally possible to study these systems and institutions as the outcomes of previous individual choices.

In assessing the usefulness of fur trade documents, several related issues guide our analysis:
1. How well do archival records complement ethnographic and archaeological information for the study area?

2. How well do quantitative data in account books complement qualitative information in fur trade journals and correspondence?
3. What can trade records reveal about local-level provisioning, nutritional status and economic dependency for individuals and families? Are such patterns informative of adaptations at the group or population level?
4. Do trade records indicate significant variations or specializations among individuals in economic strategy and decision making?

The above questions address rather pointedly the nature of "short-term adaptive strategies." Indeed, the time-frame for this study is compressed into a few decades in the late nineteenth and early twentieth centuries. However, it is suggested here that the fine-grained microbehavioural analysis is a necessary, if overlooked, building block for fashioning longer-term diachronic and macrogeographic studies. By meshing a number of group-specific studies based on both field and archival research, scholars have the potential for creating an enlightening new mosaic of subarctic fur trade adaptations.

The region under consideration is part of the Upper Churchill River drainage in northwestern Saskatchewan (Fig. 1), an area where we have conducted ethnographic research since 1971 (Jarvenpa 1976, 1977a, 1977b, 1979, 1980). In 1979 we embarked on a project that seeks to explain the historical development of economic and social interactions between several cultural-ethnic groups in that same region. Most of the substantive data in the present study are part of this broader effort and derive from archival work carried out in 1980–81. Over a period of several years to come, we hope to integrate this information with additional documentary material, ethnographic data and ethnoarchaeological analyses already completed (Brumbach et al. 1982).

Historically, the headwaters of the Churchill River supported intensive fur-trading activity. Early posts of independent pedlars and those of the major fur companies were situated near the divide separating the Athabasca-Mackenzie watershed from those waters draining east into Hudson Bay. As such, the area became part of the western contact zone between Athapaskan-speaking Chipewyan Indians and the Algonkian-speaking Cree. The late eighteenth-century rivalry between Montreal-based companies, particularly the North West Company, and the English Hudson's Bay Company was responsible for drawing some Chipewyan groups from their forest-tundra environment southward into the full boreal forest (Gillespie 1975:368–74; Smith 1975:413). It was here, especially along the Athabasca and Churchill River systems, that the Chipewyan came into contact with Western Woods Cree populations. Some of those Cree may have been resident in the area since late prehistoric times (Smith 1976:418, 429), but apparently other Cree groups had been moving westward with the expanding fur trade since the late seventeenth century (Ray 1974:12–23).

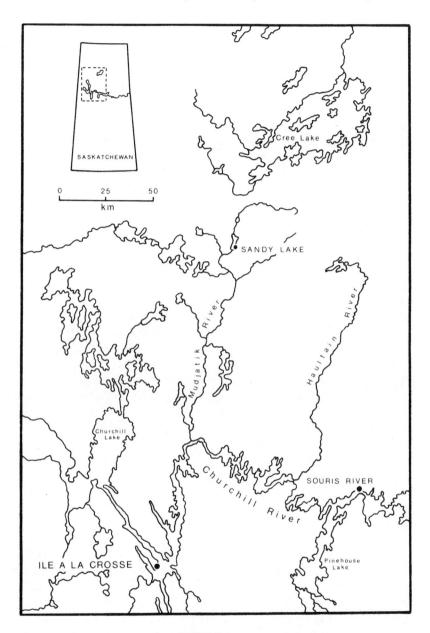

FIGURE 1:
ILE A LA CROSSE AND SELECTED HBC OUTPOSTS
IN NORTHERN SASKATCHEWAN.

Through the nineteenth century both the Chipewyan and Cree developed intimate economic relations with a growing class of Euro-Canadian fur-trade personnel at the Hudson's Bay Company's Ile à la Crosse fort and its network of secondary posts. An increasingly visible mixed-blood or Métis Cree population became a sort of rudimentary working class in the trade system (Brown 1976; Slobodin 1964), and the complexity of social life increased in the last half of the nineteenth century with the arrival and entrenchment of Roman Catholic missionaries. The early years of the twentieth century witnessed the beginnings of federal involvement in local Indian affairs with extinguishment of land title through Treaty No. 10 (1906) and the establishment of legally recognized bands and reserves. During the Depression of the 1930's there was a short-lived but dramatic influx of white trappers into the Upper Churchill region (Jarvenpa 1977b), and shortly thereafter commercial fishing became an important addition to the regional economy. By the 1940's the traditional-historical system of seasonal family nomadism began breaking down as Indian family units abandoned dispersed winter outpost communities in favour of more centralized settlements. This behaviour was a response to the diminished role of the fur-trapping economy and to a simultaneous extension of federal and provincial government control upon Indian and Métis life.

Despite the profound developments of the past four decades, however, the southern Chipewyan experienced major changes in their material adaptation in the nineteenth and early twentieth centuries. These involved a complex interplay of alterations in production and consumption behaviour, modifications in technological and economic organization, and shifts in microenvironmental distributions and annual nomadic cycles. This paper will explore the scope and direction of these changes. As is becoming apparent in historical rsearch elsewhere in the Subarctic, many of these early modifications can be profitably interpreted in terms of native response to and influence upon the Euro-Canadian-controlled fur-trade economy.

METHODOLOGICAL BACKGROUND

A component of the data-gathering phase of this study involved ethnoarchaeological surveys during the summers of 1979 and 1980 (Brumbach et al. 1982). A total of forty-one archaeological sites were located and investigated in the Upper Churchill region. The majority of these were extensively documented by mapping and photographing structures and features, through systematic artifact inventory, and by the interpretive testimony of forty-four native informants who either had lived at the sites in question or who had lived and travelled in the area when the settlements were extant. Many of these people, ranging from thirty-four to ninety-four years of age, spent portions of their childhoods and early adult years in one or more of the seasonally occupied log cabin communities and outpost settlements that we investigated archaeologically. All of these individuals were able to provide certain kinds of contextual information on the social and economic characteristics of these communities, and a few individuals who served as on-site interpreters were able to combine testimony regarding general life experience with highly specific explanations of the construction and function of facilities, implements, and features that they had once used.

In the northern periphery of our survey region (the Mudjatik River drainage and Cree Lake, Fig. 1) we documented twenty-three settlement areas and habitation locales, the bulk of these representing outposts and all-native communities occupied by wintering families of Chipewyan between the 1890's and the early 1950's. Eighteen additional sites in the southern expanse of our survey region (the Churchill River between Lac Ile à la Crosse and Pinehouse Lake) include similar kinds of outposts and domestic native settlements, but some of these date from earlier in the nineteenth century. Moreover, the latter sites often harboured a complex amalgam of Cree, Métis Cree, and Chipewyan residents. Many of the outposts were under the management of the Hudson's Bay Company district headquarters at Ile à la Crosse, and others were operated by the Revillon Frères company and free traders. In addition, Euro-Canadian trappers established encampments throughout the region.

To complement and corroborate the ethnoarchaeological material, we have been examining fur-trade records held in the Hudson's Bay Company Archives in Winnipeg and Ottawa. Most attention has been directed to the post journals, correspondence records, business account books, and district reports for Ile à la Crosse. Through the nineteenth century the Ile à la Crosse headquarters and its secondary posts comprised the Hudson's Bay Company's English River District, the official management unit embracing the Upper Churchill region. Bishop and Ray (1976) have outlined the advantages of combining archival research with ethnographic study for interpreting cultural change in the central Subarctic, and Ray and Freeman's (1978) innovative quantitative analysis of the early eighteenth-century Hudson's Bay Company trade underscores the importance of the business account book data in understanding spatial and temporal variation in the volume of trade and rates of exchange, the operation of unofficial exchange rates, the impact of competition, and the motivations of traders and Indian clientele.

Gaining inspiration from the forementioned works, we have oriented much of our archival study to retrieving annual commercial profiles for a sample of Indian customers. At this point, the data base includes trade transactions for twenty-six Chipewyan, Cree, and Métis Cree individuals trading out of the Ile à la Crosse, Souris River, and Sandy Lake posts for selected periods between 1889 and 1909. This period was chosen because it corresponds reasonably well with the occupation date for many of the archaeological sites. Moreover, the individual accounts, and supporting data such as stock inventories, fur returns, and tariffs, are the most complete for this time period. The following sections of this paper are devoted to an analysis of the Chipewyan customer accounts. A major interpretive goal is to assess the usefulness of account book data for modelling microbehavioural processes in trophic exchange and economic specialization, processes that can be wedded to archaeological and informant evidence in understanding Chipewyan material adaptations.

DISTRIBUTION AND NOMADIC CYCLES OF UPPER CHURCHILL CHIPEWYAN IN THE NINE-
TEENTH CENTURY

At some point in the early nineteenth century the upper reaches of the Churchill River began crystallizing as an approximate boundary or contact zone, with the southernmost bands of Chipewyan to the north and groups of Western Woods Cree immediately to the south. *Thilanottine* ("men of the end of the head," or "those who dwell at the head of the lakes") (Petitot 1883:651; Smith 1975:413) became a regional badge of identification for the entire population of southern Chipewyan along the Churchill River and westward toward the Cold Lake vicinity of present-day Alberta. Apparently, those southern Chipewyan who specifically became associated with the Ile à la Crosse trading sphere became known as *kesyehot'ine* or "poplar house peo-ple," in literal reference to early traders' forts built at Ile à la Crosse of poplar or aspen logs (Curtis 1928:3; Jarvenpa 1980:43–44).

Contemporary Chipewyan of the Ile à la Crosse region, including reserve communities such as Patuanak and Dillon, still identify themselves as *kesyeh-ot'ine,* and they generally distinguish themselves from *hoteladi* (literally, "northerners"), other Chipewyan band-communities immediately to the north in the region between Cree Lake and the east end of Lake Athabasca. The Chipewyan considered in this study were part of the *kesyehot'ine* regional population and trading sphere. Consistent with the flexible organization of hunting societies in this part of the Subarctic, however, there has been no sharp spatial or social boundary between *kesyehot'ine* and *hoteladi.* This is apparent in the overlapping historic wintering ranges of the two groups, in recent inter-marriage, in close kinship ties between communities such as Patuanak and Black Lake (immediately east of Lake Athabasca) (Sharp 1975:73), and in the relative ease with which individual Chipewyan shift regional identities (Jarvenpa 1980:44).

1. *A Native Perspective.* The nineteenth-century trade documents for Ile à la Crosse provide extensive information on the arrivals and departures of

Chipewyan families from the post, but they contain little information on general population distribution and movement. However, the traditional oral accounts of the Chipewyan illuminate some of these matters. Moise McIntyre, a Treaty Chipewyan of the English River Band, recalls his boyhood experiences in the early 1940's when he was captivated by the narratives of an elderly affinal relative, Sarah Bell:

> I know all these stories because when I was young I used to listen to what the old people told me, you know. There was this one old woman. I used to call her "grandma," but she wasn't really my grandmother. She was 75 years old, and I was only 13 when I sat by her to hear her stories. I used to roll cigarettes for her, and she would tell me what things were like when she was a girl.

Born in approximately 1870, Sarah Bell recalled a system of nomadic movements that was still operating when she was a young child in the mid-1870's. In essence, there were two major travel circuits or annual nomadic cycles that had become habitual for most of the Chipewyan in the northern Saskatchewan region:

A. *The Southern Cycle.* The southern nomadic round included Chipewyan who made a traditional summer trading rendezvous at Ile à la Crosse. These people, including Sarah Bell's extended family and other kin, wintered in small multi-family encampments in the vast area between the headwaters of the Foster River and Cree Lake. Prior to spring break-up, they positioned themselves near groves of birch trees where new bark canoes could be assembled. With the disappearance of the ice, families descended the Mudjatik River in canoe caravans and reassembled in late June at Big Island, the primary summer gathering place near the Ile à Crosse post. The aggregation at Big Island lasted about one month and served as a renewal of kinship and friendship bonds for Chipewyan from throughout the area. It was also the period for exchanging furs at the post for credit and outfits for the next winter's hunt. During July, the families based at Big Island also fished intensively for whitefish at favoured locations near the mouth of the Beaver River and at "Buffalo Narrows," the channel connecting Churchill Lake with Peter Pond Lake.

According to Sarah Bell's narrative, in early August the Chipewyan had largely completed the summer rendezvous at Ile à la Crosse. Small travelling units, usually composed of four to six closely related families, began moving south and southeastward from Ile à la Crosse by canoe. In many instances, the canoe travel parties represented families that wintered in the same locale. Typically, they ascended the Beaver River and entered Lac la Plonge by way of the Rivière la Plonge. From that point they utilized a portage, still referred to as the "Chipewyan Portage," to move farther south into Dore Lake, and, eventually, the headwaters of the Smoothstone River. This was the southern extremity of the annual cycle. From that point the families moved northward once again, descending the Smoothstone River to its outlet in Snake Lake or Pinehouse Lake. Here, they had rejoined the main flow of the Churchill River and continued moving northward in September and October by ascending the Foster River to its headwaters at the Foster Lakes. Occasionally, the Souris River (or Belanger River) was ascended as an alternate northward route. The Chipewyan tried to reach the Foster Lakes prior to the general freeze-up between late October and mid-November. From that point small family clusters dispersed westward and northwestward toward Cree Lake for the long period of winter hunting and trapping. This was the northern extremity of the travel circuit, and in the spring the cycle began anew.

B. *The Northern Cycle*. Sarah Bell was familiar with another major travel circuit involving Chipewyan who generally traded at posts outside the Ile à la Crosse district and summered near the edge of the barren lands. However, those people spent their winters hunting and trapping in the vicinity of Black Birch Lake and the general region west and southwest of Cree Lake. This was the southern extension of their nomadic round, and after spring break-up these Chipewyan would assemble at the headwaters of the Clearwater River. They descended that river westward to its confluence with the Athabasca River and the site of Fort McMurray. Apparently, some families had a brief summer trading rendezvous at Fort McMurray while others travelled farther north on the Athabasca River to trade at Fort Chipewyan. From this point Moise McIntyre could not recall Sarah Bell's precise delineation for the travel circuit, but he indicated that the people moved some distance north of Lake Athabasca where they remained near the margin of the tundra hunting barren ground caribou for food and winter clothing. His account does not specify what length of time the Chipewyan families remained in the forest-tundra north of Lake Athabasca. However, their dependency upon caribou for regular clothing material suggests that they may have positioned themselves along major fall-early winter migration corridors in order to harvest large numbers of southward-moving animals in October and November. After this phase, the people began moving southward, paralleling, it would appear, the extreme southern or winter distribution of the Beverly herd of barren ground caribou (*Rangifer tarandus groenlandicus*) in Saskatchewan (Kelsall 1968:109–18). They travelled south, perhaps by way of a thoroughfare like the Cree River, to the vast area southwest of Cree Lake where once again small family groups dispersed for mid-winter trapping and hunting. Thus, the annual circuit was completed.

The annual movements reconstructed from Sarah Bell's memory are schematically analogous to two attached gears. The southern "gear" or cycle moved in a counterclockwise direction. The northern cycle turned in a clockwise direction, and the two cycles loosely meshed or overlapped in the winter hunting grounds around Cree Lake. The geographical limits of the two circuits embraced an area that was approximately 700 linear kilometres on a north-south axis and 450 kilometres on an east-west axis. It is the region bounded roughly between 55°N and 60°N latitude and 105°W and 112°W longitude. Moise McIntyre observed that the overlapping winter ranges provided opportunities for limited intermarriage and social interchange between the two regional groups. Nonetheless, it is apparent that most Chipewyan maintained a long-term affiliation with one regional population or the other, and as Moise McIntyre noted, the relative distinctiveness of the two socio-spatial systems was symbolically reinforced by the enthnonyms *hoteladi* and *kesyehot'ine* for northern and southern, respectively.

Sarah Bell impressed upon Moise McIntyre the fact that the long annual round of the *kesyehot'ine* was coming to an end in the mid-1870's. Her childhood experiences recount the last time that her family and many other Chipewyan utilized the extensive counter-clockwise circuit. In interpreting the abandonment of the long cycle, Moise McIntyre suggested that the impact of the Roman Catholic church upon population movements began in the 1870's. Indeed, there is evidence that staging of Christmas masses at the Ile à la Crosse mission became a regular religious holiday for natives during the last quarter of the nineteenth century. Religious instruction during the summer coincided with the annual trading rendezvous and would not have disrupted the scheduling or location of movements for the remainder of the year, but a mid-winter religious gathering would have abbreviated the annual round. Perhaps a more influential factor was the establishment of a network of secondary or seasonally operated outposts of the Ile à la Crosse parent post.

2. *A Documentary Perspective.* The Hudson's Bay Company Archives indicate that such outposts as Island Lake and Souris River were established about 1877 and 1875, respectively, and the major secondary post of Portage la Loche had been built earlier. A decentralization of trade services at that time probably helped create new semi-permanent population centres for the Chipewyan. For example, the Souris River post was situated at the northern end of Pinehouse Lake on the Churchill River (Fig. 1), a short distance west of the Foster River outlet. This location intercepted the northward fall migration path of the *kesyehot'ine,* and thus the post may have served to draw some of those families into a more restricted and southerly wintering range near the Churchill River. Such behaviour, no doubt, was reinforced by the seasonal operation of the Souris River post, providing increased accessibility to imported food, clothing material, tools, and implements in the fall, winter, and spring months prior to the annual summer trade at Ile à la Crosse. Other *kesyehot'ine* began restricting their winter ranges in proximity to the Portage la Loche and Island Lake posts to the northwest.

The remote Cree Lake district never harboured a major winter outpost. It is assumed that the *hoteladi* who previously wintered in that region similarly began to modify their annual circuit and re-orient their wintering range in proximity to other outposts operated as outliers of the HBC parent posts at Fort McMurray, Fort Chipewyan, and Fond du Lac. This assumption receives some support in the outgoing correspondence of the Ile à la Crosse post manager in 1891 who, in trying to re-establish Chipewyan hunters in the Cree Lake vicinity, noted that the general region between Cree Lake and Wollaston Lake had not been "visited" in over fifteen years (HBCA B.89/b/14 fo.111).

Generally, the post journals and allied fur-trade documents provide little information on precise travel routes, camp locations, or winter spatial ranges for the southern Chipewyan. However, the Ile à la Crosse post journals chronicle the periodicity and volume of Chipewyan visits to the fort, and these patterns can be used to interpret the structure of trading adaptations in the nineteenth century. It should be noted that initially cordial relations between North West Company and Hudson's Bay Company (hereafter referred to as HBC) traders in Ile à la Crosse in 1790–91 (Tyrrell 1934:122–363), quickly turned to a bitter rivalry. Competition for the Indian trade put the HBC at a marked disadvantage for many years and culminated in the destruction of the HBC's facilities in 1811 (HBCA B.89/a/1 fos.1–12; HBCA B.89/a/2 fos.1–38). After the absorption of the North West Company by the HBC in 1821, the latter firm enjoyed a virtual monopoly on trade in the area for the rest of the nineteenth century.

A. *1839–1840.* An HBC census conducted in 1838 lists a total of 489 "Chepewyan" attached to the Ile à la Crosse post, including 108 adult males, 119 wives, 107 sons, 103 daughters, and 52 allied "followers and strangers" (HBCA B.239/z/10 fos.52a–57a). Missionization had not yet begun, and the activities of these people were still largely mediated by their relationship to the Ile à la Crosse traders. The post journals for the period 1839–40 (HBCA B.89/a/19; HBCA B.89/a/20) make little mention of the Chipewyan through March and early April of 1839, but five Chipewyans arrived at the post on 21 April. On 28 April a "whole band of Indians" appeared at Ile à la Crosse, although their identity as Chipewyan or Cree is not specified. By 18 May the year's fur packet was prepared and shipped out to York Factory. References to the Chipewyan are rather sparse through the summer months. In late May a few individuals arrived from Serpent Rapids or Snake Rapids, about ninety linear kilometres northeast of the post on the Churchill River. A Chipewyan man passed through Ile à la Crosse on 1 July to search for his brother on the Beaver River, and a few other Chipewyan came to the fort with furs and provisions in July and early August.

Post activity began to accelerate with the arrival on 12 August of a band of Chipewyan "from below," presumably a location downstream on the Churchill River. That group ascended the Beaver River two days later, but the 21 August entry reported that an unspecified number of Chipewyan were camped at Big Island, about two kilometres east of the fort. The major outfitting of Chipewyan families for the winter hunt occurred rather quickly in September. "Debt" was given to 114 individuals, and they departed the post by 30 September. After that point, references to the Chipewyan once again become intermittent. During October a few individuals appeared with furs and ducks and reports of other fresh meat available for trade. There is no further mention of the Chipewyan until two boys arrived with "10 skins fur" on 25 December. On 20 January 1840 two Chipewyan youths again travelled to Ile à la Crosse seeking ammunition. Then, on 27 January, as an ominous portent of what would become customary behaviour, four "starving" Chipewyan appeared at the post requesting company supplies of fish. Sporadic visits by small parties continued through February of 1840, suggesting that even during the pre-church era at least some of the Chipewyan winter camps were situated within a few day's travel of Ile à la Crosse.

B. *1849–1850.* In the late 1840's the French Catholic order of Oblates of Mary Immaculate established a mission at Ile à la Crosse, but the Ile à la Crosse HBC journal for outfit 1849–50 (HBCA B.89/a/27) indicates that the spatial and economic organization of the Chipewyan had changed little over the previous decade. For example, on 31 May 1849 a group of Chipewyan assembled near the Beaver River travelled to the fort, and the following day the clerk was "very busy with the Indians giving them ammunition for the summer." Similar transactions occurred on 2, 4 and 5 June and by the latter date virtually all of the post's Indian clients had arrived and the fur packs were being prepared for outward shipment. The summer months passed with virtually no reference to Indians, but by mid-September Chipewyan began appearing once more. They arrived in what the traders referred to as "bands," apparently small multi-family groups conveniently identified by their male leaders or spokesmen, as in traders' references to "Janvier and his band" or "Herloo's band." With the arrival of the annual "English Brigade" of trade goods in late September, winter outfitting of Indian customers began. As the journals indicate, the equipping of clients was completed by 11 October: "We equipped Janvier's Band for the winter who are the last of our Indians. We equipped in all, about 107, thirteen less than last year."

The Chipewyan received no further mention until some arrivals on 22 December, but the journal is not clear regarding numbers of people or their departure dates. Except for a reference to an encampment at Buffalo Narrows, about fifty-five linear kilometres to the northwest of Ile à la Crosse, the wintering grounds of these December visitors are also unspecified. Throughout the late winter and early spring of 1850, occasional parties of one or two Chipewyan visited the fort with a few furs or raw meat to trade. For example, two boys arrived at Ile à la Crosse to inform the traders of the availability of meat at "Dinna you's tent" on Knee Lake, about seventy-two kilometres to the northeast on the Churchill River. Post servants were dispatched to Knee Lake, and they returned on 5 April with 800 pounds of meat. On 12 April two Chipewyan women arrived at Ile à la Crosse from the Buffalo Narrows vicinity, and significantly, by 18 April the journal noted: "The Chipewyan arriving every day with nothing and starving." No doubt, the late winter food shortages were exacerbated by the well-established habit of selling large amounts of moose meat to the post as "provisions" or "country produce." Sporadic references to trade with Chipewyan occur over the next month with one individual arriving on 9 May from Island Lake, between 95 and 160 kilometres northwest of Ile à la Crosse. By 28 May most of the Chipewyan had appeared at the post, many of them with little or no fur for trade. The available fur was packed and sent out by brigade on 3 June. In very rapid succession, the Chipewyan clients were equipped for the summer season on 3 and 4 June, and most of them had departed the Ile à la Crosse post by 5 June 1850.

C. *1864–1865.* In the post journal for outfit 1864–65 (HBCA B.89/a/35), there are only intermittent references to Chipewyan trading at Ile à la Crosse in September. Some of them were camped on "the other end of Clear Lake" (that is, the north end of Churchill Lake eighty kilometres to the northwest) by early October of 1864. Not until 28 October, however, had the Ile à la Crosse traders finished extending "debt," equipping over one hundred Indians for the winter and sending supplies to the three subsidiary posts of Cold Lake, Green Lake, and Canoe Lake. The latter two establishments were located immediately to the south of Ile à la Crosse and served a predominantly Cree clientele. Thus, the period of winter equipping was now a full month later than it had been earlier in the nineteenth century.

Sporadic arrivals and departures of Indians were reported through November, and on 25 November one of the Roman Catholic priests returned to Ile à la Crosse from a missionizing tour at Portage la Loche, presumably among the Chipewyan encamped in that vicinity. On 22 and 23 December large numbers of Indians arrived at the post, and much of 24 December was spent "working with Indians and supplying them." Apparently, these customers departed the post rather quickly. On 31 December two Chipewyan boys arrived from a downstream location, "Scap(?) Portage," with a few furs and reports of poor hunting owing to illness. At that time the journals identify "scarlet fever" as a chronic debilitator of both Indians and post servants, and on 1 January 1865, Bishop Grandin of the mission made a trip to minister to the Chipewyan at Scap Portage. Through the months of February, March, and April small parties of Chipewyan visited Ile à la Crosse on an occasional but steady basis, and most of them appear to be arriving from camps located one to three days in travel distance. For example, one Chipewyan arrived from as near as the "lower end of the lake," that is, the north end of Lac Ile à la Crosse itself. On 24 February two Chipewyan travelled from their camp on Pine River, presumably the mouth of the Haultain River about eighty linear kilometres northeast on the Churchill River. Two other Chipewyan appeared in Ile à la Crosse on 4 March, coming from the direction of Dore Lake, eighty kilometres to the southeast. On 20 March, four Chipewyan arrived from the Pine River vicinity, again with a large quantity of marten furs. An Island Lake Chipewyan appeared at the post on 23 March, and on the following day two parties of Chipewyan arrived, one from Pine River again and the other from farther east on Serpent or Snake Lake.

Chipewyan from the Pine River and Serpent Lake vicinities continued appearing in Ile à la Crosse regularly through mid-April of 1865. Two Chipewyan encamped at Little Egg Lake "on this side of the Little Athabasca River" came to the post on 18 April. Through the remainder of April and early May small parties of Chipewyan arrived in Ile à la Crosse every few days, many of them from camps at Island Lake and the Buffalo Lake Narrows to the northwest. As in previous years, the Indians were outfitted for summer hunting in early June, and the journals make very few references to the Chipewyan until mid-September, when they began assembling in Ile à la Crosse for fall and winter supplies.

D. *1889–90.* The general structure of the Ile à la Crosse Chipewyan trade for the previous fifty years can be compared with the outfit for 1889–90 (HBCA B.89/a/36). The latter year marks the onset of the period which is of greatest concern in this study. By 6 and 7 June 1889 large numbers of Chipewyan had assembled at Ile à la Crosse, and the post journals indicate that they attended local church services on 9 June. For the next three months there are very few references to Chipewyan in the area. By 7 and 8 September, however, they had re-grouped at the post where they remained until 17 September before departing for the fall hunt. A short time later on 24 September, the Ile à la Crosse staff sent out the annual shipment of freight for winter operations at the Souris River outpost. Other major outposts at that time included Canoe Lake, Green Lake, Portage la Loche, and the Narrows (Buffalo Narrows).

Small Chipewyan parties began appearing at Ile à la Crosse with some furs in late November and early December of 1889, including some people from an encampment at Island Lake. By 23 December the traders reported that: "All the Chips arrived from all sides." Some of these people departed as early as 27 December, but others remained in Ile à la Crosse until the new year. Only occasional transactions with Chipewyan are recorded through January, February, and March of 1890 with parties from Clear Lake, Buffalo Narrows, and "English River Narrows," locales in a one- or two-day travel radius of Ile à la Crosse. In contrast to years previously discussed, however, large numbers of

Chipewyan, as well as all of the outpost clerks, began gathering in Ile à la Crosse on 4 April. They attended Easter church services on 6 April and by the following day they were dispersing for their respective camps. There was intermittent activity with Chipewyan at the post in late April as some made preparations for a spring "rat (muskrat) hunt." Then, on 10 and 11 June, perhaps two weeks after the ice had melted from the largest lakes, the bulk of the area's Chipewyan population once again converged on the Ile à la Crosse post for summer provisioning.

E. *Discussion.* Although the post journals indicate some continuity in the scheduling and spatial organization of the Ile à la Crosse trade, there is a gradual increase in frequency of visits to the fort through the late nineteenth century, suggesting a general reduction in wintering ranges and mobility. By the early 1890's the southern Chipewyan or *kesyehot'ine* regularly appear at the post for the important trading-provisioning periods in September and June, but they are also assembling in Ile à la Crosse to attend the Catholic mission's Christmas and Easter services. The ability of the Chipewyan population to stage four major annual gatherings at this time is facilitated by their location in winter hunting grounds that are within one- to three-days travel distance of Ile à la Crosse. The long nomadic circuit of Sarah Bell's 1870's childhood has disappeared, and small multi-family winter communities have located themselves in proximity to a network of winter outposts that trace a fan-like wedge to the northwest (Buffalo Narrows, Portage la Loche), north (Island Lake) and northeast (Souris River) of Ile à la Crosse. Yet, the Chipewyan population itself appears to have remained rather stable in size through much of the nineteenth century. For example, an 1881 Canadian government census reported 531 Chipewyan in the HBC's English River District (PAC, Microfilm C–13, 285), as compared with the HBC's 1838 enumeration of 489 Chipewyan in the same management district (HBCA B.239/z/10 fos.52a–57a).

BUSINESS ACCOUNTS AND OUTPOST ECONOMICS

The economic adaptations of the Upper Churchill Chipewyan in the late nineteenth and early twentieth centuries can be better understood by examining in detail the trade transactions of Chipewyan customers attached to the Souris River, Wagahonanci, and Sandy Lake outposts in the period between 1889 and 1909. As previously noted, Souris River was a major winter outpost about 120 linear kilometres east of Ile à la Crosse near the juncture of Sandfly and Pinehouse Lakes on the Churchill River (Fig. 1). Known as *glunedesce* by the Chipewyan and *akposisipi* by the Cree ("mouse river"), the post was established in the 1870's and continued in operation through the 1930's. During that period, the Souris River post occupied facilities in at least four separate locations, three of which were identified in an archaeological survey in 1980. Artifactual material recovered indicated that these loci had been continuously occupied for nearly a century. Although Souris River served a predominantly Chipewyan clientele through the first decade of this century, after that point, for reasons not yet fully understood, Cree and Métis Cree from the Lac la Ronge area and elsewhere replaced the Chipewyan in that region. Indeed, a few Métis Cree families from the contemporary village of Pinehouse Lake presently maintain seasonal fishing and trapping camps in and near the historic Souris River site.

By the early 1890's the HBC referred to the original Souris River post as "Old Souris," while the name "New Souris" was bestowed upon a completely new outpost (HBCA D.25/19). In fact, the new establishment was known variously to HBC traders as "New Souris," "Souris River," "Wadaouanis," and "Wakenanci" (HBCA B.89/b/23). It is apparent that this is the post which local Indians call *wagahonanci,* or "curving river place" in Cree. The name refers to its location on a bend of the Churchill River about sixty kilometres upstream from the original or Old Souris River. It was a winter facility that served a largely Chipewyan clientele. The HBC may have opened Wagahonanci and Old Souris River for business during alternate years, but by outfit 1908–1909 the two outposts were operating simultaneously (HBCA B.89/b/23). The decision to run them concurrently was no doubt related to changes introduced by Treaty No. 10 of 1906 with the English River Band of Chipewyan and by increased competition from Revillon Frères. The latter firm had outposts near the HBC's establishment at both Wagahonanci and Souris River. However, Wagahonanci had a short lifespan and apparently closed around 1915–16. After that point, local Chipewyan gravitated toward outposts farther westward on the Churchill River at Knee Lake.

A third outpost of relevance to this study is Sandy Lake. Like the two previous facilities, Sandy Lake was a winter outpost of the HBC Ile à la Crosse parent post. It was situated at the headwaters of the Mudjatik River drainage, 185 linear kilometres north of Ile à la Crosse (Fig. 1). Known as *taitwe* (literally, "sandy lake") by the Chipewyan, the Sandy Lake post was referred to as the "Cree Lake" post by HBC traders in its early years of operation, apparently because the HBC established the facility as a means of encouraging some Chipewyan families to reoccupy the Cree Lake region immediately to the north. As noted in previous discussion, the *kesyehot'ine* modified their annual nomadic cycle in the late 1860's and early 1870's in response to the developing system of winter outposts, and part of the modification involved a retraction of their wintering range southward from Cree Lake. By the early 1890's the HBC may have perceived that the Churchill River headwaters was receiving too much fur-hunting pressure and that more distant regions needed to be resurrected for trapping. Indeed, an Ile à la Crosse Inspection Report for

1891–92 indicates that the Sandy Lake outpost was established in the summer of 1891 because that "country had not been hunted over for about 22 years and is said to be rich in both food and fur-bearing animals" (HBCA B.89/e/15).

However, other factors were influencing a re-orientation northward. One of those factors was increasing competition from independent free traders. Financial losses in the English River District during outfit 1890–91 were attributed to expenses incurred in opposing free traders, and the HBC believed that a relocation of its best hunters to Cree Lake would place them beyond the reach of independent operators (HBCA B.89/b/14 fos.66–67, 117–120). Another factor motivating the HBC's establishment of the Sandy Lake outpost was its growing conflict with Catholic priests in Ile à la Crosse regarding each institution's relationship with and control over the Chipewyan. Throughout the 1890's and the first few years of this century, the HBC believed that the mission was conducting a successful sub rosa fur trade in addition to its ecclesiastical function. Church officials complained that the HBC was exposing the Chipewyan to starvation by removing them to distant wintering grounds too early in the autumn, but the management of the HBC interpreted the priests' accusations as transparent covers for their own trading interests with the Indians (HBCA B.89/b/14 fos.135–137,244–250; HBCA B.89/b/18 fos.60–62,277–283). By the time the Sandy Lake outpost was phased out in the mid-1930's, it had occupied three separate locations on a small lake of the same name (Gwillim Lake on contemporary maps), situated a short distance south of the long portage over the height of land that separates the Churchill River drainage from Cree Lake and other waters draining northward into the Arctic Ocean (Fig. 1). All three sites were documented during the archaeological survey in 1979 (Brumbach et al. 1982).

Although the Souris River, Wagahonanci, and Sandy Lake outposts operated simultaneously after the mid-1890's, their respective account records show that there was little overlap in the clientele served. Each post maintained transactions with relatively separate sets of Chipewyan families, but these families were the historically and genetically inter-related *kesyehot'ine,* ancestral to present Chipewyan of the area. To clarify the economic position of these people at the turn of the century, we will focus upon four sample customers. Analyses of their trade transactions follow:

1. *Bernard Chayauyazie 1889–90*

The account books maintained at the Souris River post for outfit 1889–90 (HBCA B.349/d/10) list twenty-seven male names in a section titled "Indian Accounts," and of the twenty-four who had recorded transactions, twenty-three have distinctively Chipewyan names while the twenty-fourth is identified as a member of the "Selkirk Band," apparently a Saulteaux or Cree immigrant from southern Manitoba. The Chipewyan customer Bernard Chayauyazie will serve as an illustration of local economic behaviour during this time period. His complete trade transactions for outfit 1889–90 are reproduced in Table 1.

Table 1 also serves as a model of the HBC's organization of its customer account data. In some instances a post's "Indian ledger" or "blotter" is simply a daily running account with each transaction recorded in sequence order, but more frequently, as in Table 1, a post ledger will summarize the complete annual transactions in furs and goods for each customer. Of course, because many Indian families also had accounts at the Ile à la Crosse post during their traditional summer rendezvous, the reconstruction of an annual commercial profile may require the wedding of two or more post ledgers. Typically, the ledger pages are divided into four sections from left to right as follows: (1) the date, (2) a listing of the general commodities purchased and the furs and country produce sold by a client, (3) the "Debt" or total of goods in Made Beaver, and (4) the "Credit" or total of furs and country produce in Made Beaver value.

As a standard of trade, Made Beaver values for various furs and goods were relatively uniform for posts in the Ile à la Crosse district at any point in time. However, the standard was not always strictly applied, since local post managers attempted to maintain individual accounts in a condition approaching parity. That is, over the course of a trading year, it was desirable to have credits equalling debts for as many customers as possible, and accounts appear to be reconciled toward parity in large transactions where the particular Made Beaver (hereafter referred to as MB) values of a large number of furs might be generalized in the interest of balancing accumulated debts. Despite this flexibility in accounting, indebtedness was chronic among a large percentage of the clientele, and large debts could not be offset by gratuities. Although further research will clarify the issue, there is evidence suggesting that a complex of competitive trade forces in the late nineteenth and early twentieth centuries increased the HBC's operating expenses while reducing its local intake of Indian fur. The simultaneous rise of serious free traders, new companies such as Revillon Frères, and surreptitious Catholic church trade, for example, diverted some of the fur traffic from the HBC during this period and, presumably, exacerbated indebtedness among HBC clientele.

In the year under consideration, an outfit of trading goods was sent from Ile à la Crosse to Souris River on 10 September 1889, and additional supplies were shipped there on 12 October, 27 December and 6 February 1890. These goods, valued at $2,213.23, consisted largely of food staples, such as flour, bacon, sugar, and jam, as well as a general selection of clothing items, tobacco, yard goods, blankets, ammunition, knives, cooking utensils, and other domestic items. Souris River remained open for business until 31 May 1890 when the outfit was officially closed and the accounts were balanced.

As Table 1 indicates, Bernard Chayauyazie's trading began with a notation

TABLE 1: SOURIS RIVER INDIAN LEDGER WITH TRADING POST TRANSACTIONS
OF BERNARD CHAYAUYAZIE, OUTFIT 1889–1890 (B.349/d/10)

				Dr	Cr
1889					
May	31	To Balance transfer a/c at Ile à la Crosse 96			
		To (?)			
		To Debt at Ile à la Crosse ot 88	105		
1889					
Sept	14	To advances at Ile à la Crosse a/c Souris River			
		To shot¹ tea¹ mat½ tab½ powd¹ sug¹		5	
Oct	19	To capot¹⁰ cloth² tea² powd¹		15	
Dec	20	To supplies F. Magloire		53	
	24	To supplies at I.C. asf. Blotter		3	
	27	To supplies at I.C. D⁻º		11	
1890					
Jan	12	By Balance			87
				87	87
		To Balance		87	
Jan	16	flour¹¹ bolles¹ caps¹ string¹ powder²		16	
		tea⁸ tab² shawl⁶ mat¹		17	
	27	By 1 lge Castor⁸ 1 Carcajou⁵			13
		To flour¹ tea 1½		2½	
Feb	8	By 1 leautres ¹⁵			15
		Bacon² flour² limes¹		5	
	18	By 1 lge Castors⁶ Leautres¹⁰			16
		dore (sore?)¹ flour⁵ bacon¹		5	
		culotte⁴ jam½ pipe¹		6	
March	8	By 3 lge Castors²⁴ 1 matre³			27
		Flannelle⁴ tea³ savon¹		8	
		the			
		pour la viandre rayon de Castor			2
		Chemise² Bernique¹ hache²		5	
		Flannelle² Tabac¹		3	
		Gratuity			3
		l'mienne²½ caps²		3	
April	11	To tea¹		x	
	14	By 2 lge Castors¹⁶ 2 small⁶			22
		1 Marten³			3
		Gratis³			3
		brot forward		158	104
		Pekan¹²			12
				158	116
		To Balance		42	
		To powder¹² souliers (?)⁵		17	
		Tea¹ Tirvid (?)⁴ tob¹		6	
		By 1 Rerd Souliens²			2
Mai	5	Tea¹		1	
		By 6 rats¹			1
	19	½ Peau Doreale⁶			6
		To Toile (?)⁶		6	
June	5	Tea¹		1	
				74	9
				9	
May	31	To blce Transfer f IxIL fo		65	
June	10	Gratis 2 flour½ bacon			

of debt transferred from Ile à la Crosse on 31 May 1889 and a short list of provisions supplied on 4 September at Ile à la Crosse as an advance. His first purchases of goods at Souris River were not made until mid-October, and later in December he obtained supplies from a camp trader or tripper. The fact that he purchased additional supplies in Ile à la Crosse near the end of December suggests that he attended the Christmas masses at the Roman Catholic mission. His purchases of supplies at Souris River resumed in January, 1890, and he began selling his furs on a regular basis until the account was closed in June. Indeed, over the entire year, Chayauyazie made an average of two transactions per month. This suggests that his winter trapping grounds were located within one- or two-day's travel of Souris River, perhaps north or northeast of the Churchill River. The general categories and Made Beaver values of his purchases are displayed in Table 2.

Bernard Chayauyazie's production in furs is summarized in Table 3. Thus, while he produced only 119 MB in furs, he acquired 194.5 MB in trade goods (Table 2), perpetuating a substantial debt. It is noteworthy that of the identifiable expenditures, the largest share went toward purchases of imported food products (38.8 per cent or 46.5 MB), followed by clothing and textile materials (34.2 per cent), productive technology (19.6 per cent), personal effects (4.6 per cent), and domestic goods (2.9 per cent). By employing food compositon tables (Adams 1975; Szanton 1965; Watt and Merrill 1963), it is possible to convert Chayauyazie's purchased food items into caloric values as a means of assessing contribution to the diet. Table 5 reveals that his purchased food staples provided approximately 181,360.5 calories of food energy. To this reserve of energy, of course, must be added documentary evidence of edible food animals that were trapped or hunted. Thus, Table 6 converts to caloric values the six muskrats, nine beaver, and half moose which are recorded as part of Bernard Chayauyazie's fur returns. These local animal resources contributed another 440,875 calories. Added to the imported food, then, the account book data provide evidence for a total food reserve of about 622,235.5 calories.

Even if very generalized nutritional requirements are applied to the above information, there is an obvious food deficit. For example, working with the assumption of an average daily requirement of three thousand calories per individual, the combined contribution of imported food and locally procured food would have supplied 207 days of food energy. That would have provided roughly 28.4 per cent of the annual caloric needs for a family of two and only 11.3 per cent of the needs for a family of five. Since Chipewyan family size tended toward four or five individuals, it is likely that most of Chayauyazie's family's nutritional needs were satisfied by extensive hunting of moose and caribou, fishing, rabbit-snaring, waterfowl hunting, and other activity that was not systematically observed or recorded by traders.

TABLE 2. CATEGORIES OF TRADE GOODS OBTAINED BY FOUR CHIPEWYAN HUNTER-TRAPPERS.

	Bernard Chayauyazie (1889–1890)			Willibert Grandfarrand (1894–1895)			Ethengoo Campbell (1900–1901)			Deaf Isaac (1908–1909)		
	MB	% of total	% of total	MB	% of total	% of total	MB	% of total	% of total	MB	% of total	% of total
Imported food	46.5	38.8	23.9	58	24.0	20.8	58	79.5		247.5	30.2	29.0
Productive technology	23.5	19.6	12.1	48.5	20.1	17.4	0	0.0		109.5	13.4	12.8
Domestic technology	3.5	2.9	1.8	14	5.8	5.0	0.5	0.7		85.5	10.4	10.0
Clothing/textiles	41	34.2	21.1	104.5	43.3	37.5	14	19.2		324	39.5	37.9
Personal	5.5	4.6	2.8	16.5	6.8	5.9	0.5	0.7		53	6.5	6.2
		100.1			100.0			100.0			100.0	
Unknown	74.5		38.3	37		13.3	0			34.5		4.0
totals	194.5 MB		100.0	278.5 MB		100.0	73.0 MB	100.0		854 MB		100.0

TABLE 3: FUR RETURNS OF FOUR CHIPEWYAN HUNTER-TRAPPERS.

	Bernard Chayauyazie (1889–1890)		Willibert Grandfarrand (1894–1895)		Ethengoo Campbell (1900–1901)		Deaf Isaac (1908–1909)	
	No.	MB	No.	MB	No.	MB	No.	MB
Black bear			4	48	1	20		
Brown bear			1	6	1	30		
Bear			1	16				
Red Fox			2	4			1	10
X fox			1	5			1	10
Beaver	9	60	16	45			10	134
Ermine			8	1.5			1	0.5
Mink			10	9			4	38
Marten	2	6	29	87	2	6	25	635
Wolverine	1	5						
Muskrat	6	1	11	2	83	14		
Otter	2	25					1	40
Castoreum			?	2.5				
Mooseskin	0.5	6	1.5	13				
Misc. country produce	?	14						
Beaver meat		2					5 quarts	5
Meat								
totals		119 MB		239 MB		70 MB		872.5 MB

TABLE 4: ESTIMATED CALORIES DERIVED FROM IMPORTED FOOD AND
COUNTRY PRODUCE BY FOUR CHIPEWYAN HUNTER-TRAPPERS.

	Bernard Chayauyazie (1889–1890)	Willibert Grandfarrand (1894–1895)	Ethengoo Campbell (1900–1901)	Deaf Isaac (1909–1910)
Total calories: imported food	181,360.5	158,033.5	458,814	831,052
Total calories: country food	440,875	2,152,787.5	574,087.5	303,000
Total calories: both sources	622,235.5	2,310,821	1,032,901.5	1,134,052
Percent of needs: family of 5	11.3%	42.0%	18.8%	20.7%
Percent of needs: family of 2	28.4%	105.0%	47.1%	51.8%

TABLE 5: CALORIC VALUES OF IMPORTED FOODS FOR
BERNARD CHAYAUYAZIE, OUTFIT 1889–1890.

	Purchase in MB	Pounds per MB	Total pounds	Calories per pound	Total calories
Flour	19.5	5	97.5	1655	161,362.5
Bacon	4	1.5	6	2836	17,016
Sugar	1	1	1	1750	1,750
Jam	1.5	0.67(?)	1	1232	1,232
Tea	20.5	0.5	10.25	—	—
				total	181,360.5

TABLE 6: CALORIC VALUES OF COUNTRY PRODUCE OBTAINED BY
BERNARD CHAYAUYAZIE, OUTFIT 1889–1890.

	Number obtained	Edible Pounds per animal	Total pounds	Calories per pound	Total calories
Beaver	9	30	270	1010	272,700
Muskrat	6	2.5	15	625	9,375
Moose	0.5	400	200	794	158,800
				total	440,875

The ecological implications of utilizing durable trade goods also merit closer examination. For example, Bernard Chayauyazie invested 41 MB, or 34.2 per cent of identifiable purchases, in clothing and textile materials in 1889–90 (HBCA B.349/d/10; HBCA B.89/d/338). These goods included one shawl, one shirt, one "culotte" (trousers), one pair of shoes, one "capot" (overcoat or cloak), and twenty-one to twenty-four yards of flannel and unidentifiable yard goods. This does not appear to be an appreciably large clothing inventory, and, indeed, the Chayauyazie family may have been small. No doubt, the shawl was used by an adult woman while the shoes, shirt, trousers and the capot most likely were worn by an adult male. The yard goods probably served as the basis for skirts, dresses, and other apparel for a woman and any children. Even this relatively modest use of commercial clothing material may have functioned to relieve the pressure on the Chipewyan population to obtain adequate animal hides for clothing. Footgear, mittens, hats, jackets, and other small apparel were still manufactured from home-processed moose and caribou hides and furs, but the possibility of tailoring complete winter parkas and leggings from caribou hides had quickly passed among the southern Chipewyan. The significance of this development was twofold: (1) By the 1890's the trapping range of most *kesyehot'ine* had retracted southward near the Churchill River. More time was available for pursuing fur-bearing animals, but the people were now beyond the southern wintering range of barren-ground caribou, a traditional source of clothing. (2) By importing large amounts and varieties in clothing and textiles, the HBC reinforced a gradual shift in Chipewyan hunting behaviour from the pursuit of large mammals desirable for native apparel and food to a more intensive pursuit of small fur-bearing mammals desirable in European dress.

Productive technology, or tools and materials used directly in the quest for food and fur, form another general class of trade goods (Table 2). Chayauya-zie's purchases of shot, powder, ball, and caps were integral in the system of hunting large food mammals and waterfowl with muzzle-loading firearms. As the southern Chipewyan became regular residents of the full boreal forest environment near the Churchill River, their dependency upon solitary mammals like the moose increased. Firearms increased the efficiency with which these animals could be hunted by individual hunters or small hunting parties, and, in turn, made available more time for fur-trapping activity. Of course, other imported goods, such as Chayauyazie's axe, file, string, and matches, also increased the efficiency of human labour in an immediate sense. All of these short-term technological enhancements must be appraised in terms of the human labour costs involved in acquiring, maintaining, and replacing such goods, and in terms of the longer-run environmental stresses of increased extractive efficiency upon local animal populations.

2. *Willibert Grandfarrand 1894–95*

Bernard Chayauyazie's economic behaviour can be compared with another Souris River Chipewyan client, Willibert Grandfarrand. For the outfit 1894–95, forty-four customers are listed in the Souris River accounts. Of these names, twenty-seven appear to be Chipewyan (including two women), while the remaining seventeen have names generally associated with Cree or Métis Cree families. Based upon the structure of the accounts, thirty-one customers, including all the Chipewyan clients, appear to have trapping and hunting livelihoods. The other accounts belong to trippers, camp traders, and other servants and staff associated with the post (HBCA B.349/d/24; HBCA B.89/d/403 fo.74).

The account books reveal that Willibert Grandfarrand purchased supplies and received some gratuities in Ile à la Crosse on 15 and 18 June 1894. By 10 September he had returned to his wintering grounds near Souris River, and between that time and 3 December he made six transactions at the outpost. As is the case with many of the account ledgers, there is no record indicating that the customer actually visited the outpost for each transaction rather than being serviced by a camp trader in Grandfarrand's bush residence. Both practices were common. Also, there is no record that Grandfarrand travelled to Ile à la Crosse during the Christmas period. In 1895 the Souris River accounts indicate that he traded once in January, twice in February, once in March, five times in April and on four occasions in May. An entry dated 18

May credited him with 20 MB for making a trip to Ile à la Crosse, presumably assisting the Souris River staff in some capacity.

Willibert Grandfarrand's expenditures for trade goods totaled 278.5 MB in value (HBCA B.349/d/24; HBCA B.89/d/403 fo.74) (Table 2), only slightly exceeding the 266.5 MB he received in credit for furs, country produce, and minor labour. As noted in Table 3, his furs accounted for 239 MB in credit at Souris River, a significantly larger production than that realized by Bernard Chayauyazie. Undoubtedly, a number of factors could have affected such an increase, including improved weather conditions, growth of animal populations (particularly beaver, mink and marten), greater trapping expertise, or more extensive support from family members. At this stage of analysis, such factors must be treated as a conjectural "black box." For example, there is no direct information regarding the size and composition of family units associated with the outpost customers.

In addition to his fur returns, Willibert Grandfarrand received 4 MB in credit for four days of labour, plus the 20 MB for his spring canoe trip to Ile à la Crosse, and 2.5 MB for an accounting overcharge yielding a total credit accumulation of 265.5 MB. In addition, he was given some food rations as "gratuities," but these were *not* computed as credit by the traders. The 265.5 MB in credit was applied in exchanges with the HBC to obtain trade goods valued at 278.5 MB. As illustrated in Table 2, 241.5 MB of those expenditures are clearly identifiable in the accounts. Of the identifiable goods, Grandfarrand invested the largest share of his earnings for clothing and textiles (43.3 per cent or 104.5 MB), followed by imported food (24 per cent or 58 MB), productive technology (20.1 per cent or 48.5 MB), personal effects (6.8 per cent or 16.5 MB), and domestic goods (5.8 per cent or 14 MB).

The estimated caloric values for the imported foods and the locally hunted mammals which apear in Grandfarrand's accounts are presented in Tables 7 and 8 respectively. Compared to Bernard Chayauyazie's intake of food energy, it is apparent that Grandfarrand obtained somewhat less from imported sources (about 158,034 calories) and considerably more from local animal resources (about 2,152,788 calories; See Table 4). Indeed, hunting and trapping activity alone provided 718 days of food energy, if we apply the standard of three thousand calories per person per day. The bulk of that energy was supplied by six bears, with moose and beaver providing significant secondary sources. It is interesting that Grandfarrand obtained much of his store credit by trapping marten (*Martes americana*), a member of the weasel family that is not utilized as food. However, this trapping income was converted into purchases of store food which did supply approximately fifty-three additional person-days of food energy. Taken together, the imported and local food resources provided an estimated total 2,310,821 calories, or about 770 person-days of food energy. Thus, the documented economic behaviour for Willibert Grandfarrand indicates that he could have satisfied 105 per cent of the annual caloric needs of a small two-member family or 42 per cent of the needs of a larger five-member family unit (Table 4). While his food acquisition appears to be four times as great as that indicated for Bernard Chayauyazie, it must be remembered that much hunting, and virtually all reciprocal sharing of large food mammals between families, was never recorded in any trade documents.

Despite their differences in food procurement, it is noteworthy that Chayauyazie's and Grandfarrand's absolute expenditures for imported food are quite similar (46.6 MB versus 58 MB, Table 2). They both purchased essentially the same amount of commercial foodstuffs. However, Grandfarrand's larger cash income was applied toward greater purchases in all other categories of trade goods, including a sizeable outlay of 104.5 MB (43.3 per cent of his income) for clothing and textile materials.

3. *Ethengoo Campbell 1900–1901*

A third Chipewyan customer profile is illustrated by the accounts of Ethengoo Campbell, who conducted business with the Wagahonanci outpost during the outfit 1900–1901. Of the twenty-four customer names listed in the Wagahonanci account books for outfit 1900–1901, twenty are recognizable as Chipewyan family names (sixteen male, 4 female), while the remaining four male names are associated with Cree or Métis Cree families (HBCA B.349/d/28). If each male hunter-trapper was affiliated with a family averaging four to five members, the Chipewyan population associated with the outpost numbered between sixty-four and eighty people.

It is interesting that our sample customer, Ethengoo Campbell, had only four contacts or transactions with the post during the trading year. These were on 25 October, 1 November, 12 November and 4 December 1900 (HBCA B.349/d/28 fos.11–45). Compared to Bernard Chayauyazie and Willibert Grandfarrand, this is an abbreviated trading record. Other customers traded at Wagahonanci throughout the late winter and spring months, indicating

TABLE 7: CALORIC VALUES OF IMPORTED FOODS FOR
WILLIBERT GRANDFARRAND, OUTFIT 1894–1895.

	Purchase in MB	Pounds per MB	Total pounds	Calories per pound	Total calories
Flour	14.5	5	72.5	1655	119,987.5
Bacon	7.5	1	7.5	2836	21,270
Sugar	3	1	3	1750	5,250
Tea	29	0.5	14.5	—	—
Tallow	1.5	1	1.5	3682	5,523
Molasses	1	1 (?)	1	1525	1,525
Prunes	0.5	1	0.5	1100	550
Biscuit	1	2	2	1964	3,928
				total	158,033.5

TABLE 8: CALORIC VALUES OF COUNTRY PRODUCE OBTAINED BY
WILLIBERT GRANDFARRAND, OUTFIT 1894–1895.

	Number obtained	Edible pounds per animal	Total pounds	Calories per pound	Total calories
Bear	6	225	1320	1010	1,333,200
Beaver	16	30	480	1010	484,800
Muskrat	11	2.5	27.5	625	17,187.5
Moose	1.5	400	600	794	476,400
				total	2,152,787.5

that the post was open for business past December. Furthermore, Ethengoo Campbell appears in the accounts of subsequent years, showing that he had not died or emigrated from the region in 1900. The servants at the Wagahonanci post were extensively involved in "tripping" or "camp trading" as a way of conducting business with a clientele scattered over a large territory. It is possible that some of Ethengoo Campbell's transactions with camp traders were not entered into the post ledger.

A more plausible explanation of Campbell's abbreviated record is the possibility that some of his fur production was siphoned off by independent traders who were beginning to percolate northward. This is suggested by the rather brief accounts for most of the Wagahonanci customers of the period and by the outward correspondence of the Ile à la Crosse HBC manager Thomas Anderson. In a letter to James McDougall of the HBC, Prince Albert, on 8 December 1900, he complained that a new company policy of not advancing credit (or "giving debt") to Indians was having a disasterous impact on HBC trade for the entire English River District: "The Opposition got at least two thirds of all the fur caught in this quarter enabling them to return here again with far larger Supplies to oppose us" (HBCA B.89/b/18 fos.177–178).

As indicated in Table 3, Ethengoo Campbell's recorded fur production was valued at a meager 70 MB, and there is no documented evidence of income from country produce or labour. His furs were exchanged with the HBC for trade goods valued at 73 MB. Of those expenditures the largest share represented imported food (79.5 per cent or 58 MB), followed by clothing and textiles (19.2 per cent or 14 MB), domestic articles (0.7 per cent or 0.5 MB) and personal items (0.7 per cent or 0.5 MB). No earnings were spent for productive technology (Table 2). Table 9 converts Campbell's inventory of store-purchased food into caloric values, and Table 10 presents the caloric values of the hunted food animals which appear in his accounts. The two sources represent a total food energy value of approximately 1,032,902 calories (Table 4). Divided by the standard of three thousand calories per person per day, the total reserve would have provided about 344 days of food energy. A food supply of those dimensions could have supplied about 47.1 per cent of the

TABLE 9: CALORIC VALUES OF IMPORTED FOODS FOR ETHENGOO CAMPBELL,
OUTFIT 1900–1901.

	Purchase in MB	Pounds per MB	Total pounds	Calories per pound	Total calories
Flour	54	5	270	1655	446,850
Bacon	1	1	1	2836	2,836
Sugar	1	1	1	1750	1,750
Tallow	1	1.5	1.5	3682	5,523
Syrup	1 tin	1 (?)	1 (?)	1855	1,855
				total	458,814

annual caloric needs of a small two-member family of 18.8 per cent of the needs of a family of five. Thus, Campbell's recorded food supply was mid-way between those of Bernard Chayauyazie and Willibert Grandfarrand. Clearly, the two bears and 270 pounds of flour constituted the bulk of his larder.

Individually, muskrats had a rather low trade value, but procured in quantity, they became significant resources for subsistence and exchange (Table 3). For example, Campbell's eighty-three muskrat furs were valued at only fourteen MB or about six pelts per MB. However, six pelts or one MB could be exchanged for five pounds of flour representing 8,275 calories of food energy, and the six muskrats themselves yield another 9,375 calories. Thus, as items of exchange for food imports and as directly consumable food, large numbers of muskrats served as a convenient backup subsistence resource in the fall and spring months.

4. *Deaf Isaac 1908–1909*

The final commercial profile outlines the activities of a Chipewyan man named Deaf Isaac, who maintained an account at the Sandy Lake outpost for the outfit 1908–1909 (HBCA B.342/d/10 fos.1–124). While there is no post journal available for Ile à la Crosse during that year, the 1909–11 journals indicate that during the first decade of this century an additional winter outpost had emerged along the Churchill River at Dipper Lake. There were also secondary posts at Clear Lake and Buffalo River near the Churchill River headwaters. Thus, while some Chipewyan families were reorganizing their wintering grounds along the Churchill River, others were continuing to winter in more northern regions. Outgoing correspondence from the Sandy Lake post in 1910 specifically identifies the southern and eastern margins of Cree Lake, and the Poor Fish River country to the east of Cree Lake, as wintering grounds for some of its Chipewyan clients (HBCA B.255/b/1).

The Sandy Lake account books for 1908–1909 list sixty-three separate customer names, but it is possible that a few of these are alternate spellings of the same names. Of this total, thirty-one customers appear to be Chipewyan, including twenty-seven males and four females who may represent widows. The total Chipewyan population serviced by the post may have been in the

TABLE 10: CALORIC VALUES OF COUNTRY PRODUCE OBTAINED BY
ETHENGOO CAMPBELL, OUTFIT 1900-1901.

	Number obtained	Edible pounds per animal	Total pounds	Calories per pound	Total calories
Bear	1	220	440	1010	444,400
Muskrat	83	2.5	207.5	625	129,687.5
				total	574,087.5

neighbourhood of 135 individuals. Another twenty-two customers have names that are commonly associated with Cree or Métis Cree families, and half of these customers may have been servants or labourers attached to the outpost, while the other eleven were members of bush-oriented hunting families. The ten remaining names have no native association and may have included four outpost staff workers and six free traders who maintained accounts with the HBC.

Deaf Isaac and his wife, who appears in the accounts as "Mrs. Isaac," traded at the Sandy Lake post during its open period between 7 October 1908 and 5 June 1909. They made forty-five recorded transactions, for an average of five contacts per month over the nine-month season, suggesting that this family wintered in close proximity to the post. It should be noted, however, that the Sandy Lake fur returns for that year (10,296 MB) exceeded the value of returns at Sandy Lake and Souris River in the previous sample periods by several times (HBCA B.342/d/10). This increase in value did not reflect an intensification of local fur production but rather a dramatic rise in the price of *marten* from an average of 3 MB per pelt in 1890 to 25 MB per pelt in 1908. Thus, the exceptionally high fur income generated by Deaf Isaac in 1908-1909 (872.5 MB) was achieved with a smaller pelt production, and less investment in extractive activity, than that of Willibert Grandfarrand in 1894-95 (239 MB). As illustrated in Table 3, most of Deaf Isaac's fur returns were marten pelts. In addition to furs, Deaf Isaac exchanged five quarts of meat of an unspecified animal for trade goods valued at 5 MB.

It is interesting that very little of Deaf Isaac's large income was used as credit "cushion" (18.5 MB). As was common with less affluent clients, most of his 872.5 MB in earnings were channelled toward purchases, but in this instance, at a higher level in quantity and variety in trade goods. Of his 854 MB in expenditures, 819.5 MB can be identified in the accounts with the largest share going toward purchases of clothing and textiles (39.5 per cent or 324 MB), followed by imported food products (30.2 per cent or 247.5 MB), productive technology (13.4 per cent or 109.5 MB), domestic goods (10.4 per cent or 85.5 MB), and personal effects (6.5 per cent or 53 MB) (see Table 2). This account reflects the greater purchasing power enjoyed by the Isaac family, since the MB values of most trade goods were not increasing at the same rates as fur values.

Deaf Isaac's expenditures for clothing alone surpassed the *total* expenditures of the other sample customers. This included significant increases in purchases of ready-made apparel: three shirts, two pairs of trousers, one pair of overalls, one capot, one set of suit clothes, an "F.C. coat," underwear, and men's hose. Large quantities of yard goods (88.25 yards, excluding 50 yards of duck) and trimmings were also purchased. These included the more common materials, such as print, cotton, flannel, and duffel most likely destined for the home manufacture of clothing. Also included were significant quantities of more exotic, and perhaps prestigious, velvets, velveteens, merino, tartans, and plaids. Some of these latter products, such as black merino and black velvet, probably served as women's dress materials. Overall, such purchases indicate an increase in European-style apparel among the Chipewyan, although, no doubt, the use of such clothing was restricted to religious holidays in Ile à la Crosse and other special occasions.

Other unusual purchases separate Deaf Isaac from the previous customers. For example, on 4 November 1909 he purchased for 63 MB a set of commercially manufactured dog harnesses and two sets of sleigh bells. In addition to the common purchases of shot and other materials used with older muzzle-loading firearms, he also acquired six boxes of factory-loaded cartridges. The cartridges were of several different calibres (38–55, 44–40, and .308), indicating that Deaf Isaac's family maintained a rather varied hunting technology, including three breech-loading rifles.

Table 11 converts Deaf Isaac's inventory of imported food items to caloric values, and Table 12 presents the caloric values of hunted food animals that appear in his accounts. Despite his fur-trapping success, however, relatively little food energy was acquired from local sources. The record of ten beaver, yielding about 303,000 calories, is the lowest recorded energy supply from locally procured animals of the four sample customers (Table 4). On the other hand, Deaf Isaac's account exhibits the greatest variety and cumulative weight in imported food of the four Chipewyan customers and included the first appearance, in this sample, of tinned condensed milk and lard. The lard particularly represented an important substitute for locally procured animal fat, and it combined a high caloric value with advantages of portability and storability. Thus, the documents indicate a total food energy reserve of 1,134,052 calories for Deaf Isaac's family in 1908–1909. This can be translated to 378 days of food energy by applying the constant of three thousand calories per person per day. A food supply of that magnitude would have satisfied 51.8 per cent of the annual caloric requirements of Deaf Isaac and his wife or about 20.7 per cent of the caloric needs of a larger five-member family. This food supply is comparable to that recorded for Willibert Grandfarrand and falls midway in the range of variation for the four customers.

TABLE 11: CALORIC VALUES OF IMPORTED FOODS FOR DEAF ISAAC, OUTFIT 1908-1909.

	Purchase in MB	Pounds per MB	Total pounds	Calories per pound	Total calories
Flour	82.5	3.33	275	1655	455,125
Bacon	8.5	1	8.5	2836	24,106
Sugar	16.5	1	16.5	1750	28,875
Jam	14	1 (?)	14	1232	17,248
Tea	17	0.5	8.5	—	—
Tallow	9	1-3.5	27	3682	99,414
Lard	51.5	ca. 1	47	4091	192,277
Syrup	3	0.67 tin	2 (?)	1856	3,712
Milk	10	0.67 tin	5.25 (?)	667	3,502
Chocolate	2.5	0.5	1.25	2288	2,860
Currants	3	1	3	1311	3,933
Salt	3	0.33	1	—	—
				total	831,052

TABLE 12: CALORIC VALUES OF COUNTRY PRODUCE OBTAINED BY DEAF ISAAC, OUTFIT 1908-1909.

	Number obtained	Edible pounds per animal	Total pounds	Calories per pound	Total calories
Beaver	10	30	300	1010	303,000
				total	303,000

Unlike Bernard Chayauyazie, Willibert Grandfarrand, and Ethengoo Campbell, Deaf Isaac sold neither bear nor moose hides, both animals representing commonly hunted food animals. In fact, one of Deaf Isaac's purchases at the Sandy Lake outpost was a "piece of mooseskin" (HBCA B.342/d/10 fol. 124). This would appear to be a rather unusual purchase for a bush-oriented hunting family. Indeed the packing accounts for the Sandy Lake 1908-1909 outfit reveal that only two mooseskins were freighted in with other merchandise (HBCA B.89/b/23). Even if it is assumed that the rising price of marten furs resulted in intensified trapping of that species, such specialization would not have precluded procurement of large food mammals since the hunting of large game is often opportunistic in nature. It is possible that moose populations were decreasing during that period. Given the high price of marten, and Deaf Isaac's ability in capturing twenty-five of them for 635 MB in credit, he was able to meet his family's needs at the outpost without selling mooseskins or other country produce.

CONCLUSIONS

The material adaptation of the *kesyehot'ine* in the nineteenth and early twentieth centuries involved a complex interplay of shifting microenvironmental distributions and annual nomadic cycles, changing technoeconomic organization, and alterations in production and consumption behaviour. As elsewhere in central subarctic Canada, these adaptations were heavily affected by native response to and influence upon the fur market economy of the English-controlled Hudson's Bay Company. The relationship between the southern Chipewyan and the major HBC post at Ile à la Crosse in the early (after 1821) and mid-nineteenth century was unfettered by major trading competition or other European institutions, and a short-term economic symbiosis emerged. Annual summer trading rendezvous corresponded well with the conventional concentration period of band populations, and the focused summer trade did not disrupt the long nomadic cycles that were linked to traditional winter hunts of barren ground caribou. With the expanding interests of the Roman Catholic church, increased free-trader competition, and the development of a winter outpost network by the HBC, the Chipewyan in the late nineteenth century retracted generally southward from the caribou wintering range, shortened their annual travel circuits to accommodate a higher visiting frequency to secondary outposts, and intensified social and economic interactions with Europeans.

· Of course, the outpost system and competitive economic conditions meant that opportunities for trade, and the availability and variety in imported goods, were increasing in the late nineteenth century. For the southern Chipewyan, however, accessibility to commercial markets and trade merchandise was not an unqualified benefit. As noted above, one obvious trade-off for participating in the growing market economy was the virtual abandonment of barren ground caribou-hunting. Because the southern Chipewyan were the "primary producers" or hunter-trappers in the local fur industry, the elimination of any major subsistence resource was presumably a stressful change. From a strictly interspecies ecological perspective, then, the width of the southern Chipewyan "niche," as indicated by subsistence resource variety (Hardesty 1975, 1977:109–20), was decreasing in the late nineteenth century.

This study has emphasized the utility of business account book records as a quantitative complement to qualitative information in fur trade journals and correspondence and as a complement to an array of ethnographic testimony and archaeological materials retrieved in anthropological field research. Account book data at the level of individual customers can be treated as glimpses into the microbehaviour of subsistence provisioning, fur production, and goods exchange. Patterning in the energetic and economic behaviour of individuals, in turn, provides a basis for interpreting adaptive processes common to the entire southern Chipewyan population. The customer accounts suggest the increasing importance of imported food products as caloric substitutes for locally procured animal food and the significance of imported textiles as substitutes for locally manufactured animal hide and fur clothing. Simultaneously, in the late nineteenth century, the Chipewyan were making large expenditures for certain kinds of imported productive technology, such as firearms, which would make subsistence hunting more efficient at a time when people were becoming more dependent upon solitary mammals like the moose. Fur production and expenditures for imported goods were mutually reinforcing factors. Locked together in a positive feedback relationship, they further reduced the time expended in acquiring local food energy. Thus, while the Chipewyan continued to be regarded by Ile à la Crosse traders as the hunters par excellence of the fur industry, they were losing energetic self-sufficiency. Flour, and later lard, became the staple imported sources of food energy.

Although further information is needed in this area, there is evidence that Chipewyan participation in the fur market economy affected the social context of food procurement and food distribution. Certainly, the reciprocal sharing among closely related families of large food mammals, such as moose and caribou, persisted through the nineteenth and early twentieth centuries and is customary behaviour in many contemporary communities. Yet, some Chipewyan in the nineteenth century served on an occasional basis as "fort hunters," providing meat for the servants and managerial staff at Ile à la Crosse. Other Chipewyan regularly exchanged substantial quanitites of moose and caribou meat as "country produce," and it thereby became a commodity for trade in the same manner as furs. It is plausible that the marketability of large food mammals led to a certain degree of individualization in food production and food distribution. The partial collapse of reciprocal sharing networks, coupled with the siphoning off of locally hunted meat to post traders, would appear to account for otherwise incongruous situations at Ile à la Crosse when some Chipewyan families arrived "starving" while others were trading large quantities of moose meat. Hickerson (1956; 1971:183–89) has related individualization in food production and distribution to chronic starvation among Chippewa fur trappers in early nineteenth-century Minnesota. Of course, cyclical declines in animal populations would have magnified the impact of such behaviour, making the traditionally "lean" period of late winter in northern Saskatchewan even more stressful.

Another value of the customer account data is the potential insight they hold for understanding intra-cultural variation in behaviour, individual economic strategies and decision-making processes. In this regard, the present study is only exploratory. A small sample of Chipewyan customers was examined to illustrate basic scheduling of transactions, the variation in commodities traded, and the implications of such commodities for patterns of resource procurement and food consumption. Generally, the customer profiles exhibit a similar commercial adaptation of trading beaver, marten, and mink fur for key food staples like flour. Yet, within this general framework are notable individual variations. Ethengoo Campbell's concentration upon muskrat production, a resource with a low unit value but potential for high-quantity returns and associated food value, is one distinctive variation. Deaf Isaac's exchange of marten pelts, during a period of heightened fur prices, for an extensive stock of clothing and textiles is another variation in marketing, one that may reflect an embryonic acquisition of capital for enhanced prestige and status.

In closing this discussion, it is worth relating a comment which Sarah Bell once made to Moise McIntyre as she summarized her 1870's experience on the long nomadic circuit of the *kesyehot'ine:*

> It didn't seem like work in those days. It was a lot of fun. Always moving. Always seeing something new. The time would go fast. I could hardly believe it when spring time would come again. It wasn't like work. It was like an adventure to me.

A different emphasis on the past is provided by Eugene George, a fifty-five year-old member of the English River Band, who recalls the winter hardships of his parents and grandparent's relatives before the turn of the century:

> Things were hard in those days, you know. Lots of time people had to go without food. Sometimes starve that way, in the winter time. One time my relatives couldn't find food, no game animals, you know. And one of them was sick real bad with the flu. Hard to travel that way, and then the dogs had nothing to eat. Dogs can't do any work without food. They have to eat. Well, they left that place and started walking and made a camp near a lake where there was a beaver trap. The old man of the family told the people that if there was nothing in his trap they would have no food, and they could all starve to death. And after the old man left, you know, one of his boys got real sad: "I just looked at my brother lying there. Sick. No food. My brother looked so pitiful." Like, I'm telling you, things were hard.

Perhaps the realities of *kesyehot'ine* economic life in the late fur trade period lie somewhere between these two perspectives.

Acknowledgements: This study is based largely upon field and archival research supported by a National Endowment for the Humanities grant (RO–00157–80–0320) and an Urgent Ethnology Contract (UE10–23–79) from the National Museum of Man, National Museums of Canada. We extend our gratitude to the Hudson's Bay Company for permitting us to examine and quote from their original documents in the Provincial Archives of Manitoba and from their microfilm collections in the Public Archives of Canada. Mrs. Shirlee Anne Smith, Hudson's Bay Company Archivist in the Provincial Archives of Manitoba, and her staff provided considerable assistance for which we are grateful. An early version of this paper was presented as part of the symposium, "Economic Adaptations of Natives in the Subarctic Fur Trade," at the 1981 meetings of the American Society for Ethnohistory, and we thank our fellow participants for sharing information and insights. The Chipewyan people of Patuanak and Cree Lake, Saskatchewan, deserve special thanks for their collaboration in this project and for their keen interest in their past.

References Cited

Adams, Catherine
  1975 Nutritive Value of American Foods in Common Units. Agricultural Handbook No. 456. Washington, D.C.: U.S. Government Printing Office.
Barlett, Peggy F.
  1980 Adaptive Strategies in Peasant Agricultural Production. Annual Review of Anthropology 9:545–73.
Bennett, John W.
  1976 The Ecological Transition: Cultural Anthropology and Human Adaptation. New York: Pergamon Press.
Bishop, Charles A., and Arthur J. Ray
  1976 Ethnohistoric Research in the Central Subarctic: Some Conceptual and Methodological Problems. Western Canadian Journal of Anthropology 6:116–144.
Brown, Jennifer
  1976 A Demographic Transition in the Fur Trade Country: Family Sizes and Fertility of Company Officers and Country Wives, ca. 1759–1850. Western Canadian Journal of Anthropology 6:66–71.
Brumbach, Hetty Jo, Robert Jarvenpa, and Clifford Buell
  1982 An Ethnoarchaeological Approach to Chipewyan Adaptations in the Late Fur Trade Period. Arctic Anthropology 19(1):1–49
Curtis, Edward S.
  1928 The Chipewyan. *In* The North American Indian. Vol. 18, pp. 3–52. Norwood.
Gillespie, Beryl C.
  1975 Territorial Expansion of the Chipewyan in the 18th Century, *In* Proceedings: Northern Athapaskan Conference 1971. A.M. Clark, ed., pp. 350–88. National Museum of Man Mercury Series, Canadian Ethnology Service Paper No. 27. Ottawa: National Museums of Canada.
Hardesty, Donald L.
  1975 The Niche Concept: Suggestions for Its Use in the Studies of Human Ecology. Human Ecology 3:71–85.
  1977 Ecological Anthropology. New York: Wiley.

Hickerson, Harold
    1956   The Genesis of a Trading Post Band: The Pembina Chippewa. Ethnohistory
            3:289–345.
    1971   The Chippewa of the Upper Great Lakes: A Study in Sociopolitical Change. *In*
            North American Indians in Historical Perspective. E.B. Leacock and N.O. Lurie,
            eds., pp. 169–99. New York: Random House.
Hudson's Bay Company Archives (HBCA)
        HBCA B.89/a/1,2,19,20,27,35,36,39. Ile à la Crosse Post Journals, 1805–1911
            passim.
        HBCA B.89/b/14,18,23. Ile à la Crosse Correspondence, 1891–1910 passim.
        HBCA B.89/d/338,403. Ile à la Crosse Accounts, 1890–1900.
        HBCA B.89/e/15–16 Ile à la Crosse Reports, 1892–1894.
        HBCA B.255/b/1. Buffalo River and Sandy Lake Correspondence, 1907–1911.
        HBCA B.342/d/10. Sandy Lake Accounts, 1908–1909
        HBCA B.349/d/10,24,28. Souris River Accounts, 1889–1901 passim.
Jarvenpa, Robert
    1976   Spatial and Ecological Factors in the Annual Economic Cycle of the English River
            Band of Chipewyan. Arctic Anthropology 13:43–69.
    1977a   Subarctic Indian Trappers and Band Society: The Economics of Male Mobility.
            Human Ecology 5:223–59.
    1977b   The Ubiquitous Bushman: Chipewyan-White Trapper Relations of the 1930's. *In*
            Problems in the Prehistory of the North American Subarctic: The Athapaskan
            Question. J.W. Helmer et al., eds., pp. 165–85. Archaeological Association of the
            University of Calgary.
    1979   Recent Ethnographic Research: Upper Churchill River Drainage, Saskatchewan,
            Canada. Arctic 32:355–365.
    1980   The Trappers of Patuanak: Toward a Spatial Ecology of Modern Hunters. National
            Museum of Man Mercury Series, Canadian Ethnology Service Paper No. 67,
            Ottawa.
Kelsall, John P.
    1968   The Migratory Barren-ground Caribou of Canada. Department of Indian Affairs
            and Northern Development, Ottawa.
Netting, Robert McC.
    1974   Agrarian Ecology. Annual Review of Anthropology 3:21–56.
Orlove, Benjamin S.
    1980   Ecological Anthropology. Annual Review of Anthropology 9:235–273.
Petitot, Emile
    1883   On the Athabasca District of the Canadian North-West Territory. Proceedings of
            the Royal Geographical Society and Monthly Record of Geography 5:633–655.
Public Archives of Canada (PAC), Microfilm Collections
    1881   Census, 192—The North West Territories, Q—S.D. Cumberland District North,
            C–13, 285.
Ray, Arthur J.
    1974   Indians in the Fur Trade: Their Role as Hunters, Trappers, and Middlemen in the
            Lands Southwest of Hudson Bay, 1660–1870. Toronto: University of Toronto Press.
Ray, Arthur J., and Donald Freeman
    1978   'Give Us Good Measure': An Economic Analysis of Relations between the Indians
            and the Hudson's Bay Company before 1763. Toronto: University of Toronto Press.
Sharp, Henry S.
    1975   Introducing the Sororate to a Northern Saskatchewan Chipewyan Village. Ethnol-
            ogy 14:71–82.
Slobodin, Richard
    1964   The Subarctic Métis as Products and Agents of Culture Contact. Arctic Anthropol-
            ogy 2:50–55.

Smith, J.G.E.
  1975 The Ecological Basis of Chipewyan Socio-territorial Organization. *In* Proceedings: Northern Athapaskan Conference 1971. A.M. Clark, ed., pp. 389–461. National Museum of Man Mercury Series, Canadian Ethnology Service Paper No. 27. Ottawa: National Museums of Canada.
  1976 On the Territorial Distribution of the Western Woods Cree. *In* Papers of the Seventh Algonquian Conference, 1975. William Cowan, ed., pp. 414–35. Ottawa: Carleton University.
Szanton, Jules G.
  1965 Food Values and Calorie Charts. New York: Frederic Fell.
Tyrrell, J. Burr, ed.
  1934 Journals of Samuel Hearne and Phillip Turnor between the Years 1774 and 1792. Toronto: Champlain Society.
Watt, B.K., and A.J. Merrill
  1963 Composition of Foods. Agricultural Handbook No. 8. Washington, D.C.: U.S. Government Printing Office.

Notes on Contributors

CHARLES A. BISHOP is professor of anthropology at State University of New York College, Oswego. He has conducted fieldwork among the Northern Ojibwa and the Six Nations Iroquois and has done extensive archival research. He is author of *The Northern Ojibwa and the Fur Trade*, "The Emergence of Hunting Territories among the Northern Ojibwa," "The Emergence of the Northern Ojibwa: Social and Economic Consequences," and other articles.

HETTY JO BRUMBACH is assistant professor of anthropology at Rensselaer Polytechnic Institute. She has carried out fieldwork in the northeastern United States and subarctic Canada. Her publications include "'Iroquoian' Ceramics in 'Algonkian' Territory," "Early Ceramics and Ceramic Technology in the Upper Hudson Valley," and "An Ethnoarchaeological Approach to Chipewyan Adaptations in the Late Fur Trade Period" (with Robert Jarvenpa and Clifford Buell).

ROBERT W. JARVENPA is associate professor of anthropology at State University of New York, Albany. He has conducted extensive fieldwork among Chipewyan, Cree and Metis groups in Canada and among subarctic farmers in Finland. He is author of *The Trappers of Patuanak: Toward a Spatial Ecology of Modern Hunters*, "Intergroup Behavior and Imagery; The Case of Chipewyan and Cree," "Ethnoarchaeological Perspectives on an Athapaskan Moose Kill" (with Hetty Jo Brumbach), and other publications.

CAROL M. JUDD is a historian who has published several articles on the fur trade, most recently "Native Labor and Social Stratification in the Hudson Bay Company's Northern Department, 1770-1870." She also is an editor (with Arthur J. Ray) of *Old Trails and New Directions: Papers of the Third North American Fur Trade Conference*.

SHEPARD KRECH III is research associate in anthropology at the American Museum of Natural History and associate professor of anthropology at George Mason University. He has conducted ethnographic work among the Northern Athapaskan Kutchin and Afro-Americans and has done extensive archival research. His most recent publications include "Ethnography and Ethnohistory in the Subarctic," "Northern Athapaskan Ethnology in the 1970's," *Praise the Bridge That Carries You Over: The Life of Joseph L. Sutton,* and an edited volume, *Indians, Animals and the Fur Trade: A Critique of Keepers of the Game.*

TOBY MORANTZ is research associate at the Centre for Northern Studies and Research at McGill University. She has done extensive archival research on the James Bay Cree. Among her recent publications are *Partners in Furs: A History of the Fur Trade in Eastern James Bay 1600-1870* (with Daniel Francis), "The Fur Trade and the Cree in James Bay" and "L'importance de caribou durant 200 ans d'histoire à la baie de James (1600-1870)."

ARTHUR J. RAY is professor of history at the University of British Columbia. He is a geographer whose publications on the fur trade include two books, *Indians in the Fur Trade: Their Role as Hunters, Trappers and Middlemen in the Lands Southwest of Hudson Bay, 1660-1870* and (with Donald Freeman) *"Give Us Good Measure": An Economic Analysis of Relations Between the Indians and the Hudson's Bay Company Before 1763,* and numerous articles.

Index

Abitibi, 28; Iroquois raids against, 60
Abitibi River, 83, 89
Accounts books, analysis of, xv, xvii, 109,
    118-28, 143n, 147-48, 151-52, 160-80
Achmet, 89; death of, 91
Adaptation, analysis of, 147
Adaptive processes, analysis of, 147, 179
Adaptive strategies, analysis of, 147-48
Albanel, Father Charles, 27, 30
Albany River, 28, 30-32, 43
Alcohol, trade of. *See* Trade goods
Algonquians, 25, 49; and stories of Iroquois,
    74
Algonquin, 25
Allouez, Claude-Jean, 26
American Society for Ethnohistory, ix
Anderson, Thomas, 173
Archaeology, 59, 150, 152, 178; findings on
    diet from, 70; findings on habitation sites
    from, 70; ignoring data from, 55, 71; use
    .of data from 22, 55, 69-72, 147, 161-62
Arctic Drainage Lowlands, 101; as ecozone,
    101-2. *See also* Ecological zones
Assiniboine, 4, 17n, 36; hostility with Black-
    foot, 5
Athabasca District, 13-14, 129, 133, 137
Athabasca River, 148, 154
Attawapiskat Cree, 30

Bands, 157; composite, 73; local or micro-,
    64; macro-, 64; patrilocal, 73; regional,
    64, 103; territories of, 6, 29, 102-3; trad-
    ing, 109. *See also* Social groups; Socio-
    territorial organization
Barlett, Peggy F., 147
Bayly, Thomas, 28, 31
Beale, Anthony, 42
Bear, 62, 101, 108, 110, 113, 167, 174-75
Beaulieu, 133
Beaver, 2, 4, 6-7, 18n, 30, 38, 42, 58, 61-62,
    70-71, 73, 85, 101, 110-12, 120, 122, 167,
    171, 176-77, 179; decline or scarcity of, 5,
    46, 114; marking of lodges of, by Slaveys,
    104; need for preserving, 130-31, 133; not
    killing young of, 26; overhunting of, 43-
    44, 104, 114, 130-31; trade of pelts of, 32,

63, 92; trade of pelt capotes or of coat,
    42, 126-27; traditional use of pelts of, 3,
    26, 29, 32, 63, 104; used for subsistence,
    103; ways of hunting, 104, 108, 113-14,
    126. *See also* Beaver lodges, concepts of
    ownership of
Beaver Indians, 103, 143n
Beaver lodges, concepts of ownership of, xii,
    26, 46-47, 49, 104
Beaver River, 153, 156-57
Bedzebethaw, 109-10, 133
Belanger River, 154
Bell, Sarah, 153-55, 160, 180
Bennett, John W., 74, 147
Berries, edible, 101
Big Island, 153, 157
Bishop, Charles A., xi-xiii, xv, 57, 63, 65, 68-
    69, 81, 138, 151
Bison, 2, 4, 101; diminishing numbers of, 5
Black Birch Lake, 154
Blackfoot, 4, 17n; hostility with Assiniboine,
    5
Black Lake, 152
Bosseux, 139-40
Bosseux's son, 141
Bride service. *See* Kinship, marriage, and
    residence patterns, features of
Buffalo Narrows, 153, 157-60
Buffalo River, 174
Button, Thomas, 31

Campbell, Ethengoo, 166-68, 177, 180; anal-
    ysis of trade of 172-75
Canadian Pacific Railroad, 19n; and compe-
    tition in Rupert's Land, 11-12
Canadian Shield, 22, 31; climate of, 58; pro-
    ductivity of, 58-59
Cannibalism, 40, 132. *See also* Starvation
Canoe Lake, 158-59
Canoes, 92; arriving to trade, 65-66; reveal-
    ing social organization, 65-66; trade of,
    38, 83
Canushirthew, 66
Caribou, 2, 6, 8, 29, 31, 38, 42-43, 58-59, 70-
    71, 101, 107, 114; Beverly herd of, 154;
    declining numbers of, 44, 46; habits of